THE QUEEN'S BUSH SETTLEMENT

Black Pioneers 1839-1865

LINDA BROWN-KUBISCH

NATURAL HERITAGE BOOKS

TORONTO

Published by Natural Heritage / Natural History Inc.
P.O. Box 95, Station O, Toronto, Ontario M4A 2M8
www.naturalheritagebooks.com

National Library of Canada Cataloguing in Publication

Brown-Kubisch, Linda
The Queen's Bush Settlement : Black pioneers, 1839-1865 /
Linda Brown-Kubisch.

Includes bibliographical references and index.
ISBN 1-896219-85-3

1. Blacks — Ontario — Waterloo (County) — History —19th century.
2. Blacks — Ontario — Wellington (County) — History —19th century.
3. Queen's Bush Settlement (Ont.) I. Title.
FC3100.B6B76 2004   971.3'4400496   C2003-905508-6

Cover and text design by Sari Naworynski
Edited by Jane Gibson
Printed and bound in Canada by Hignell Book Printing, Winnipeg

Front cover photo: Crumbling tombstones in what is left of the Peel Township AME/BME Cemetery. Photo by Linda Brown-Kubish.
Back cover photo: Courtesy of the Wellington County Archives.

THE CANADA COUNCIL | LE CONSEIL DES ARTS
FOR THE ARTS | DU CANADA
SINCE 1957 | DEPUIS 1957

ONTARIO ARTS COUNCIL
CONSEIL DES ARTS DE L'ONTARIO

Natural Heritage / Natural History Inc. acknowledges the financial support of the Canada Council for the Arts and the Ontario Arts Council for our publishing program. We acknowledge the support of the Government of Ontario through the Ontario Media Development Corporation's Ontario Book Initiative. We also acknowledge the financial support of the Government of Canada through the Book Publishing Industry Development Program (BPIDP) and the Association for the Export of Canadian Books.

For Michael, Nicholas and Kaitlin.
With a special thank you to Ian Easterbrook.

Table of Contents

ACKNOWLEDGEMENTS

Over the years I have incurred many debts. Many people have generously helped me in all phases of this book. I am particularly indebted to Susan Hoffman and Ryan Taylor, my former colleagues at the Grace Schmidt Room of Local History at the Kitchener Public Library, Kitchener. It was their encouragement and help that enabled me to begin this research project. During my research trips to Kitchener, Pat and Reinhold Kauk opened their home to me, for which I am truly grateful. Doing research long distance is always difficult, but whenever I needed a local source checked Francis Hoffman provided the information. Lisa Lee, Melba Jewell, Pat Jewell and Ted Jewell graciously shared their memories and knowledge of their ancestors with me. Ian Easterbrook, past-President of the Wellington County Historical Society, has remained a constant source of encouragement and was extraordinarily generous in sharing his own research material with me. Ian and Katherine Lamb also read the manuscript and made many useful suggestions. Any errors, factual or interpretive, however, are purely my own.

My research was aided immeasurably by helpful staffs at many different libraries, archives, and historical societies in the United States and in Canada. I am greatly indebted to the staff of the Inter-library Loan Department at Ellis Library, University of Missouri-Columbia, who were resourceful in locating and securing for me many sources. My gratitude must particularly go to the staffs of the Kitchener Public Library, Kitchener; the Wellington County Museum and Archives, Fergus; the Wellesley Historical Society, Wellesley; the Canadian Baptist Archives, Hamilton; the Regional History Collection, D.B. Weldon Library, University of Western Ontario, London; North American Black Historical Museum and Cultural Centre, Amherstburg; the Buxton National Historic Site and Museum, North Buxton; the John Freeman Walls Historic Site, Maidstone Township; the Amistad Research Center, New Orleans;

the Maine Historical Society, Portland; the New Hampshire Historical Society, Concord; and the Rembert E. Stokes Learning Resources Centre, Wilberforce University, Wilberforce, Ohio.

Parts of Chapters 1 and 2 first appeared as articles in *Wellington County History* and *Ontario History*, and are used with their editor's permission. Finally, I would like to acknowledge the Amistad Research Center and the New Hampshire Historical Society for permission to quote from their manuscript collections.

My greatest debt, however, is to my family, who suffered through my graduate studies and then tolerated my continued interest in the Queen's Bush as I completed the manuscript. My husband, Michael, undertook the formidable task of editing the original manuscript. His ruthless pen and keen judgment greatly improved the work. My son, Nicholas, and my daughter, Kaitlin, have my sincere thanks many times over.

Preface

Nestled in the rural countryside of Wellington County near Glen Allen is a small abandoned cemetery, known as the Peel Township Black Cemetery. There are probably hundreds of graves in this cemetery, but natural weathering, neglect and vandalism have destroyed most of the stones. Only a few are remaining and even those are almost unreadable. Years ago the broken stones were mended with iron rods, that have now rusted, and then set in a slab concrete in a straight line. While well-meaning, the attempt to restore the tombstones probably contributed even more damage to the crumbling stone. These gravemarkers are the only physical reminder of a once thriving and important Black community known as the Queen's Bush.

Walking through the cemetery causes one to wonder what the community was like. How did it originate and what caused it to fade away? I became interested in the Queen's Bush while employed at the Kitchener Public Library in Kitchener, Ontario. The staff of the Grace Schmidt Room of Local History frequently received queries about the community's inhabitants, especially those who had been fugitive slaves. Because of this experience, my interest began to focus on the fate of fugitive slaves in Ontario, which developed first into an article then into a thesis for a masters degree in history. Still fascinated by the topic, I expanded my thesis into a work suitable for publication.

When I began my research on the Queen's Bush, I questioned how much information I would be able to locate. Previously published references to the community indicated that few documents would be available, because most fugitive slaves had never had schooling opportunities and thus were illiterate and incapable of leaving written records. Indeed, very few residents of the Queen's Bush left correspondence or other documents, which could tell of their experiences in their new homeland. Moreover, very few American abolitionists, who travelled to the province, actually visited the community — not because the community was unknown, but because the frontier settlement was north of the more southerly transportation routes. Roads leading into the settlement were little more than wilderness trails and were impassable during most of the year. One consequence of this invisibility is that the residents of the Queen's Bush have been ignored throughout history, although they represented one of the largest Black communities of its time. Until now, the Queen's Bush has only been briefly mentioned in historical accounts of the Black experience in Ontario. More attention has focused on the organized communities of Wilberforce, the British-American Institute, the Elgin Settlement and the Refugee Home Society.

As I discovered bits and pieces of information about the community, I realized that there was, indeed, a wide variety of material available. Public documents including tax records, land deeds, marriage records, death records, and obituaries revealed a wealth of information about the Queen's Bush inhabitants. The 1851 and 1861 Canadian census for Wellington and Waterloo counties provided a foundation for the study of the community. From this source, I compiled a list of residents, including their ages, religion and birthplaces, which my former colleague Ryan Taylor entered into a database that could then be printed out alphabetically, by religion or by place of birth. In the late 1820s, these early Black settlers began to petition the provincial government for land grants and assistance in securing titles to their farms. These records, too, provided a valuable source of information. Another major resource is the letters and reports written by the American missionaries, who resided in the community between 1839 and 1853. A combination of all of these sources provides a remarkable glimpse at the community.

In telling the story of the Queen's Bush settlement, I have sought to explore several questions: who were its residents? how did the community develop? what was the relationship between the Black residents and the missionaries? and what caused the demise of what was once one of the largest Black communities in Ontario? Finally, a word about what this study does not attempt. In seeking to find information about the Black residents I only touched briefly on the white settlers who also lived in the community.

Gathering the pieces of the puzzle about the Queen's Bush has taken more than twelve years, but there are still many questions that remain unanswered. very little is known about the everyday lives of these pioneers. I wish I had been able to uncover more information about individual families. Perhaps, in the future more biographical data will come to light. Despite the limitations of this book, I hope the reader will find the story of the settlement in the Queen's Bush and its Black inhabitants to be as engrossing and fascinating as I have.

List of Abbreviations

AAS	American Anti-Slavery Society
ABA	Amhertsburg Baptist Association
ABFMS	American Baptist Free Mission Society
ACS	American Colonization Society
AMA	American Missionary Association
AMAA	American Missionary Association Archives
AME	African Methodist Episcopal
AMEZ	African Methodist Episcopal Zion
ASC	Anti-Slavery Society of Canada
BAS	British Abolition Society
BME	British Methodist Episcopal
CABA	Canadian Anti-Slavery Baptist Association
KPL	Kitchener Public Library
ME	Methodist Episcopal Church
RHS	Refugee Home Society

An Overview of the Black Experience in Canada West

Farewell, old master
Don't come running' after me,
I'm on my way to Canada
Where colored men are free.[1]

Slavery And The Introduction of Blacks Into Canadian Society

BEFORE 1763, CANADA WAS A FRENCH colony known as New France. Although Blacks were present in New France prior to 1628, this year marks the arrival of the first slave whose life is adequately documented. In 1628, a young slave boy was brought to the colony by the English and sold to David Kirke. The following year, the boy was baptized and assumed the name Olivier Le Jeune. It appears that Le Jeune was a domestic servant for the majority of his life, but it is likely that by his death in 1654 he had been emancipated. It does not appear that Le Jeune's arrival precipitated a massive importation of slaves, for no other Black slaves are known to have resided in New France until the late 1600s.[2]

The goals of the Company of New France, which owned the colony, were markedly different from those of the British colonies further south. It was not concerned with colonization, but solely interested in reaping a quick profit from the fur trade. Since fur trading was essentially an individualistic enterprise, there was little need for slave labour. In any event, Native Americans, who practised slavery by enslaving prisoners from other tribes, easily met the need for slaves. Frequently, these slaves, called *Panis*, were sold to the French as domestic servants or agricultural labourers. But without an economy in which slavery could profitably expand, the practice was slow to develop.[3]

In contrast to the institution of slavery practised in the British colonies, slavery in New France was less abusive. Those colonists who could afford slaves were mostly wealthy merchants and government officials who imported them as domestic servants. Most of them received relatively humane treatment, frequently adopting their owner's surname and remaining with the family until their death. Furthermore, the Catholic Church, while condoning slavery, did not view slaves in the same way as British colonists did. Slave status was not thought to be inherent in man, but was a temporary condition arising from an unfortunate turn of events. The Catholic Church's tempered views encouraged slaveholders to treat their slaves humanely. There is little evidence of widespread brutal treatment of slaves, and punishment for crimes was the same for slaves as for freemen.[4]

In the late seventeenth century, in an effort to expand the colony's economy and reduce the chronic labour shortage, the governor of New France, Marquis de Denonville, began to encourage the importation of slaves. King Louis XIV encouraged Denonville's plan, but with reservations, limiting the use of slaves to agricultural production. He also warned that slavery would not be economically profitable because slaves would not acclimate to the harsh northern climate. However, the outbreak of King William's War in 1689 made international shipping difficult and consequently very few slaves were actually imported. In 1704, France declared that her colonies existed only to provide natural resources, which forced New France to continue to depend primarily on its fur trading economy. Under these conditions, the institution of slavery expanded at a very slow rate. Indeed, by 1759 only 3,604 slaves lived in New France and, of this number, only 1,132 were Blacks.[5]

In 1763, the Treaty of Paris ended the French and Indian War and Britain assumed control of the colony. The British continued the practice of slavery, but it took on a new form. British law and custom regarded slaves as property without any rights whatsoever. English civil and criminal law replaced French legislation, depriving slaves of the few rights previously guaranteed under the French Code Noir. However, the Quebec Act of 1774 reinstated French civil law in Quebec. Once the Constitutional Act of 1791 divided Quebec into two provinces, Lower Canada maintained French civil law, while governmental officials introduced British civil law into Upper Canada. However, British criminal law applied to both Canadas and it was these laws that governed the institution of slavery.[6]

During the American Revolutionary War, British military officials regarded slavery as a significant economic weakness in the southern colonies. Hoping to attract labourers and to disrupt the southern economy, the British offered freedom to those slaves who would desert their owners and join the war effort. The number of slaves who accepted the proposition was lower than had been anticipated and corrupt military officers sold many of those who did side with the British back into slavery. All too often there was no difference between free Blacks, those who had volunteered to serve with the British forces, and slaves who had been captured as a result of the war. For instance, in Quebec in 1778 members of the Light Infantry Chasseurs of Brunswick seized and sold a slave owned by a French merchant, while Loyalists in New York captured slaves to sell on the Montreal auction block. It is difficult to determine how many Blacks actually arrived in Upper Canada during the Revolutionary War, but it is clear that British attitudes and unscrupulous behaviour actually contributed to the expansion of slavery.[7]

In 1781, Governor Sir Frederick Haldimand ordered Sir John Johnson, who had invaded the American colonies numerous times, to conduct a census of all Blacks that had been brought into the province. According to Johnson's calculation, only fifty Blacks whose slave status appeared questionable lived there. This number most likely reveals a lack of concern as well as an indication of the difficulty in securing an accurate count. Haldimand's only recourse was to try to prohibit the unauthorized entry of slaves from the American colonies. However, despite his efforts, a substantial number of Blacks had entered Canada by the end of the American Revolution. Many were slaves owned by Loyalists who had fled the rebel colonies; some were fugitive slaves who had sought freedom behind British lines, while yet another group consisted of Jamaican Maroons, who had been exiled to Nova Scotia by the British government.[8]

The white response to the post-Revolutionary War immigration of Blacks changed the pattern of slavery. A noticeable shift occurred primarily in the type of work newly imported slaves performed. They were no longer restricted to domestic service, but provided a greater variety of skilled labour as blacksmiths, caulkers, carpenters and coopers. Tavern and hotel owners employed slaves as waiters, while others became surveyors or construction workers building roads across the frontier. The nature of manumission, (freeing slaves from bondage) also changed. Manumitted slaves frequently became apprentices to their former owners in order to learn a trade. In some cases, slaves acquired freedom after agreeing to remain as paid employees. Nevertheless, the changes had little influence on the relatively less brutal system of slavery practised in the colonies of Canada.[9]

Upper Canada became the first province in British North America to seriously consider the abolishment of slavery and Lieutenant-Governor John Graves Simcoe became the driving force behind the anti-slavery movement. In 1793, due to Simcoe's encouragement, the

House of Assembly passed a bill that banned the importation of slaves. The bill confirmed the status of slaves already living in Upper Canada, but decreed that children of slaves born after the enactment would become free at age twenty-five. Amidst such anti-slavery sentiment the institution of slavery gradually declined. In 1833, the British Parliament passed a bill for the abolition of slavery throughout its empire, which officially went into effect on August 1, 1834.[10]

Canada as a Safe Haven:
The Arrival of Fugitive Slaves and Free Blacks

After the War of 1812, American soldiers, who had fought in Upper Canada, returned home relating their impressions of the British government's attitude towards slavery. By the 1820s most Canadian slaves had been emancipated and, unlike their American counterparts, enjoyed full equality under the law. Canadian free Blacks could vote, serve on juries, own property and serve in the military. Upper Canada soon became mythologized in southern slave quarters as a safe haven. Consequently, small, unorganized groups of fugitive slaves determined to escape from their lives of bondage sought freedom there. Networks of information describing escape routes, employment opportunities and the egalitarian society in Upper Canada directed the modest but constant stream of fugitive slaves northward.[11]

Gradually, the so-called Underground Railroad developed to assist fugitive slaves in their flight to freedom. The primary "secret" escape routes led through Ohio, Pennsylvania and New York, and then across the Detroit River or Lake Erie into Upper Canada. Along the way both Blacks and whites from both sides of the border guided a very diverse group of individuals, the vast majority of which were young men. In their analysis of runaway slave notices published in newspapers in five states between 1838 and 1860, historians John Hope Franklin and Loren Schweninger found that males constituted

eighty-one per cent of those sought by their owners. Among this
group, seventy-four percent were in their late teens and early twenties. Women were less likely to run away, but sixty-eight per cent of
those who did were also in their teens and twenties. It is likely, that
once enslaved men and women married and had children they considered it too difficult and risky to attempt an escape although there
are some remarkable stories of mothers with their children successfully fleeing to freedom.[12]

The majority of these fugitives came from the Upper South and
most had spent some time in a free northern state where they "received
some valuable experience by working in a free-soil economy and
adapting to a colder climate."[13] Others chose to emigrate directly to
Upper Canada. Many of them arrived there in deplorable condition,
starved, exhausted and without proper clothing. Destitute, many
ended their journey as soon as they reached Upper Canada, settling
mostly in the cities along the border such as Amherstburg, Hamilton,
Windsor and St. Catharines. Jermain Wesley Loguen,[14] in a letter
dated May 8, 1856, to Frederick Douglass,[15] reminisced about his
arrival in Hamilton in 1835. He stated that he arrived "penniless,
ragged, lonely, homeless, helpless, hungry and forlorn – a pitiable
wanderer without friend or shelter, or a place to lay my head."[16]

The availability of employment, cheap housing and the presence
of relief organizations contributed to the establishment and growth
of Black communities in the border towns. Toronto in particular
became a centre of Black culture.[17] The proximity of the border not
only guaranteed easy access to the United States, should fugitive
slaves decide to return, but it also enabled them to maintain ties with
free Black communities in the northern states. With time Blacks settled in communities further inland such as, Chatham, Brantford and
London. Nevertheless, wherever they settled they entered trades and
professions, purchased land and businesses, organized benevolent
societies and established churches and schools. Many individuals
sought temporary refuge and employment in urban areas, but as

soon as they had earned enough they purchased land for farming. Ultimately, the freedom and prosperity enjoyed by these early emigrants prompted many free Black Americans, who had grown weary of their second-class status in the northern states, to emigrate as well.[18]

American free Blacks were essentially caught in a "no man's land" between slavery and freedom. Their status as free men was a precarious one in a white society, which tended to view slavery as the natural condition of Blacks, thus most of them encountered legal, as well as political, economic and social discrimination. By 1840 ninety-three percent of the northern free Black population lived in states which completely or practically denied them the right to vote. While white males enjoyed the right to vote regardless of their economic status, most states either required property qualifications for Blacks or completely disfranchised them. Whites there also used segregation to prevent Blacks from assimilating into northern society – segregation which pervaded all institutions of society including churches, jails, hospitals, schools, parks, theatres, public transportation and even cemeteries. Economically, Blacks were restricted to menial, semi-skilled or domestic employment. Men made a living as labourers, porters, barbers or coachmen, while women worked as seamstresses, cooks or washerwomen.[19]

Free Blacks often complained bitterly and openly about their treatment and rejected the contention that they were truly free. Many felt that regardless of their education, conduct or wealth, they still faced discrimination and enjoyed, at best, a second-class status. Samuel Ringgold Ward,[20] a former slave and social activist described the sense of powerlessness of many free Blacks when he wrote that prejudice:

> was ever at my elbow. As a servant, it denied me a
> seat at the table with my white fellow servants; in the
> sports of childhood and youth, it was ever disparag-
> ingly reminding me of my colour and origin; along
> the streets it ever pursued, ever ridiculed, ever

> abused me. If I sought redress, the very complexion
> I wore was pointed out as the best reason for my
> seeking it in vain.[21]

Through different strategies, including the establishment of mutual aid societies and participation in the anti-slavery movement, Blacks attempted to provide for their individual self-expression and to achieve full and equal citizenship within the United States. When these goals continued to be unattainable, many Blacks considered emigration as an alternative to the continual struggle against racism. The positive image of Canada as a land of freedom and opportunity, and the relative ease of getting there, motivated many to seek a better life under the protection of the British government. The enactment of the Fugitive Slave Law in 1850, however, contributed more to the promotion of Black emigration than any other event. The law capitulated to the southern slaveholder's demand for the return of runaway slaves and stipulated that captured fugitive slaves or free Blacks had no recourse to a trial as long as the claimant provided proof of ownership. Northerners were required to assist with the capture and return of runaway slaves or face a fine or imprisonment. Many Blacks, regardless of whether they were born free or who had long since escaped from slavery, fled to Canada.[22]

Emigration to Canada had begun as an alternative to slavery or racial oppression, but it later often took on an important symbolic role. With each escape to Canada, the fugitives made an implicit anti-slavery statement by discrediting pro-slavery claims that slaves were content with their lives in bondage. By prospering in Canada, Blacks furthermore disproved claims that their race was inherently inferior and could not exist equally with whites. Contemporary newspaper articles, speeches, and interviews show that the fugitive slaves were very much aware of the symbolism of their actions. For instance, delegates to the 1851 North American Convention of Colored People held in Toronto stated:

every refugee in Canada is a representative of the
millions of our brethren who are still held in
bondage; and the eye of the civilized world is looking down upon us to see whether we can take care of
ourselves or not.[23]

To assist the influx of immigrants, Blacks organized their own
benevolent and mutual aid societies. The Society for the Protection
of Refugees, St. John's Benevolent Association, the Queen Victoria
Benevolent Society and Daughters of Prince Albert were among the
many groups formed in Toronto. Famed Underground Railroad conductor, Harriet Tubman,[24] helped to establish the St. Catharines
Fugitive Aid Society, while mutual-aid organizations called True
Band Societies were formed in Amherstburg. In Chatham, the
United Daughters of Zion provided a dollar a week to sick or disabled
members. Another prominent women's organization called Love and
Charity had ninety members by 1861 and offered similar monetary
assistance to its members.[25]

Significant documentation shows that Blacks who sought freedom
in Upper Canada before the 1830s were generally tolerated. The white
response to their arrival appears to have been generally sympathetic
because Blacks "were a novelty and as such received friendly treatment."[26] However, by the end of the decade there was a perceptible
shift in public opinion towards people of African ancestry, and
whites became less tolerant of them. The late historian, Robin
Winks, attributed the shift in white public opinion to several specific
developments. In the 1830s, the number of Blacks emigrating to
Upper Canada rose dramatically and, while most Canadians generally opposed slavery, they were not in favour of a massive immigration of Blacks. Moreover, many, once in Canada, displayed
ambivalence towards their newly-adopted home. Many pledged their
devotion to Queen Victoria, served in the militia and purchased land,
but quickly returned to the United States when the opportunity

arose. Many whites, therefore, viewed Blacks merely as temporary residents and considered them primarily as a cheap source of labour. However, their value as labourers diminished with the arrival of large numbers of Irish immigrants, who were also willing to provide cheap manual services. Public opinion also changed because the extradition of fugitive slaves had developed into a political conflict between Canada and the United States. Many Canadians became concerned about the legal implications of their offer of assistance to fugitive slaves.[27]

Beginning in the 1840s, as a result of an increase in the number of fugitive slaves and the concomitant white hostility, Blacks and whites began to establish organized self-help communities that would provide a transition from slavery to freedom. They hoped that these communities would enable fugitive slaves to lead independent, self-reliant lives through educational and vocational training, which would allow them eventually to assimilate into mainstream white society. The three organized communities were the British-American Institute, the Elgin Settlement, and the Refugee Home Society.[28]

As the Upper Canadian Black population increased, many American abolitionists also moved northward to offer their services as teachers and to establish relief stations. These missionaries remained philosophically and financially associated with the American anti-slavery movement. They maintained close ties to American anti-slavery organizations and depended on their financial support to sustain schools and missions. Information available on these missionaries also suggests that they had remarkably similar backgrounds. Most were young New Englanders with strong religious convictions, who shared a belief in evangelical reform activity and personal sacrifice. Their motivation to be missionaries was rooted in the ideology of evangelical abolitionism and they wanted to see an end not only to slavery, but to the ignorance and superstitions it had created. In their view, slavery was a corrupt and sinful institution which had denied Blacks of the ability to be independent, moral people. Although fugitive slaves had broken from the bonds of their masters, the missionaries believed that they needed to be freed from the morally degrading effects of slavery, which could only be achieved through education, both intellectual and religious. As Christians, the missionaries believed it was their duty to regenerate the ex-slaves and prepare them for the responsibilities they would face as free, independent citizens.[29]

Despite their good intentions, most missionaries encountered hostility and resistance from the very people whom they were trying to help. Religious rivalry, paternalistic attitudes, moral rigidity and subtle racism all combined to create a climate in which conflicts became inevitable. In their preoccupation with moulding Blacks into their ideal model of middle-class Christians, the missionaries often failed to realize how their attitudes only alienated the Black community. While they welcomed the schools and relief assistance provided by the missionaries, they would not tolerate the control the teachers tried to inflict over their lives. Another issue that created animosity was the system of solicitation and the management of donations, referred to as the "begging system." With no central relief organization, missionaries or hired agents travelled across Canada and the United States soliciting money and clothing. This system of fundraising created a passionate debate among Blacks and missionaries. Some Blacks felt deeply embarrassed by the practice – it was, after all, begging – and sought to demonstrate that it was unnecessary and corrupt. They were appalled by the fact that unscrupulous men, Black and white, often solicited funds under the pretense of being agents for fugitive slaves only to keep the money for themselves. They feared that such fraud would damage the anti-slavery symbolism of the Black experience in Canada. While others supported the begging system they argued that since the donations had been sent for their benefit, they should control their distribution, not the missionaries. The missionaries, on the other hand, believed that they had solicited the donations and therefore should be able to use them as they saw

Mary Ann Shadd,
social activist,
newspaper editor
and educator,
c. 1845-1855.
Courtesy of the
National Archives of
Canada, C-029977.

fit. Often they used donated clothing in lieu of cash to purchase supplies or services needed to operate their missions, which occasionally
led to charges of misappropriation and even theft.[30]

Delegates at Black conventions held in 1847 in Drummondville,
and in 1852 in Amherstburg and New Canaan, adopted resolutions
against the begging system.[31] Black activist, Mary Ann Shadd,[32] an
outspoken opponent of the begging system, regularly lashed out
against those who perpetuated its practice. Shadd suggested that
dependency on missionaries for relief assistance would create a class
of beggars and provide whites with an opportunity to maintain a
sense of superiority and power over Blacks. She reminded them that
many had gained their freedom at great cost and therefore they
should not submit to the authority of the missionaries. To do so, she
thought would merely be a change "from physical shackles to those of
a moral and religious character."[33]

Sectarian controversies were yet another source of friction. White missionaries and ministers were unable to fully appreciate or understand the devotion of Blacks to their own style of religion, which they considered too superstitious, showy, inappropriate and loud. The missionaries were especially determined to change the religious practices, which included African traditions of shouting, singing and dancing. Moreover, many Black denominations, including the African Methodist Episcopal (AME) and Baptist churches publicly condemned slavery and refused fellowship with slaveholders or any church that condoned slavery. Consequently, very few white ministers were allowed to preach before Black congregations, which prompted many missionaries to accuse religious leaders of promoting hatred and prejudice against whites.[34]

Another factor, contributing to the poor relationship included articles published in the anti-slavery press to attract funding for their operations. Opening paragraphs typically described fugitive slaves as ignorant, destitute and helpless. As one missionary stated, "the colored inhabitants come fully up to my expectations with regard to ignorance, destitution, and all that can combine to make them a degraded race."[35] Following paragraphs then offered brief reports of the fugitive slaves' achievements, industry and self-reliance. Concluding remarks often focused on the difficulties of missionary life, the lack of teaching supplies and the urgent need for donations. Many Blacks had access to American anti-slavery publications and were outraged at the unflattering depictions. It was true that the majority of fugitive slaves had arrived in Canada destitute and without an education, but many of these same individuals had taken control of their own lives and were struggling to build a new life for themselves. They were extremely proud of the measure of success they had gained through hard work and determination.

Criticism of the missionary movement in Canada West also came from American newspapers. An editorial writer of the New York newspaper, *Colored American,* rejoiced that fugitive slaves found a safe haven in Canada West but objected to the amount of money sent to Canada to support them when many Blacks were still held in bondage and faced racial oppression in the United States. Instead, the author advised American philanthropists to "first look at home and spend our charities there."[36]

The Churches

The willingness to assist fugitive slaves varied enormously across white Canadian denominations. In contrast to the anti-slavery sentiment of their American counterparts, Quakers in Canada West did not establish any relief organization for fugitive slaves. This attitude may have stemmed from a conviction that, once in Canada West, the fugitive slaves' troubles were negligible. Due to congregational independence, individual Baptist churches could form their own positions towards slavery and consequently did not hold a united view on the issue. Not surprisingly, the Baptist churches in the western half of Canada West, which had the largest black congregations, provided the most material and spiritual assistance to Black newcomers.[37]

The Anglican Church actively sought to assist fugitive slaves. Knox College in Toronto, the church's institution of higher education, admitted Black students and encouraged white graduates to become involved in projects assisting fugitives. The missionary branch of the church, the Colonial Church and School Society, established a school in London in 1854. Initially the school was a success, but closed in 1859. Despite this support, however, very few Blacks joined the Anglican Church. Educational qualifications and the knowledge of complex catechisms restricted the number of Blacks eligible to assume ministerial positions. Moreover, many Blacks perceived the worship services to be too ritualized and formal.[38]

The character of white churches also contributed to a preference for segregated churches because Blacks sought a more emotional and spontaneous religious service. The majority of Blacks practised fundamentalist Protestantism and generally attended Methodist and Baptist congregations. The revivalist nature of these denominations, with their emphasis on repentance and on the personal experience of conversion, offered a more egalitarian religion.[39]

The AME, the Baptist and the Wesleyan Methodist denominations were among the earliest Black churches in Upper Canada. The AME church had originated in 1816 in Philadelphia, Pennsylvania, in reaction to white discrimination of Black Methodist Episcopal church members. In 1828, the New York AME Conference appointed Jeremiah Miller as missionary minister to Upper Canada in response to a petition by Black parishioners for pastoral care. Interest in the church increased and, on June 10, 1837, church members drafted a second petition requesting a permanent minister. Church officials dispatched Reverend Richard Williams to St. Catharines, and he went on to establish churches in Niagara Falls, St. Davids, Toronto, Malden, Hamilton and Brantford.[40]

Baptist theology, which held the belief in the worth of each individual regardless of colour and personal responsibility to God, appealed to many Blacks and many early Baptist churches in Upper Canada had biracial congregations. In 1821, residents of Colchester, in Essex County, founded one of the earliest Black Baptist congregations in Upper Canada. Elder William Winks, the first ordained fugitive slave in Upper Canada, served as the congregation's minister. In 1826, Reverend Washington Christian organized the First Baptist Church in Toronto and later went on to establish churches in St. Catharines and Hamilton. By 1841 Baptist churches were scattered across the province and, in an effort to unify the congregations, church delegates from Amherstburg, Sandwich and Detroit, Michigan, organized the Amherstburg Baptist Association (ABA). Over time ABA delegates adopted resolutions proclaiming that no Black person should adhere to a religious denomination that supported slavery or apologized for the practice. Congregations were also encouraged to establish Sabbath Schools and hold monthly anti-slavery and temperance meetings. In 1849, the ABA became an auxiliary to the American Baptist Free Mission Society (ABFMS), a white organization dedicated to aiding fugitive slaves. However, dissatisfaction with the activities of the ABFMS lead to a schism and ultimately the establishment of the Canadian Anti-slavery Baptist Association (CABA). This group advocated that control of the church should be kept within the province and encouraged fellowship with other anti-slavery denominations. Whites who objected to the Black presence in Canada West often used this schism to further their own interests, pointing out that if Blacks could not cooperate with each other they could not be expected to live harmoniously with whites. Realizing the destructiveness of the schism, Black ministers met in Amherstburg in 1857 and decided to merge the ABA and the CABA under the name Amherstburg Anti-slavery Regular Baptist Association. By 1860 the organization consisted of twenty Canadian and American churches with over a thousand members.[41]

In 1843, American abolitionist who were members of the Methodist Episcopal (ME) church accused their denomination of condoning slavery after church officials refused to expel slaveholders. In protest, the abolitionists led a secession movement that ultimately led to the establishment of the Wesleyan Methodist church. Within two years, 15,000 ME church members had joined the ranks of the new denomination and, in 1845, church leaders organized the Wesleyan Methodist Missionary Society. Within a year its members had collected $125 and clothing valued at $80, which they forwarded to fugitive slaves in Upper Canada. The denomination's abolitionist views and interest in the fate of fugitive slaves appealed to Canadian Blacks who increasingly converted to Wesleyan Methodism.[42]

Undoubtedly the Black church was an indispensable institution in the development of the fugitive slaves' independence and self-reliance. Beyond its spiritual and social roles, it provided the opportunity for Blacks to acquire important social and economic skills.

The Press

Whites used the press as a legal means of assaulting Blacks and as a voice to disseminate their objections to their immigration into Canada. Editorials, articles and advertisements reveal blatant racism towards Blacks, especially as they became more visible in Canadian society. One of the most racist newspapers was the Toronto *Colonist.* With utter disregard for Black or white public opinion, it launched frequent assaults against the Black community, stating on at least one occasion that slavery was an appropriate institution for Blacks and that a poll tax should be enacted to halt the influx of fugitive slaves.[43]

While many rebuttals to racist articles did appear in white newspapers, the white press largely ignored Black issues. Forced to endure demeaning and condemnatory statements, dissatisfaction with the white press grew, leading eventually to the establishment of Black newspapers. Established in Toronto in March 1845, the *British American* was the first newspaper founded by and specifically for fugitive slaves. It failed to survive its first month, but other publications soon followed.[44]

The *Voice of the Fugitive,* founded by fugitive slave Henry Walton Bibb,[45] circulated across Canada West and the United States. In the first edition of the *Voice of the Fugitive*, Bibb expressed his editorial policy:

> We shall advocate the immediate and unconditional abolishment of chattel slavery everywhere, but especially on American soil. We shall also persuade, as far as it may be practicable, every oppressed person of color in the United States to settle in Canada, where the laws make no distipetion [sic] among men, based on complexion, and upon whose soil no slave can breathe. We shall advocate the cause of Temperance and moral reform generally. The cause for education

shall have a prominent space in our columns. We
shall advocate the claims of agricultural pursuits
among our people, as being the most certain road to
independence and self-respect.[46]

A survey of the *Voice of the Fugitive* reveals that Bibb upheld his
editorial objectives. Each edition of the newspaper provided information about slavery, local and international news, as well as reports
of arriving refugees. Bibb devoted substantial space to information
about the prosperity and activities of the growing Black communities in Canada West and offered advice on a variety of topics, including the choice and care of agricultural crops, hygiene and child
rearing. However, the most powerful impact of the newspaper came
from the editorials and articles, which encouraged African Americans
to emigrate to Canada West. Bibb compared Canada West to other
possible emigration destinations and concluded that Canada West
was by far the most favourable because of its convenient proximity to
the United States, its mineral and agricultural wealth and the lack of
legal and political discrimination.[47] He aimed his message at fugitive
slaves and warned free African Americans:

think not that you are safe and out of danger while
you are under the wings of the flesh-devouring eagle
of America…. Be not flattered into the belief that
you are not liable to be pounced upon by the man-
thief, at any moment.[48]

Another publication, the *Provincial Freeman,* was founded by
Mary Ann Shadd and Samuel Ringgold Ward in 1853. Although Ward
was the official editor, at least during the first year, Shadd was the primary force behind the newspaper. Like Bibb, she concluded that
Canada West was the best destination for Black emigrants. Shadd
believed that Blacks in the United States needed to be informed about

the condition of Black residents in Canada West, to allow them to make intelligent decisions about whether to emigrate or not. Consequently, like Henry Bibb, she devoted the pages of the *Provincial Freeman* to the activities of the Black community in Canada West. Concerned about the slow rate of emigration, Shadd published an editorial in 1857 questioning the motives of Blacks who remained in the United States in "such utter darkness," when in Canada West there was "a prosperous and free government ... lands and resources capable of sheltering and sustaining, the half million free coloured people of the northern states."[49] Shadd predicted that the second-class status of African Americans in the United States would eventually become so unbearable that emigration would be the only alternative. She also encouraged newly arriving immigrants not to think of themselves as refugees, but to embrace British culture, view Canada as their permanent home and to become British citizens. To help individuals adjust to their new homeland, she regularly published articles explaining the British political and legal system.[50]

Animosity developed between Bibb and Shadd, primarily because of their differing opinions on segregation and integration, and they used their newspapers to publicly attack each other. Bibb wrote articles in the *Voice of the Fugitive* for an audience he perceived to be in exile. In contrast, Shadd's *Provincial Freeman* adamantly argued that Canada was now the fugitives' home and she promoted their full integration into Canadian society. She attacked Bibb's support of the Refugee Home Society (RHS), an organized self-help community near Windsor. She charged that the RHS endorsed segregation and encouraged the practice of begging. Other organized communities were not safe from her condemnation either, for she frequently chastised them for relying on agents to solicit funds. Instead, Shadd encouraged economic independence, which would not only personally benefit the fugitive slave, but also promote the acceptance of the Black race in white society. Furthermore, Shadd promoted the use of the judicial system to assault discrimination. Through the columns of the *Provincial Freeman*, she urged Blacks that encountered discrimination to take court action to assert their rights.[51]

Henry Bibb stopped printing the *Voice of the Fugitive* in 1853 and the *Provincial Freeman* ceased publication in 1857. In 1860, Augustus R. Green,[52] a British Methodist Episcopal (BME) minister and former editor of the *Christian Herald*, an AME church publication, tried to revive the Black press in Canada. With the encouragement of the BME church he established the *True Royalist and Weekly Intelligencer* in Windsor. The newspaper stressed the British loyalties of BME church members, but Green abandoned the project after only ten issues.[53] The *Voice of the Bondsman* was another newspaper that supported the Black cause in Canada in the late 1850s. Although its editor, John James Edmonstoune Linton,[54] was a Scottish Presbyterian, he supported Canada's Black community and condemned church fellowship with slaveholders. Linton founded the newspaper in Stratford in 1856, but it ceased publication after only two issues. Between 1854 and 1860 he went on to publish *The Challenge*. Although primarily devoted to the temperance movement, it regularly included anti-slavery articles.[55]

Education

The majority of the fugitive slaves who arrived in Canada, especially before 1850, were illiterate, having been deprived of opportunities for schooling. After arriving in Upper Canada many individuals eagerly sought an education for themselves and their children as a means of bettering their lives and allowing them to understand civil laws, to intelligently transact business deals and to demonstrate intellectual parity with whites. Many white parents, however, feared that associating with Black students would harm their children, and school boards across Upper Canada consistently restricted access to schools. By the 1830s segregated schools were entrenched in many communities.[56]

As early as 1828, Black parents voiced their discontent with the educational system. Approximately two hundred Blacks met in Ancaster to protest the lack of provincial educational opportunities for Black residents. However, their protests and petitions did not effect any changes, mainly because the provincial legislature and the General Board of Education were busy trying to develop a standard educational system for the whole province. With little support from the provincial government, Black families in many communities opened their own schools or sent their children to private mission schools. Nevertheless, the majority of these schools were inferior to white schools because of incompetent teachers, inadequate funding and supplies, as well as poor facilities.[57]

The Act of Union in 1840[58] legally authorized separate schools. The provincial government enacted the legislation to guarantee the right of Roman Catholics and other religious denominations to establish separate schools. Unintentionally, it also ensured racial segregation since many whites interpreted the act as a means to justify the segregation of Blacks. In 1850, the Separate School Act served to further limit access to public schools by stating that any group of at least five Black families could petition local school boards for their own school. Provincial Superintendent of Education, Egerton Ryerson, intended the act to promote equal education and to provide Blacks the choice of attending public schools or establishing separate schools. Instead, whites used the legislation to coerce parents into sending their children to separate schools. Toronto, Brantford and Hamilton continued to operate interracial schools, but other communities such as St. Catharines, Simcoe and Chatham adopted fully segregated school systems. In 1851, the school board of Amherstburg forced Blacks to establish their own school despite opposition. The school operated without sufficient funding and teachers were unable to provide any meaningful education.[59] Boston journalist and abolitionist, Benjamin Drew, visited the school in 1855 and described it as "comfortless and repulsive." The school texts were "miserably tattered and worn-out." Two nearly empty ink stands, containing "very little bad ink," served the entire class of thirty students. Not surprisingly, the teacher was "troubled by the frequent absences of the pupils." Regardless of complaints, white trustees deemed the school adequate.[60]

The judicial system tended to support the segregation of the school system. One of the most significant court cases in this regard was *Hill v. Camden*. In 1852, Dennis Hill, an educated and prosperous farmer in Dawn Mills, near Dresden, complained to Egerton Ryerson, Superintendent of Education, that his son was not allowed to attend the local common school. The nearest Black separate school was four miles away. A year later, when teachers denied admittance to a second child, Hill accepted Ryerson's advice and sued the school board. Chief Justice John Beverly Robinson ruled that the existence of separate schools was justifiable because white parents believed their children's association with Blacks would harm morals and habits. Furthermore, he explained that once a separate school had been established, it was to be compulsory for Black children to attend it. In the 1855 case of *Washington v. Trustees of Charlotteville*, George Washington, another Black plaintiff, accused the Charlotteville school board officials of shifting school district boundaries to exclude Black children from the local school while refusing to establish a separate school for them. This time Chief Justice Robinson ruled that if no separate school existed, Black children could not be denied access to public schools. Over the years, the ambiguity and confusion over the legality of white school boards' discrimination against Black students persisted. Courts continued to hear litigation on the issue because many Black parents argued that their taxes already supported the public schools.[61]

Many Blacks, however, were willing to accept separate educational facilities and this lack of unity probably contributed significantly to the persistence of segregation. Mary Ann Shadd, as editor of the *Provincial Freeman*, criticized Blacks for submitting passively to segregation. She pointed out that acceptance of separate schools strengthened the white resolve to segregate Blacks and the belief that their children could not complete the same curriculum as white children.[62] White abolitionists also criticized the apathy of Black parents. Benjamin Drew noted that in Sandwich (now part of Windsor), as in other sections of the province, "the colored people by accepting of that provision of law, which allows them separate schools, fail of securing the best education for their children."[63]

Ultimately, education did not provide the equality Blacks sought nor did it destroy the barriers of racism. In fact, educational discrimination was probably more rampant than any other form of discrimination in Canada West. With the establishment of segregated schools, whites promoted the exclusion of Blacks as equal participants in their society, thereby ensuring that they remained an inferior social and economic class.

Despite Canadian racist attitudes, Black leaders continued to encourage fugitive slaves to rise above the degradation they had encountered in slavery. They urged them to obtain an education and to be industrious and thrifty, in order to prove to whites that Blacks were their equals. However, Blacks quickly realized that this alone did not guarantee assimilation into white society; nor did it eradicate discrimination and resentment. Canada, therefore, was not the haven mythologized in the southern slave quarters or in the free northern states, but neither was it an institutionalized oppressive society as was the United States. At least in principle, Blacks were guaranteed the same rights and privileges as white Canadian citizens and, as a result, Canada retained its symbol as a safe haven until slavery ended in the United States.

CHAPTER 1

"We marched right into the wilderness"[1]

IN 1828, A GROUP OF FREE Blacks in Ohio packed up their belongings and moved to Upper Canada. Their exact motivation to leave the free northern state is unknown, but their departure coincided with the deteriorating living conditions for Blacks in the state. In 1802 the Ohio state legislature had abolished slavery, but in 1804 and 1807 new laws, known as Black Laws, had been enacted that regulated the movement and liberties of free African Americans. The laws were meant as deterrence to Blacks to settle in the state. They also limited the activities of Blacks already living in Ohio with the aim of encouraging them to leave. The 1804 law, "An Act to Black and Mulatto Persons," stated that Blacks could not live or work in Ohio without possessing a Certificate of Freedom issued by a federal court. After 1807 free Blacks entering the state also had to provide a $500 bond, signed by two white men, as a guarantee of their good behaviour. These repressive laws were frequently ignored, but they remained a threat to the Black community by restricting their movements and employment opportunities. By the late 1820s as the state's Black population increased, whites began to demand that the Black Laws be enforced.[2]

In November 1828, Paola Brown and Charles Jackson, spokesmen for the Ohio emigrants, petitioned the Executive Council of Upper Canada for a township to be set aside for their settlement. The petitioners acknowledged that the Oro Settlement[3] on the western shore of Lake Simcoe in the Township of Oro in Simcoe County had already been established for Black settlers. However, the petitioners believed many disadvantages were associated with the community and requested that another township be appropriated for their purposes. If the Executive Council denied their request, the petitioners asked that the government at least subsidize their move to the Oro Settlement. In response, the Executive Council stated that lots were still available in Oro Township for settlement and they did not feel it was expedient to appropriate additional land specifically for Black settlers. The government officials also refused to provide any financial assistance to the group. Paola Brown, as well as Blacks from St. Catharines, Ancaster, Brantford, Waterloo and Dumfries, submitted a second petition in late 1828. The petitioners outlined a plan to establish a land company, with Paola Brown as their agent, and requested permission to purchase a block of land in the Clergy Reserves near the Grand River. Officials rejected the second petition as well, on the grounds that the land had not been surveyed and was therefore unavailable for sale.[4]

Efforts by Paola Brown and the emigrant colony to acquire land in Upper Canada coincided with deteriorating conditions for Blacks in Cincinnati, Ohio. On June 29, 1829, Trustees of the Cincinnati Township issued a proclamation announcing that the Black Laws would be strictly enforced. Blacks who did not comply with the regulations would be banished from the state. Thus, threatened with expulsion, the Black community sent a delegation to Upper Canada to request asylum. Lieutenant Governor Sir John Colborne met with the delegation and encouraged them to emigrate to Upper Canada. By August, however, few Blacks had actually left Cincinnati or had paid their $500 bond. Determined to expel all people of African

descent from the city, white mobs swarmed through Black neigh-
bourhoods for three days, beating residents and burning their
homes. Driven from their homes, approximately two hundred individuals settled on a tract of land near the Canadian town of Lucan.
They named the settlement Wilberforce, in honor of William
Wilberforce, a member of the British House of Commons and a
leader in the anti-slavery movement.[5]

Paola Brown and his emigrant group continued on their own
search for suitable land. The settlers eventually found their way to
Crook's Tract in Woolwich Township in northern Waterloo County[6]
where they established a settlement near present-day Winterbourne.
They decided to call their new home Colbornesburg Settlement, in
honor of Lieutenant Governor John Colborne. The fertile clay loam
soil proved suitable for growing vegetables and grains, especially
wheat. The meandering Grand River and its tributaries criss-crossing
the gently rolling hills guaranteed abundant sources of water. Crook's
Tract had originally been part of a larger land grant given to the Six
Nations Confederacy for their military support to the British during
the American Revolutionary War.

In 1797, William Wallace purchased Block 3, a twelve-mile square
tract, which included Woolwich and Pilkington townships, from
Thayendinage, better known as Joseph Brant, chief of the Mohawk
Nation. Wallace, gave the requisite securities for the land at the time
of purchase, but failed to make any further payments. As a result, the
Executive Council, which had the responsibility of managing the
Indian Lands, confiscated all but 7,000 acres from Wallace in 1807.
The remaining property formed a triangular section in the southeast
corner of Woolwich Township. In 1821, Wallace lost this tract of land
as well, when the Commissioners of Forfeited Estates confiscated it
as punishment for his support of the Americans during the War of
1812. James Crook, of Flamboro West, purchased the tract and offered
lots for sale to settlers but, despite his efforts to attract buyers, the
area remained undeveloped for several years.[7]

On June 26, 1832, Paola Brown drafted a letter to the editor of the Toronto *Colonial Advocate* in which he described the success of the Colbornesburg Settlement. He reported that the community, with the help of friends from Flamboro West, had recently begun construction on the first Black church in the area, which would also serve as the community's school. At the dedication ceremonies community members elected to name their new church Brown Chapel, in honor of Bishop Brown[8] of the African Bethelite Societies. Encouraged by their success and prosperity, Paola Brown extended an invitation to other Blacks to join the residents of Colbornesburg Settlement in their venture. He advised interested settlers that lots in Crook's Tract could be purchased from James Crook on reasonable terms and promised to keep the *Colonial Advocate* informed about the community's progress. The following October, the newspaper reported that Brown, on behalf of the Colbornesburg Settlement, was in Quebec to solicit donations to pay for the completion of the church.[9]

The 1832 assessment rolls provide a more detailed account of the community of Black pioneers, which by that time consisted of nine households totalling thirty-four people. John Brown, Jacob Williams, Josephus Mallot, Solomon Conaway, John Johnson, Paola Brown, Daniel Banks, Lewis Howard and Griffith Hughes were listed as the heads of the households. Jacob Williams, Paola Brown and Daniel Brown were listed as unmarried, while five families had a total of eighteen children under the age of sixteen. One family included a female over sixteen. All of the settlers, except John Brown, lived in Broken Front Concession 2, just north of Cox's Creek. Brown and his wife claimed one hundred acres in lot 18 in Broken Front Concession 1. They owned two milch cows, a team of oxen, and had twenty-six acres planted in crops. The tax assessor considered Brown's holdings more valuable than that of his neighbours. Assessed at £63, his property was the highest valued farm in the community. The remaining families claimed seventy to one hundred and fifty acres, but at most they had only three or four acres cleared and planted with crops.

Their farms were assessed between £11 and £33. None of the settlers possessed horses, but three families owned oxen which were better suited to the strenuous work of logging and breaking virgin soil.[10]

Although, the Colbornsburg Settlement was on the edge of the frontier, it was widely known. American abolitionist, Benjamin Lundy, noted its existence in his diary written during his 1832 tour of Upper Canada when he investigated the economic and social conditions of fugitive slaves. Writing in his diary on January 15, while visiting Brantford, Lundy wrote:

> A settlement of colored people is located a few miles to the north of this place, which goes by Woolwich. There is said to be a considerable number of emigrants from the United States there and they are represented as doing well.[11]

Although he did not include the community on his itinerary, Lundy was obviously referring to the Colbornesburg Settlement in the Township of Woolich.

By 1833 the composition of the settlement had begun to change. By the time newcomers Morris Jackson and Lewis Crague had arrived, over half of the original settlers, including Jacob Williams, Solomon Conaway, Daniel Banks, Lewis Howard and Griffith Hughes, had left the community. By the following year, Jonathan Butler was the only Black residing in Woolwich Township. Since he lived west of the Grand River, it is probable that he had not been a member of the Colbornesburg Settlement.[12]

The residents of the Colbornesburg Settlement scattered across the province. Josephus and Lucinda Brown Mallot, along with their children, relocated to nearby Bloomingdale, while Paola Brown moved to Hamilton, where he became a leader in the Black community. In 1833, several families moved approximately eighteen miles north of Waterloo, a small village in Waterloo County, to the southern fringe

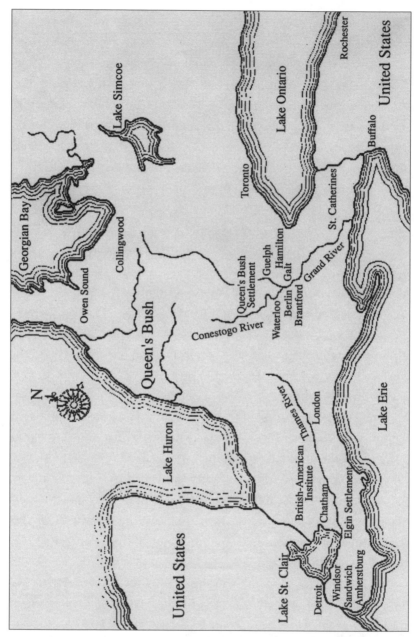

Map of the southwestern Canada West in the 1840s, showing the location of the Queen's Bush Settlement and other major Black communities. Courtesy of Linda Brown-Kubish.[13]

of yet unclaimed government land known as the Queen's Bush. It is believed that the group included Solomon Conaway, his wife and five children; Lewis Howard, his wife and six children, and Daniel Banks. The group settled illegally as squatters and served as the catalyst for the establishment of a new Black settlement also called the Queen's Bush. The wilderness area chosen for the new settlement spread along the boundary line of what today are the Townships of Wellesley in Waterloo County and Peel in Wellington County. At the time the land was heavily timbered with maple, beech, elm, birch and ash, and abundant numbers of deer, rabbits, muskrats, squirrels, fox, bears and wolves roamed the forest. The streams and rivers teemed with fish. Wild ducks and geese lived along the waterways. Most importantly, the land with its rich soil, numerous rivers and creeks proved to be an excellent area for agricultural pursuits.[14]

Eventually additional Black settlers found their way to the small but growing Queen's Bush. They, too, settled illegally as squatters, but with hard work, determination and luck, they hoped in a year or two to achieve a measure of success, a good home, a productive farm and economic stability. They looked to the future and hoped that when the land became available for sale they would have the financial resources to purchase their illegally held farms.

Travel to the Queen's Bush, however, was difficult and exhausting. Early settlers had to make their way along roads from Hamilton through the villages of Brantford, Preston and Berlin (now Kitchener) and Waterloo. The trail leading directly into the Queen's Bush was little more than a blazed narrow path filled with tree stumps that zigzagged through the dense forest. Early travellers to the remote area had to cut a path through the dense trees and underbrush to accommodate their wagons and pack animals. After spring and fall rains the trail further deteriorated into a quagmire of mud making it virtually impassable. More than one settler found it impossible to drive his team and wagon through and eventually had to walk the distance into the settlement.[15] One visitor remarked that he had "never before travelled such a miserable road as that of the Queen's Bush; what, between stumps, stones, railbridges, made of trees laid crossways, swamps, and gullies, we were shaken almost to death."[16] Despite the poor transportation route, each succeeding year more families arrived in the Queen's Bush in search of land.

Establishing a farm in the wilderness of the Queen's Bush proved to be an extremely difficult, dangerous and lonely undertaking. Many newcomers probably had agricultural experience, but it is unlikely that they were familiar with living in the wilds and relying solely on hunting, fishing and the gathering of plants, such as wild leeks and cow cabbage, for their dietary needs. The job of clearing the land for settlement was also a daunting challenge. Trees had to be felled and removed, buildings erected and fields tilled so that crops could be planted. All of this required stamina, strength, determination and, most important of all, family co-operation. Typically, the clearing of land began with the removal of underbrush to create an open space. Then trees under six inches in diameter were cut close to the ground, while larger ones were cut approximately three feet above the ground. The larger logs were used to erect buildings and fences. Families fortunate enough to own teams of oxen used them to haul the logs, but more often than not the clearing was done with just human muscle and an axe. The brush and leftover logs were burned and as the flames died down clouds of grey, billowing smoke spread through the community. When the fire died out, settlers gathered and piled the charred, smoking remains of the first burning and repeatedly lit fires to the partially burnt logs. Ashes from the burnt timber were then spread evenly over the scorched clearings. Gardens and cash crops were planted between the stumps and roots. Since it was impossible to use a plow amidst the stumps, roots and rocks, the land was essentially tilled with heavy hoes and hand rakes. Seeds were planted by hand. The work was time-consuming and often only three or four acres of land could be cleared and cultivated in a given year. It usually took another five years before the tangled roots and stumps had decayed sufficiently so that they could be wrenched from the ground. Only when the fields had been completely cleared could the land be worked with teams of oxen or horses.[17]

The first homes built by the settlers were usually crude temporary shelters. One early settler who arrived in the Queen's Bush in the middle of the winter constructed his first shelter from a hollowed-out log. A smaller piece of wood laid cross-wise inside the log served as his pillow. Despite the adverse conditions, the hardy settler slept in his makeshift wooden bed on the frozen ground without any bedding until he could build a more suitable home. Most settlers lived in log shanties, which typically measured approximately 2x3 metres (about 6x9 feet). The front of the shanty was approximately two and a-half metres high (about 75 feet), but sloped to the rear to a height of one metre (about 3 feet). Frequently, shanties had no windows and a small hole in the roof served as a chimney. Furnishings in these early homes often consisted of old trunks and barrels, which served as tables and chairs. Pegs lined the walls upon which settlers hung their clothing. Family members often slept on tanned animal hides laid down on the dirt floor in front of a fire. As the economic circumstances of individual families improved, a one-storey log cabin might replace the shanty. The size and furnishings of the cabin naturally varied, but in general the log cabins were bigger and more elaborate with finished doors and windows. Roughly hewn planks replaced the dirt floors and furniture included, handmade chairs, tables, and beds. Fieldstone fireplaces provided greater warmth and less of a hazard than an open fire.[18]

John and Eliza Little, who arrived in the Queen's Bush on a cold wintry day in February 1841, exemplified the past experiences of many of the fugitive slaves living in the community. John Little, born into slavery near Murfreesboro in Hertford County, North Carolina, was proud of the fact that "there is no white blood in me; not a drop. My mother's father was imported from Africa, and both my grandparents on the father's side were also imported."[19]

Typical bush clearing with log house. Courtesy of the National Archives of Canada, C-044633.

Little did not provide the name of his first owner, but simply described him as "a reasonable man for a slaveholder."[20] The unidentified slaveholder owned seven slaves, which included Little, his mother and five younger siblings. Little spent the first twenty-three years of his life labouring on his master's farm until he was sent to Murfreesboro to be sold at auction. He reminisced that he "felt miserably bad to be separated from my mother and brothers and sisters. They too felt miserably about it."[21] Little's mother desperately tried to protect her son from being permanently separated from the family. Every Sunday, her only day of rest, she walked to neighbouring farms, often a distance of several miles, to plead with the owners to purchase her son so that he would at least remain in the area. Ultimately, two of Little's sisters were sold to slaveholders in Georgia. John Little was somewhat more fortunate, for another Hertford County slaveholder identified only as "S.E." purchased him. A wealthy planter, S.E. owned seventy slaves and had gained a notorious reputation as a slave breaker. Little described his new owner as "a hard-hearted, overbearing scoundrel: the cries and groans of a suffering person, even if ready to die, no more affected him, than they would one of my oxen in the field."[22]

Life changed drastically for Little on S.E.'s plantation where he encountered a harsher form of slavery. The day began before sunrise with the blowing of a horn calling the field hands to work. There was no opportunity to prepare breakfast; food left over from the previous night's supper was eaten while walking to the overseer's house where they received their assigned tasks for the day. They worked from sunup to sundown. Their only rest period was the noonday meal. According to Little his master believed that, "a nigger could always find time to eat and smoke and shuffle about, and so he wouldn't allow it [a rest break] to us."[23]

After three weeks at his new home, Little requested a pass to visit his mother, which S.E. refused to grant. Slaves could not legally leave their master's plantation without a pass and a slave found away from his home without proper authorization faced severe punishment. Ignoring the risk, the independent-minded slave defied his master and visited his family. After discovering Little's disobedience, S.E. ordered his overseer to administer five hundred lashes with a bull-whip to the rebellious slave. Little was given one hundred lashes before the overseer stopped. Little remembered that the flogging hurt "horribly, but after the first one hundred, sensation seemed to be beaten out of my flesh."[24] S.E. cursed Little for defying his authority and then struck him twice on the head with his cane. Humiliated, Little admitted that the blows from his master's cane were worse than those from the bullwhip. The overseer continued the flogging until Little's back right down to the calves of his legs were raw, bleeding flesh. Not wanting to kill a valuable slave, the overseer finally released him into the care of the other slaves, who were instructed to sprinkle salt on the wounds, which worsened and prolonged his agony. Little was taken to the plantation's blacksmith shop and fitted with iron shackles. That night his feet were placed in wooden stocks to prevent him from running away and two slaves stood guard with instructions to kill him if he tried to escape. Early the next morning the remaining lashes were administered and on the third day S.E. ordered fifty additional blows from a bucking-paddle. Battered and broken, Little fainted after three blows. To compound the pain, the iron shackles gradually rubbed deep sores to the bone on his ankles, which became seriously infected. Wracked with pain, Little wished he "could die, but could not."[25]

Despite the brutal flogging, which left massive scaring on his back, John Little remained strong-willed and defiant. S.E. finally concluded that Little was "too stubborn for him to subdue," and sent him to the Norfolk, Virginia, jail to await passage to New Orleans where he would be sold at the slave market.[26] While confined in the jail Little contracted measles. To avoid a major outbreak of the contagious disease, the jailor isolated the slave in the kitchen. Little took advantage of the situation and as soon as he recuperated he escaped by climbing over the jailhouse wall. Unaware of the freedom he could find in the northern states, Little returned to Hertford County where he camped in a secluded area of the woods near his mother's home. Despite S.E.'s offer of $50 for his capture, dead or alive, Little managed to elude his master for nearly two years. For the sum of $10, a free Black man revealed Little's hiding place to a group of local slave catchers and the men ambushed Little while he lay sleeping. While trying to escape, Little was hit by a bullet in his right thigh and finally collapsed, bleeding badly. The slave catchers took him to the county jail where his wounds were treated, although the bullet lodged deep in his thigh was never removed. As punishment, S.E. sold Little to a slave trader from Madison County in western Tennessee, where the rapidly expanding production of cotton had created an insatiable demand for slaves.[27]

In Madison County the slave trader hired Little out to T.R., who proved to be a more humane master and the slave slowly adjusted to his new home. In Jackson, the county seat and a major port on the

Forked Deer River, Little met his future wife, Eliza, a native of
Petersburg, Virginia. As a child she had been separated from her parents when her master's death resulted in the sale of his slaves as part
of the estate settlement. Eliza became the property of T.N., her
master's son, while her parents were sold to another local slaveholder. This forced separation from her parents was traumatic, but
she was at least able to visit her parents periodically. However, a year
later Eliza's parents were once again sold, this time to a distant slaveholder. Fearing that she would never see her daughter again, Eliza's
mother visited her one last time and poignantly said, "Good bye, be a
good girl; I never expect to see you any more."[28]

On T.N.'s plantation, Eliza worked as a domestic servant and frequently received beatings from her mistress. She bore several
disfiguring scares on her body as reminders of the violent abuse. In
one incidence, the woman threw pieces of a broken china plate at
Eliza and "one piece cut into the sinew of the thumb, and made a
great knot permanently. The wound had to be sewed up."[29] Another
time Eliza was beaten with a stick of wood that cut a deep gash over
her right eye. The wound never healed properly leaving a jagged scar.
And yet another cruel beating with a pair of heavy iron tongs
knocked Eliza unconscious.[30]

At age sixteen, Eliza married John Little. However, slaveholders
rarely regarded slave marriages as legally binding even if ministers
performed them. Indifferent to the Little's marriage vows, T.N. sold
Eliza shortly after the wedding to F.T., another Madison County
planter. Her new master assigned her to work as a field hand. The
back breaking labour was much harder than what she had been
accustomed too. Initially, her hands became blistered and bloody
from lifting and swinging the large, heavy hoes. With time her hands
became calloused and hardened, but she never adjusted to working
in the hot sun all day, the exposure often making her sick.[31]

Shortly after being separated from Eliza, John Little was sent to the
Memphis slave market to be sold once more. Fearing that he would

never see his wife again, he escaped and headed back to his home and wife, "as a man had a right to do."[32] Slave catchers quickly seized the runaway and imprisoned him in the local jail. Still refusing to passively submit to white authority, Little escaped once again. This time he broke through the jailhouse roof during the night after the guards had fallen asleep. With his legs shackled in iron chains, Little fled through the woods on his hands and knees. At daybreak he discovered a blacksmith shop and stole a rasp to cut the chains. Little eventually made his way back to Madison County where he hid out in the vicinity of his wife's home. They tried to maintain some semblance of a marriage, but after several months Eliza finally convinced her master to purchase her rebellious husband for eight hundred dollars. F.T. probably yielded to Eliza's request to prevent her from running away with her husband. John Little joined his wife, but before long he was in trouble again, this time for talking to another slave during working hours, an offense to be punished by three hundred blows from a paddle. Once again Little fled and hid in the woods, but by now he had become aware of the freedom Blacks could find in the northern states. The enticing prospect of freedom and a place to create a new life for themselves prompted John and Eliza Little to begin planning their escape north. Tragically, Willis, a fellow bondsman betrayed the couple by disclosing their plans to F.T., who flogged Eliza hoping that, she would expose the whereabouts of her husband. Eliza refused to betray her husband and managed to escape. After joining her husband they began their long dangerous journey through unfamiliar territory northward to Canada. It was a time of fear and uncertainty for the two fugitive slaves, who faced almost insurmountable odds. Ignorant of geography they were often lost, fatigued, and without food. Suspicious of everyone, the Littles avoided contact with both whites and Blacks. Before reaching the Ohio River they crossed enumerable creeks and rivulets that crisscrossed the river bottoms. In order to safely cross each stream, Eliza Little straddled a log with their meagre belongings strapped to her back in a pack. Her husband pushed the log as he swam through the dark, murky water. In her precarious position Eliza knew that she faced certain death if she fell into the swift running current. As soon as they had successfully crossed one stream, another one would be in their path. Despite the constant dangers the couple continued on, preferring the possibility of death to enslavement, and never considered the option of giving up.[33]

John P. Parker, an ex-slave who worked as an Underground Railroad conductor for fifteen years in the river port town of Ripley, Ohio, frequently assisted fugitive slaves from Tennessee. In his autobiography, Parker noted that it was more difficult for slaves to escape from Tennessee than from other border states. He stated that:

> Men and women whom I helped on their way came from Tennessee, requiring weeks to make the journey, sleeping under the trees in the daytime and slowly picking their dangerous way at night. How they crossed the numerous creeks that lay waiting for them like a trap was unbelievable to me. As a matter of fact, they became backwoodsmen, following the north star, or even mountains, to reach their destination, the Ohio River. Once there they felt they were in view of their promised land, even if they had no way to cross into it. Few had shoes, and these were so worn out by the time they reached me, the soles were held together by twine – making loose fitting sandals.[34]

After travelling for three months, with several close encounters with slave catchers, the Littles finally reached Chicago, exhausted and barefoot. In the bustling port city they received aid from sympathetic abolitionists who paid for their fare to Detroit. From there the couple sailed across the Detroit River to the Canadian town of Windsor. The

Littles were finally free and safe, but their problems were far from over. Employment opportunities in the small border town were limited and they were unable to find work. They "heard of the Queen's Bush, where any people might go and settle, colored or poor, and might have a reasonable chance to pay for the land."[35] The couple decided to try their luck in the Queen's Bush, but had difficulties locating this more remote backwoods community. The Littles travelled first to Buffalo, New York, and then back to Canada West before they finally received more accurate directions in St. Catharines. In Hamilton they purchased supplies and then began their fifty-five mile trek to the Queen's Bush in search of a permanent home. In later years Little described his arrival in detail stating that:

> We had not a second suit of clothes apiece; we had one bedquilt and one blanket, and eighteen dollars in money. I bought two axes in Hamilton, one for myself, and one for my wife; half a dozen plates, knives and forks, an iron pot, and a Dutch oven: that's all for tools and furniture. For provisions I bought fifty weight of flour, and twenty pounds of pork. Then we marched right into the wilderness, where there were thousands of acres of woods which the chain never run round since Adam. At night we made a fire, and cut down a tree, and put up some slats like a wigwam. This was in February, when the snow was two feet deep.[36]

John and Eliza Little chose a favourable site of one hundred acres north of the Conestogo River on what would later become lot 20, concession 1 in Peel Township. Their nearest neighbours were two miles away. In the dead of winter amidst drifts of snow, the Littles worked alone to clear an open space in the dense forest and erected a small hut. They sliced shingles from cedar trees growing in the nearby swamp for a makeshift roof, but without sufficient blankets and bedding they had to keep a fire burning every night. Their small hut may have been crude, but for the first time in their lives the Littles had a home that they could call their own. They were their own masters and no longer had to fear separation, brutal floggings or the threat of being captured and re-enslaved.[37]

Farming the land provided the Queen's Bush settlers with a degree of self-reliance and independence. But they also had to endure many hardships, disappointments and dangers. Families who were from the southern slave states had to adjust to the long, cold Canadian winters with freezing winds and snow. Frosts, droughts and diseases could destroy crops. The settlers also had to stave off wild animals that damaged crops or killed their livestock. John Little reminisced that:

> Wolves, any quantity, were howling about us con-
> stantly, night and day – big, savage wolves, which
> alarmed the people. Some men carrying meat, were
> chased by them. In the spring, plenty of bears came
> about us after sheep and hogs. One day my wife and
> I were walking out, and we saw four bears in the
> cherry-trees eating the fruit. My wife went for my
> gun, called some neighbors, and we killed all four.[38]

To survive the privations of the wilderness settlers depended on each other for survival. Newcomers often received gifts of field beans and potatoes from their neighbours. New arrivals, especially those who were fugitive slaves suffered from a shortage of agricultural equipment, seed and livestock. They borrowed whatever they could from their neighbours, but they also relied on aid from sympathic merchants in the nearby villages. Henry Stauffer Huber,[39] a Mennonite merchant in Bridgeport, was well-known for his abolitionist views and assisted many families.

*Henry Stauffer Huber,
a Mennonite merchant,
assisted many Queen's
Bush families.*
Courtesy of the Kitchener
Public Library.

Upon his arrival in the Queen's Bush, John Little obtained seed on credit from local merchants on the promise that he, in turn, would help them during the harvest season. Using only hoes and hand rakes, Little and his wife raised 110 bushels of spring wheat and 300 bushels of potatoes their first year. Families also joined together in communal work groups to clear the land, erect cabins, or harvest crops. Moreover, it was not uncommon for several families to live together sharing resources and manpower until individual homes could be built and crops planted. John Brown and John B. Brooks were among those early settlers who formed partnerships. They arrived in the community on April 15, 1843, and within three years the two men had built a substantial log house and had eight acres of land under cultivation.[40]

The Black settlers in turn helped those whites who arrived in the Queen's Bush and who faced the same daunting challenges. William Nell recalled that his family, recent immigrants from Ireland, had arrived in the Queen's Bush late one night in 1847 after a four-day wagon journey from Toronto. Tired and hungry, they had come upon a small, crude log shanty in a clearing just north of Hawksville owned by a Black logger named Keath. The family had no food to spare, but had given the Nells shelter for the night. William Ghent, another early white settler, had constructed his new home with the help of his Black neighbours, whom he praised as "reliable and honest."[41]

The Queen's Bush settlers produced a variety of crops such as, barley and oats with wheat being the primary cash crop. They also raised cattle, horses, sheep, and hogs; planted orchards and a variety of garden crops, including turnips, potatoes and beans. Families also took advantage of the sugar maple trees in the forest and produced maple sugar every spring.[42]

Women were primarily responsible for the management of the household and care of the children. They preserved fruits and veg-etables, spun wool into thread, wove cloth on handmade looms, quilted, made soap and candles from lard, raised poultry and cured meat. However, many women like Eliza Little, also assisted their hus-bands with clearing the land, planting, cultivating and harvesting the crops. Because they had been raised in slavery where men and women often shared the same tasks, neither John nor Eliza Little thought it unusual for her to assist her husband in such gruelling work. Eliza Little was proud of the fact that she was able to handle an axe and other agricultural implements as well as her husband. Reflecting on their initial years on their farm and how Eliza had worked as his equal, John Little remarked, "I did not realize then; but now I see that she was a brave woman."[43] Young children were respon-sible for less strenuous daily chores, such as gardening, feeding live-stock, gathering eggs, and milking, while older children helped with the more difficult farm work. But everyone worked in the fields when needed, especially during the planting and harvesting seasons.[44]

Lumberjacks were in great demand on the frontier and many Blacks were eager to work for wages. For the more prosperous white settlers, hiring Black loggers offered an affordable and quicker means of clearing and working their farms. However, during the early years of settlement in the Queen's Bush very little currency was available, so a barter system developed. In exchange for their labour, many loggers received food and lodging. However, the low wages and uncertain working conditions created a precarious life for them. One Black logger reported that he only received a small ration of flour and meat each day, and that his family often suffered because of a lack of food "and at one time were obliged to live for several days on boiled meat."[45]

As more prosperous settlers moved into the Queen's Bush, Blacks found work as farm labourers during the planting and harvest seasons. One visitor to the community in August 1847 noted that groups of Black men could be seen each morning walking to nearby farms with their sharpened scythes slung over their shoulders. The harvesters received a dollar a day plus meals. The money enabled them to purchase livestock and other necessary supplies for their farms, but it also meant that they were not able to clear and work their own farms as quickly as their employers. During his initial months in the Queen's Bush, John Little worked as a farm labourer two days a week in order to purchase agricultural supplies. He devoted the remainder of the week to clearing and cultivating his own land.[46]

The timber trade and the production of potash were by-products of farming and constituted important secondary industries in the community. Many residents sold timber to sawmills in nearby towns. Others made a profitable income from the production of potash, the potassium salts obtained by leaching and heating wood ashes. Potash was an ingredient in the manufacture of soap, dyes, bleach, glass and saltpeter; and was in great demand, especially in Great Britain's textile factories.[47]

Whatever commodity the settlers produced, they faced the challenge of transporting it to the nearest markets, often an extremely difficult task. For many years the roads into the Queen's Bush existed only as narrow trails filled with tree stumps making them almost impassable with wagons. Waterloo, one of the closest villages, was approximately eighteen miles southeast of the community and a round trip with a team of oxen hitched to a jumper took two days. A jumper was a long, low sleigh with a box attached to hold goods and many settlers used it instead of a wagon, even in the summer, because it slid smoothly over ruts and around stumps. In the spring and fall the trails became quagmires of mud, forcing farmers to carry their wheat or other goods in packs loaded onto their backs.[48]

Blacks who settled in the Queen's Bush came from very diverse backgrounds and experiences. James Curry had been born a slave in 1816 in Person County in the north-central section of North Carolina, near the Virginia border. His mother, Lucy, was the daughter of a white man and a slave woman. Lucy, along with her brother, sister-in-law, and their combined children were owned by Moses Chambers;[49] one of Person County's most prominent citizens and landholders. Shortly after Curry's birth, his father, Peter Burnet, a free Black man, accompanied a white man on a business trip to Alabama. Once away from family and friends who could verify Burnet's free status, the man sold him into slavery. Curry never saw his father again. Lucy later married a slave on the Chambers farm and bore six more children.

As a young child, Curry worked in the Chambers household as a servant and probably performed innumerable daily chores including running errands, tending fires and assisting his mother in the kitchen. Although, it was illegal to educate slaves in North Carolina, the Chambers children taught Curry how to read and write. Reading opened new doors for the young boy and thereafter he was seldom without a book. On Sunday mornings, after the Chambers family had left home to attend church, Curry regularly read their family Bible. In later years Curry reminisced that it was from his master's Bible that he:

> learned that it was contrary to the revealed will of
> God, that one man should hold another as a slave. I

had always heard it talked among the slaves, that we
ought not to be held as slaves; that our forefathers
and mothers were stolen from Africa, where they
were free men and free women. But in the Bible I
learned that "God hath made of one blood all
nations of men to dwell on all the face of the
earth."[50]

When Moses Chambers discovered that Curry could read, he forbade
any further lessons, but the boy never waivered in his pursuit of an
education. His mother encouraged her son's efforts and even managed to obtain a spelling book, so that he could continue his rudi-
mentary education.[51]

When Curry turned sixteen, Chambers assigned the teenager to
work as a field hand. Curry helped the other slaves on the farm to
cultivate tobacco, cotton and wheat, spending the winter months
working with his uncle in the hatter's shop. At age twenty, Curry
married and although he was reasonably happy, he longed to be free.
The only obstacle that prevented him from running away was his
attachment to his wife and family. However, in May 1838, shortly after
he turned twenty-two, Curry received a horrendous beating from the
overseer who managed the Chambers' farm. Incensed, Curry firmly
resolved that he "would no longer be a slave. I would now escape or
die in the attempt. They might shoot me down if they chose, but I
would not live a slave."[52]

Curry and his two half-brothers were tempted to run way immediately, but they cautiously decided that they would wait until the
following month when Chambers would be away on business.
Shortly after Chambers' departure for Alabama, the overseer threatened Curry with yet another flogging. Determined never to be
beaten again, Curry and his half-brothers fled immediately. They
quickly crossed the Virginia state line in a northeasterly direction,
and headed for Petersburg. Curry had been to the city on numerous

occasions and knew the route through the Virginia countryside. But
after passing Petersburg, the three men were dependent solely on
rather vague instructions they had received from other slaves. After
travelling for several days, the fugitives were approximately forty-five
miles south of Washington, D.C. when slave catchers discovered
them one night as they cooked their evening meal over a campfire.
Reflecting on the moment when the slave catchers arrived at their
campsite, Curry stated that:

> when hearing a noise in the bushes, we looked up,
> and beheld dogs coming towards us and behind
> them several white men, who called out 'O! you
> rascals, what are you doing there? Catch him! Catch
> him!' The dogs sprang towards us. My feelings I
> cannot describe, as I started, and ran with all my
> might. My brothers, having taken off their coats and
> hats, stopped to pick them up, and then ran off in
> another direction, and the dogs followed them,
> while I escaped, and never saw them more. I heard
> the dogs barking after them, when I had got as much
> as a mile from where we started. Oh! then I was most
> miserable, left alone, a poor hunted stranger in a
> strange land – my brothers gone. I know not how to
> express the feelings of that moment.[53]

Lost and alone, Curry continued his northward course. At
Alexandria, Virginia, he crossed the Potomac River and reached
Washington, D.C. where a Black family gave him shelter for several
days. Just before dawn on July 19, he crossed the state line into
Pennsylvania "with a heart full of gratitude to God, believing that I
was indeed a free man, and that now, under the protection of law,
there was none who could molest me or make me afraid."[54] Curry
hoped to find a sanctuary in Chambersburg, but a Black woman

warned him that local whites were not sympathic to fugitive slaves and would return him to slavery if captured. The woman advised Curry to settle further north, so he moved on to Philadelphia where he found relative safety and employment with a Quaker family. Nevertheless, he still felt vulnerable and moved once again to Fall River, Massachusetts, where Quaker abolitionists, Samuel and Elizabeth Chace, gave him a temporary refuge. Samuel Chace was a cotton manufacturer and his wife was the president of the Fall River Ladies Anti-slavery Society. While living with the family, Elizabeth Chace wrote Curry's biography and submitted the work to William Lloyd Garrison, editor of the *Liberator,* a Boston-based anti-slavery newspaper. Impressed with the biography, Garrison published it on the front page of the January 10, 1840, issue of his newspaper under the title, "Narrative of James Curry, A Fugitive Slave."[55]

Fearing that his freedom still remained precarious, Curry left the Chace home in late 1839 and moved to Upper Canada. Not long after his escape, Curry's mother, Lucy, also ran away and made her way north. Miraculously, mother and son were reunited in Toronto. By 1843, Curry had settled in the remote Queen's Bush where he established a farm, but his main source of income came from the production of potash. In one year alone he produced seventeen barrels, which he sold to a merchant in Dundas near Lake Ontario.[56]

Moses and Nancy Prater were among several fugitive slaves in the Queen's Bush who had received assistance from Reverend Charles T. Torrey [57] during their escape to freedom. Torrey lived in Baltimore, Maryland, where he worked as a Congregational minister, newspaper editor and Underground Railroad conductor. The Praters had also lived in Baltimore as the slaves of Dick Snowder. When Snowder sold their son to an Alabama slaveholder, they refused to accept the separation with resignation. In 1844, the couple ran away with Torrey's help. While the exact escape route taken by the Praters is unknown, it is known that one of Torrey's regular escape routes from Baltimore traversed northeastern Maryland across the state line to the vicinity of Peachbottom in York County, Pennsylvania. From there other Underground Railroad conductors escorted the fugitive slaves to Philadelphia and then onto New York and Canada. It seems possible that this may have been the same route taken by the Praters.[58]

At least one resident, Sophia Burthen, had lived as a slave in Upper Canada. Burthen had been born in Fishkill, New York, the daughter of slaves, Oliver and Dinah Burthen. When Sophia was a young girl, her owner's sons-in-law, Daniel Outwaters and Simon Knox, kidnapped her along with her sister and took them to Niagara where they were sold to Joseph Brant, the Mohawk leader. Nothing more is known of her sister, but Burthen became one of the many slaves owned by Brant.[59]

Sophia Burthen lived a nomadic life with the Mohawk people as they migrated across the Grand River region dividing their time across Mohawk, Ancaster and Preston areas. She remembered hunting deer with Brant's children:

> We would let the hounds loose, and when we heard them bark we would run for the canoe – Peggy, and Mary, and Katy, Brant's daughters and I. Brant's sons, Joseph and Jacob, would wait on the shore to kill the deer when we fetched him in. I had a tomahawk, and would hit the deer on the head – then the squaws would take it by the horns and paddle ashore. The boys would bleed and skin the deer and take the meat to the house.[60]

Sophia Burthen's life with the Mohawks, however, was far from idyllic. She described her mistress, Catharine Brant, as a barbarous creature who often beat her and as a result she bore numerous scars on her body. Most noticeable was the long jagged scar over her eye the result of a knife cut. Sometime before his death on November 24, 1807, Brant sold Burthen to Samuel Hatt, of Ancaster, for one hundred

*Joseph Armstrong
was born a slave
in Maryland in
1819. In 1837, he
escaped from
slavery and even-
tually settled in
Peel Township. In
1905, E. H. Good
of Waterloo
photographed
Mr. Armstrong
in Glen Allan.*
With permission
from *The London
Free Press.*

dollars. Burthen served Hatt for seven years until neighbours confided to her that she was being held illegally as a slave. Sophia later married Robert Pooley,[61] a Black farmer in Waterloo Township, but by 1851 he had deserted her to live with a white woman. In her old age, Sophia Pooley moved to the Queen's Bush where she lived primarily upon the charity of friends.[62]

Joseph Armstrong, born in Maryland on June 28, 1819, was also a fugitive slave. Armstrong's first owner had been Jacob Martin, who in 1835 sold him to Jacob Baer. At age 18, Armstrong decided to end his life of bondage and ran away. Slave catchers tracked him as far as Harrisburg, Pennsylvania. Fearful of being captured and re-enslaved, Armstrong fled to Canada West. He initially settled in Brantford's Black community but, by August 1843, he had moved to the Queen's Bush. Armstrong was a strong, robust man and well known in the community by his nickname, "Uncle Joe." In his later years, Armstrong required the aid of a cane to walk, but he remained a powerful looking man. His white hair and full, neatly-trimmed beard accentuated his dark, wrinkled skin giving him the appearance of a venerable old patriarch.[63]

Other residents of the Queen's Bush, such as John Francis, were ex-slaves who had purchased their freedom. Francis had been born a slave in Virginia and while he was still a child, his mother was sold to another slaveholder. Angered by the separation, eleven-year-old Francis and his father ran away from their master. They escaped by boat and sailed north along the Atlantic coast. One night, shortly after their escape, the weather turned stormy. Torrential winds furiously pitched the boat until the runaways thought for sure they would be capsized into the turbulent ocean. They survived the storm, but then suffered ten days without fresh drinking water. Dehydrated and near death, they risked landing the boat to search for water and food. On shore, the two fugitives were captured and re-enslaved. Francis was sold twice before he finally purchased his own freedom. In 1843, at age twenty-eight, he moved to the Queen's Bush where he and his Canadian-born wife, Ann, began farming.[64]

Former Cobornesburg Settlement resident, Josephus Mallot, who moved to the Queen's Bush sometime between 1840 and 1843, had been born a slave in Alabama. Mallot had worked as a cook on Mississippi River steamboats and by saving the tips that he had received from passengers, he had been able to purchase his freedom. Once a free man, Mallot had moved to Ohio, where he married his wife before moving to Canada West.[65]

Thomas Elwood Knox, had been born free and lived in Pittsburgh, Pennsylvania. Frustrated by racial discrimination, bigotry and oppression, he emigrated to Canada in 1844. Three years later he established a farm in the Queen's Bush. Knox acknowledged that there was less racism in Canada West than in the United States, but he admitted that he "would rather have remained in [his] native country."[66]

James and Mary Ann Hart had been born in Maryland in 1821. In 1844, the couple lived in New York where their oldest daughter

Elizabeth M. was born but, by 1847, the family had settled in the Queen's Bush. The family's motivation to leave the relative safety of a northern state remains a mystery, but the precarious nature of their freedom may have spurred them northward. According to a correspondent for the *Elmira Signet* newspaper, the family had even created a new identity for themselves by changing their surname from Smith to Hart to ensure their safety from their former owner.[67]

Little information has been found for other Queen's Bush residents but, despite their individually unique experiences, it is likely that they a common bond of shared hope for a better life on the Canadian frontier. Some Queen's Bush inhabitants, like John Little, even saw their wilderness homes as a means of isolating themselves from white society. Bitter over how he had been previously treated, Little declared:

> I felt thankful that I had got into a place where I could not see the face of a white man. For something like five or six years, I felt suspicious when I saw a white man, thinking he was prying round to take some advantage. This was because I had been so bedeviled and harassed by them. At length that feeling wore off through kindness that I received from some here, and from abolitionists, who came over from the States to instruct us, and I felt that it was not the white man I should dislike, but the mean spirit which is in some men, whether white or black.[68]

By the late 1830s the Queen's Bush community comprised an area eight by twelve miles in what would eventually become the southern section of the Township of Peel in Wellington County and the northern half of the Township of Wellesley in Waterloo County. However, the highest concentration of settlement occurred in the southern half of Peel Township between Concessions 1 and 6. Although many regarded the Queen's Bush as a fugitive slave community, its residents during the ensuing years would continue to be a diverse group of people, that included, not only runaway slaves, but free Blacks from the United States, Canadian-born Black and white settlers. The community's Black residents maintained a network of family and friends with other Black communities in the province and in the United States. These links of communication provided a foundation of mutual support in adapting to their new homeland and, in many cases, to their new-found freedom. These networks also enticed a growing number of settlers of African descent to the community, who sought solidarity with other members of their race. Beginning in 1839, American abolitionists were also attracted to the community in their desire to assist fugitive slaves. These missionaries created an additional link between the community and the American anti-slavery movement. Ultimately, they would have a profound effect on the community.

CHAPTER 2

"Many are the trials we have to encounter"[1]

IN 1839, REVEREND WILLIAM A. RAYMOND, a tall, slender young man with a robust constitution, arrived in the Queen's Bush to open a school for the community's children. Raymond had been born on October 27, 1815, in Ashby, Massachusetts. His friends described him as "a man of cheerful piety, strong faith, great self-denial and devotedness."[2] His travelling companion was his new bride, Eliza Ruggles, a petite young woman who shared his missionary zeal. Although, a wagon maker by trade, Raymond had dreamed of becoming a minister and once confessed to a student: "I thought of but little else than of becoming a great and popular preacher – successful evangelist."[3] To achieve his lifelong goal he enrolled at Amherst College in 1835 where he took classical and theological courses. During this time Raymond volunteered as a teacher in the local Black community conducting Bible classes on Sunday. He quickly became convinced that his life's ambition would be to serve as a minister and teacher there.[4]

Although Massachusetts was a free state and many whites regarded slavery as evil, it still was not socially acceptable for races to interact. The faculty of the college advised Raymond to terminate his association with the Black community, especially when rumours began to circulate that a young, unmarried Black woman he had befriended was pregnant. Tainted by scandal, Raymond returned to his home where he related his circumstances to a female friend. After due consideration she offered to accompany Raymond back to Amherst and live with the young woman, believing that such an arrangement would end the malicious rumours. Raymond accepted the offer and the two friends travelled to Amherst from Ashburnham, a distance of forty-five miles. News of their lengthy, unchaperoned trip only added to the gossip and Raymond's growing reputation as a philanderer. Local newspapers noted the incident, which further outraged the college's faculty and led to Raymond's dismissal. Stedman W. Hanks, a classmate who later became the minister of the John Street Church in Lowell, Massachusetts, defended Raymond's commitment to the Black community, noting that if his friends had been white, no one would have been concerned.[5]

Undaunted, Raymond left Amherst and enrolled at Oberlin Collegiate Institute (present-day Oberlin College) in Ohio, where he continued his classical and theological studies. At Oberlin, Raymond met Hiram Wilson, a staunch abolitionist who had been born in September 1803 in Acworth, New Hampshire. In 1834, Wilson was one of seventy-four students who had left the Lane Seminary, near Cincinnati, Ohio, because of the faculty's less radical anti-slavery views. The group of students, known as the Lane Rebels, went on to attend the more liberal Oberlin Collegiate Institute. While a student, Wilson helped to organize the Ohio Anti-slavery Society and the Oberlin Anti-slavery Society. On September 14, 1836, Wilson graduated from Oberlin's Theological Department and was ordained a Congregational minister the following day.

After graduation he left for Upper Canada to gain a first-hand perspective on the economic and social conditions of fugitive slaves. Upon discovering that schools were badly needed in the Black communities there, he began to recruit Oberlin students as teachers. One of his first recruits, Joseph Lawrence, established a school in Amherstburg, although he died just ten weeks after his arrival in February 1837. Diana Samson, another Oberlin student and one of Wilson's first female recruits, became his replacement at the school. In the spring of 1837, Wilson attended the annual meeting of the American Anti-slavery Society (AAS) as a representative of Upper Canada. Impressed with his dedication and efforts, AAS officials hired Wilson to work as the organization's agent in Upper Canada. Wilson's association with the society lasted only a year but, by May 1839, he had arranged for fourteen teachers to teach in ten different schools with a total of three hundred students – a considerable accomplishment in such a short span of time. Eventually, Wilson's work attracted the attention of a group of Rochester, New York, philanthropists who organized the Canada Mission to help pay teacher salaries, purchase school supplies, and construct schoolhouses.[6]

In 1838, during one of his recruiting visits to Oberlin, Hiram Wilson met William Raymond and convinced him to join his group of teachers in Upper Canada. Thrilled by the offer, Raymond seized the opportunity to resume his missionary work. After visiting several Black communities, Raymond decided his services were needed most in Brantford, a small hamlet on the banks of the Grand River. The village had been established in 1830 by the Mohawks under the leadership of Joseph Brant, following the American Revolutionary War. During the war the Mohawks had fought as British allies and in return had received a strip of land six miles wide on both sides of the Grand River from its source to its mouth at Lake Erie. Brantford's original Black population were slaves that the Mohawks had brought with them to Upper Canada. Ironically, Brant also permitted fugitive slaves from the United States to settle in the area. Among the earliest Black settlers were John Boylston, Adam Akin, James Anderson and Samuel Wright.[7]

In January 1832, Benjamin Lundy, an American abolitionist and editor of the *Genius of Universal Emancipation*, travelled to Upper

Canada to report on the living conditions of fugitive slaves. He hoped that the information gathered during his investigation would help American Blacks in their decisions to emigrate to Upper Canada. From Hamilton, Lundy took the stage to Brantford, which he found to be a neat and thriving village. Lundy noted in his diary that a sizeable Black population resided in the village and that many Mohawks, Blacks and whites had intermarried. Nevertheless, Lundy noted that discrimination against Blacks was widespread in the community. He felt American emigrants despised Blacks and still retained "all the prejudices here that they formerly held against the colored people in their native country. And the latter, being admitted to equal privileges with them under this government, are accused of being saucey."[8]

Blacks attended the local Baptist church, however white worshippers demanded that they sit at the rear of the church in the "Negro pews." Brantford's white community also denied Black children access to the local school forcing parents to establish their own educational facility in 1837. The school achieved such a high level of instruction that many whites applied to have their children enrolled until finally both schools merged.[9]

When William Raymond arrived in Brantford in 1838, he taught reading, writing and arithmetic and offered Sabbath School classes for the children on Sunday. Typically, Sabbath School programs began with hymn singing, followed by prayers and a Scripture lesson devoted to a biblical hero or event. Catechism lessons with questions read by the teacher and answered by the students were also part of the instructions. Despite his busy teaching schedule, Raymond conducted religious services for adults at the school. A regular member of these meetings was a twenty-two-year-old woman named Eliza Ruggles. Born in 1817, she was the daughter of William and Mary West Ruggles, of Dempsey Corner, Kings County, Nova Scotia. Mary Ruggles had died during the birth of her daughter and shortly thereafter William Ruggles moved to Brantford, where he purchased land and built a sawmill. He married Sally Johnson and in 1821 sent for his daughter who had remained in Nova Scotia with relatives. Unfortunately, just before Eliza arrived in Brantford her father passed away, but Sally Johnson Ruggles took Eliza in and raised her as if she were her own child.[10]

In later years Hiram Wilson recalled meeting Eliza Ruggles in 1837 during one of his many visits to Brantford. The pious young woman had made a lasting impression on Wilson and he remembered that:

> she was in an inquiring state of mind & disposed to set her face towards the heavenly canaan. I directed her as well as I could. We knelt down & prayed. In a convulsed state she sobbed aloud – melted down & gave her heart to the Lord on the spot.[11]

William Raymond and the religious-minded Eliza Ruggles became friends and before long a loving romance developed between the two. Sally Ruggles, however, vehemently opposed the courtship. Undoubtedly, she hoped her stepdaughter would someday make a more prosperous match. Ignoring her disapproval, the determined couple eloped with the help of Black employees who worked on the Ruggles farm. They were married in St. Catharines and shortly thereafter moved to the Queen's Bush.[12]

The Raymonds were the first missionary teachers in the Queen's Bush and they both taught in their newly established school. During this same time period Raymond's brother Ari, a minister under the sponsorship of a Boston Congregational Church, began teaching in Oro Township's Black community near present-day Edgar in Simcoe County. Ari Raymond and his wife, Eliza Ann, arrived in Oro Township in October 1838 and settled on lot 10, concession 3 where they built a log schoolhouse that also served as a church. Ari Raymond became well known for his missionary work within the Black community and was highly regarded for his patience and self-denial. In 1865, after serving the community for twenty-seven years as

William A. and Eliza Ruggles Raymond. Courtesy of the Nova Scotia Archives and Records Management, Berringer Family Fonds, MG1, Vol. 127, No. 17.

a minister and teacher, Raymond, by then in poor health, returned to his former Massachusetts home.[13]

William and Eliza Raymond's tenure in the Queen's Bush, however, was short-lived, for in the winter of 1840 William Raymond learned about the appeal for teachers to educate the Africans involved in the celebrated Amistad Affair.[14] Raymond decided to apply for the position, but his aspirations seemed impossible for his savings amounted to only twenty-five cents, certainly not enough money to pay the necessary travel expenses to the United States. The fare for passage across Lake Erie alone amounted to two dollars. One cold winter's night Raymond trudged through the snow to the home of Thomas Vipond, a Primitive Methodist minister. Vipond had been born in England in 1810 and lived with his wife, Mary Ann, and family in what would later become Wellesley Township in Waterloo County. An abolitionist, he had helped many early Black Queen's Bush settlers and had gained the reputation of being their devoted friend.[15]

William Raymond explained his desire to return to the United States and asked Vipond for a loan to finance the trip. Although sympathic to his plans, Vipond was equally penniless and unable to help.

While the two friends discussed Raymond's financial dilemma, a wolf entered the yard and attacked Vipond's dog. Hearing the snarling, the men opened the door and the two fighting animals tumbled inside the cabin. The men quickly killed the wolf and the seven-dollar bounty fee for the pelt enabled Raymond to proceed with his plans. Gilbert O. Field replaced Raymond at the Queen's Bush school until at least 1843, but nothing is known about his work in the community.[16]

The early Black immigrants in Upper Canada brought their own religious beliefs, practices and traditions. One of the earliest Black churches to be established in Upper Canada was the AME church. In 1840 it had a membership of 256 people, but by the following year it had almost doubled to 448. In response to this rapid growth, AME church officials convened in Toronto on July 21, 1840, to organize the AME Upper Canadian Conference. Bishop Morris Brown,[17] of Philadelphia, Pennsylvania, chaired the meeting along with Elder Edmund Crosby,[18] missionary to Upper Canada, and Deacon George Weir,[19] of Rochester, New York. Nine Canadians who were ordained ministers, or who had an interest in the ministry, also attended the meeting. They included: Jacob Dorcey, Samuel H. Brown, William H. Edwards,[20] James Harper,[21] Alexander Helmsley,[22] Jeremiah Taylor,[23] Daniel D. Thompson,[24] Peter O'Banyon,[25] and Henry Bullard.[26] Dorcey and Brown eventually served as ministers in the Queen's Bush, but all of these men would play instrumental roles in organizing and ministering to congregations throughout the province.[27]

During the meeting, the men focused most of their attention on organizing the new conference according to the AME Discipline. They established circuits in London, St. Catharines and Brantford, with a station in Toronto. Four itinerant ministers were dispatched to preach in the churches with instructions to travel the countryside and organize new congregations in their assigned areas. The ministers also discussed the needs of Blacks living in Canada and were especially concerned about the economical and moral status of former slaves. The ministers hoped that if members of their race could overcome

Morris Brown, originally of South Carolina, became a Bishop in the African Methodist Episcopal Church.
From Payne, Daniel A., *A History of the African Methodist Episcopal Church,* published in Nashville, Tennessee, in 1891, by the Publishing House of the African Methodist Sunday School Union, 1891.

the evil influences of slavery and become educated, industrious, law-abiding citizens, they would earn the respect of whites. More importantly, they could refute racist claims that Blacks were an inferior race. The ministers unanimously agreed that education had to be one of their highest priorities and, as such, they adopted resolutions pledging to promote schools and Sabbath Schools. They also advocated total abstinence of alcohol and encouraged ministers to establish temperance societies. Over the years, education and temperance would be a recurring topic discussed at AME meetings.[28]

With a limited number of qualified ministers and a vast territory to cover, the remote Queen's Bush settlement was not included in the original circuits. However, in March 1841, an aspiring minister named Jacob Dorcey responded to the community's request for a minister, and settled on land that surveyors later designated as the north half of lot 18, concession 1 in Peel Township. In May, the editor of *Der Morgenstern,* the German-language newspaper published in Berlin, approximately twenty miles southeast of the settlement, announced that Black residents had erected a church south of the

Baptist minister,
James Sims, ministered
to both the Black and
white residents of the
Queen's Bush.
Courtesy of the Waterloo
Historical Society
Collection, Kitchener
Public Library.

Conestogo River. The exact location and denomination of the church is unknown, but it is likely that Dorcey participated in the planning and construction of the sanctuary. At the second annual meeting of the AME Canadian Conference held in Hamilton on July 2, 1842, church officials acknowledged Dorcey's ministerial work and accepted him into full church membership. They also assigned him to the St. Catharines circuit along with the more experienced the Reverend William H. Edwards. Officials also extended their territory to include Detroit, Michigan, and the Queen's Bush community. In 1844, after serving the minimum requirement of four years as a local preacher, Dorcey became an ordained deacon.[29]

James Sims was another early minister who settled in the Queen's Bush. After leaving their home in Scotland, Sims and his family settled in the Queen's Bush Clergy Reserve as squatters in the spring of 1838. He spent his initial years clearing a homestead and supported his family by occasionally working as a labourer in the surrounding villages and hamlets. While employed as a construction worker at Ferrie's Flour Mill in Doon, Sims became a member of the Baptist church in the community of Blair. On October 5, 1841, Sims became an ordained minister and began travelling throughout Waterloo and Wellington counties as an itinerant preacher. He was also associated with the American Baptist Free Missionary Society between 1846 and 1849. An esteemed minister, Sims performed marriages, conducted funerals, baptized new members and offered support to Black and white residents in the Queen's Bush region.[30]

In 1842, those squatters who had settled on the edge of the frontier in the Queen's Bush Clergy Reserve hoping for economic improvement, realized that "civilization" had begun to catch up with them. A massive migration into Canada was taking place with immigrants, primarily from England, Scotland and Ireland, eager to buy plentiful and inexpensive agricultural land. In order to make more land available to the ever-increasing number of settlers, the government announced that it would open Crown and Clergy reserves for settlement. This put Black and white squatters, without any legal right to the land, at the risk of having to leave their homes. Many families still had not achieved any kind of economic stability and consequently did not have the capital to purchase their farms. With their homes and livelihood at stake, the inhabitants of the Queen's Bush united in an effort to secure what constituted the very basis of their existence. James Durand, member of the Parliament for Canada West, received a letter in the fall of 1842 drafted by the Queen's Bush inhabitants, in which they humbly stated:

> We are aware that an apology for our boldness of squatting into the Queens Bush the way we have, should be reasonably looked for. We would therefore beg leave to state to you that we are, most of us, Emigrants who came to this country without the means of buying land, either cultivated or wild, –

and that we had therefore no means of making a living except as Day Labourers, which is, by the way, no very easy way of getting a living, but to which we would have still cheerfully submitted, could we got places to live with our families and constant employment; but we could get neither one nor the other. It is true, we owe many obligations to the older Settlers of Waterloo and Woolwich for employment and temporary places of residence; but a strong emigration, as you are no doubt well aware, cannot, for any length of time, be supported, or support itself, in this manner. Taking these things into consideration, we thought it would be best for ourselves and Families, if we could go into the woods and cultivate the soil, which we saw was, at any rate, as long as it was unsettled, of no more use than being a rendezvous of the wolf and bear, – contemplating at the same time, once to buy the land we have taken in possession, should it be sold upon such conditions that we could buy it. And we are sincerely glad that there is a prospect of its being surveyed out. At the same time, we would beg to state that a report is abroad that the late Lord Sydenham should have recommended that no wild land should be sold anymore, except for Cash. We will by no means question the propriety of this plan, in a general point of view; but in our case, it would be hard indeed, as it would be impossible for most, if not all of us, to buy our land in this way; whereas as we would have a prospect of buying it, were it to be sold upon as favorable conditions as possible, as also that the lots will not be made so large. We think that 200 hundred acres would be a good size for a lot. In the

whole we hope, and have full confidence, that you
will do the best for us you can; and we are withal
truly thankful that you have taken up our cause and
have done what you have done already.

P.S. We would prefer, by far, having the lots surveyed
out from <u>North</u> to <u>South</u> – from <u>North</u> to <u>South</u>
length ways.[31]

In April 1843, Deputy Provincial Surveyor, William Walker, and his
men trekked into the unmapped wilderness of the Queen' Bush
Clergy Reserve with their surveying equipment, axes and stakes. The
surveyors slashed trees and drove stakes to divide and mark the land
into uniform lots and concessions. By the beginning of September,
Walker and his workers had surveyed an area consisting of approximately 66,000 acres in the southernmost section of the Queen's
Bush, which became the Township of Wellesley in Waterloo County.
Walker also drew a map of the township indicating its boundaries,
natural features and other information that would be needed by
future potential buyers.[32] In June, Robert W. Kerr and his surveying
crew arrived in the Queen's Bush and further subdivided the land
tract. Kerr's team surveyed an area of 74,627 acres, which became Peel
Township in Wellington County. While surveying the township, Kerr
attempted to compile a list of all the squatters living in the area.
Although he had a guide who was familiar with the area, they were
unable to locate all of the squatters whose farms were often hidden in
the dense forest. Kerr finally gave up, after noting the names of only
thirty-three squatters.[33]

In response to the arrival of the surveyors, the Queen's Bush
inhabitants once again drafted a petition to the new Governor
General, Sir Charles Metcalfe, in hopes of securing possession of
their homes. The petition contains the names of 123 individuals of
whom fifty-one can be confidently identified as Black. This time the

petitioners proposed a solution to their dilemma and suggested that the government provide them with a land grant. The petition stated:

> ...that your petitioners, the Inhabitants of the Queens Bush now labouring under many disadvantages on account of the state of the land on which we have settled not having been surveyed, consequently we have no regular Roads and being a distance of fifteen miles to the nearest Mill, and your Petitioners being extremely poor, having lately emigrated from England, and from the Southern states where we have suffered all the horrors of Slavery, and having no means of purchasing land, your Petitioners humbly pray that your Lordship will take our case into consideration and if agreeable to your Lordship's humanity to make us a grant of Land, it will be most thankfully received by your Lordship's dutiful and Loyal Petitioners.[34]

No land grant or special consideration was given to the petitioners.

The boundary lines created by the surveyors further complicated the situation faced by the Queen's Bush farmers. New boundary lines tended to ignore already established property lines between farms. Residents soon discovered that more than one farm lay within the neat, square lots created by the surveyors. Consequently, clashes over boundary lines and ownership were not uncommon. For instance, in Wellesley Township five families claimed ownership of land that lay within the boundaries of a single lot. A similar dispute erupted between Lewis Creig and a Mr. Hale over the ownership of the east half of lot 1 on concession 5. Residents took their grievances before the surveyors, but there was little they could do. During a tour of Township of Wellelsey, Deputy Surveyor Thomas C. Jarmey advised the settlers to wait and consult the District Land Agent when the land came on the market for sale. However, in his report to the Surveyor General's office, Jarmey more candidly stated that such disputes would be difficult to resolve and would threaten the orderly settlement of the township.[35]

An additional threat was the opening of new roads, including Hurontario Street, and the Durham, Northern and Garafraxa roads, which ran north to Collingwood, Owen Sound and Meaford. These roads made it easier for the new immigrants to reach the Queen's Bush. With cash in hand and fitted out with supplies and agricultural implements, they pushed into the wilderness and staked out additional claims. Population growth, increasing urbanization, and the disappearance of the vast forests hailed a new era for the community.[36]

During these troubling times in February 1844, Fidelia Coburn, a thirty-nine-year-old woman from Maine and her escort travelled over the snow-covered roads leading northward to the Queen's Bush. A staunch abolitionist, she was on her way to the community to reopen the school for Black pupils. Born February 2, 1805, Coburn was the daughter of Eleazer and Mary Weston Coburn. Her father, a Baptist, was a highly respected businessman and justice of the peace in Bloomfield, Maine, a bustling town on the Kennebec River in Somerset County. He had been a member of the Constitutional Convention in 1820 when Maine became a state and had served in the Maine House of Representatives from 1820 to1831. He had also been a trustee of the Waterville College, president of the Somerset Anti-slavery Society and vice-president of the Maine Anti-slavery Society. Eleazer Coburn's son, Abner, was likewise very active in politics, serving in the Maine House of Representatives between 1838 and 1841 and as governor of Maine from 1863 to 1864.[37] Growing up in the Coburn household must have been an intellectually stimulating environment for Fidelia. Social issues such as education and slavery were undoubtedly topics of family discussions and must have helped to form her abolitionist views at an early age. Coburn's writing ability evidenced by her correspondence and published writings attest to

Fidelia Coburn, born in Maine in 1805, served as a missionary teacher in the Queen's Bush from 1844 to 1849.
From Cobourn, Louise, *Skowhegan on the Kennebec*, published in 1941.[38]

the quality of the education that she had received. Despite her qualifications as a teacher, the notion of a woman travelling to a foreign country to teach fugitive slaves was a remarkable plan in an era when the accepted customs dictated that women restrict themselves to the home and the care of their families. Given these social norms, Coburn's decision to defy convention and move to Upper Canada demonstrates her wholehearted commitment to aiding fugitive slaves. In the ensuing years, Coburn repeatedly received praise for her devotion and her missionary work.[39]

Coburn had actually arrived in Canada West in the spring of 1842 with an invitation from Hiram Wilson to teach at the British-American Institute, located on the Sydenham River near Chatham. Wilson had co-founded the school with fugitive slave Josiah Henson[40] and James Cannines Fuller, a Quaker philanthropist in Skaneateles, New York. However, when Coburn arrived at the Institute she discovered that the schoolhouse had not yet been completed and that there were no lodging facilities available for the teachers. Wilson's small 4x5 metre (about 13x16 feet) log cabin was the only shelter and so Coburn moved in with Wilson, his wife Hannah,[41] and two teachers from Massachusetts, Wesleyan Methodist minister, Reverend Elias E. Kirkland and his wife, Elizabeth C., also known as Fanny. Coburn and the Kirklands made the best of the cramped quarters and slept on mounds of straw in a corner of the cabin. Undaunted, the teachers enthusiastically set to work to finish the school. On December 12, after months of preparations, the British-American Institute opened with nine young men enrolled as its first students.[42]

The Canada Mission and other benevolent organizations provided financial assistance to the school, but donations were sporadic and never enough to fully sustain the school. To procure additional funding, the teachers drafted letters about their missionary operations to the editors of leading American anti-slavery publications. Throughout her career as a missionary, Fidelia Coburn wrote numerous letters to friends, relatives and newspaper editors. The earliest known published letter drafted by her, appeared in the July 13, 1842, Hallowell *Liberty Standard*. It is addressed to her cousin, a member of the Anti-Slavery Ladies Society of Maine. She announced her safe arrival at the British-American Institute and described her first impressions of Canada West, which she believed had a healthy climate and rich soil suitable for agricultural pursuits. However, much to her disappointment, she had discovered that many Canadians harboured racist attitudes towards Blacks. She also concluded that claims by organizations, such as the Canada Mission, that Blacks could receive free land grants were false.[43] She remarked to her cousin that the long held belief:

> that the land was free for fugitives to take up and do what they pleased with is far from the truth: they have none for less than $2.00 per acre, and the whites are more strongly prejudiced than in the States, as a general thing, and are very much opposed to their

remaining here. Thus you see they neither get love, nor money.[44]

Many slaves had heard stories of the freedom and equality to be found in Canada and had risked their lives during their escape. To arrive in Canada and to be treated less than an equal as promised was a shock. According to Coburn, this negative reception "chills them to the heart."[45]

Greatly concerned about the needs of Black women in Canada West, Coburn implored her cousin to exert her influence over other members of the Anti-Slavery Ladies Society of Maine and convince them to sponsor a female department at the British-American Institute. Coburn believed that classes devoted to the special needs of young girls "would do much to ameliorate the condition of our sex."[46]

On April 22, 1843, Coburn along with Hannah M. Wilson, Fanny C. Kirkland, Lorana Parker and Sybil Clary, all teachers at the British-American Institute, founded the Committee of Education in Canada West to specifically address the needs of their female students. Consistent with the traditional ideals of womanhood, the women proposed to teach sewing, cooking and basic household management. They also planned to instruct the students about their future responsibilities as wives and mothers. The committee believed that the proper education of young Black girls had been completely neglected because:

> but few of those mothers who have escaped from the oppressor's grasp are qualified to teach their daughters even those domestic duties calculated to render them comfortable, useful, or happy, as most of them have been accustomed to labor in the field when in slavery.[47]

Realizing that they had little influence over adults, the teachers also proposed to establish a boarding school for young girls between

the ages of five and twelve. The missionaries firmly believed that parents were perpetuating in their children the corrupting habits of
slavery. By requiring young girls to board at the school, they would be
under the total influence of the missionaries twenty-four hours a day
and thereby removed from "former pernicious and evil habits and
influences." The committee implored all white women to assist their
Christian sisters, who were "outcasts of American slavery; through
prayer, sympathy and alms."[48] To raise money for the project, the
committee appointed Coburn to return to Maine during the
summer of 1843 to solicit funds. By the end of her tour, Coburn had
raised over two hundred dollars and had collected several barrels of
clothing worth approximately three hundred dollars. Not having
money to purchase construction materials, the Reverend Kirkland,
four local construction workers and the students began work on a
girl's school and dormitory. Coburn kept family and friends
informed about the progress of the building through letters which
appeared in the *Liberty Standard*. On February 15, 1844, Coburn joy-
fully announced the completion of the 11x7 metre (about 36x23 feet)
building, which she described as a "distance enough from the road
for a good front yard after our New England style. The site is a most
delightful one – and a beautiful situation for a garden."[49]

Tragically, just days before the first girls were to occupy the school,
disaster struck. A young boy playing in one of the rooms started a fire
and construction workers were unable to extinguish the blaze. What
appeared to be a major reversal for the missionaries actually proved
to have positive results as Coburn reported in the *Liberty Standard*:

> the fire awakened the sympathies of the white
> inhabitants, though they have been exceedingly
> opposed, and they are offering 5, 10, and 15 dollars
> apiece to repair the loss, if I come back and take
> charge as contemplated. Indeed! it seems they are all
> turning Abolitionists.[50]

Despite the setback, the British-American Institute quickly prospered and began attracting Black families. The town of Dawn grew around the school and within a few years the population increased to almost five hundred people.[51]

In 1844, Coburn decided to leave the British-American Institute. Her reasons for doing so are unclear, but it is probable that she felt her services were more urgently needed in the Queen's Bush. She arrived in the settlement just as community members were finishing construction on a new schoolhouse, located on the east half of lot 12, concession 3, in Peel Township. The log building measured 2.5x4.5 metres (about 8x15 feet) and had an exterior chimney, but only one window covered with paper. Distressed by the darkness of the interior, Coburn's first challenge was to acquire a proper glass window for her schoolhouse. She purchased glass panes from a local sash maker who donated the frame. Despite the modest facility, Coburn had ambitious plans for the future of her schoolhouse, which she called Mount Pleasant Mission. Due to her background and abolitionist beliefs, the school soon became known as the Abolition or Yankee School.[52]

Initially, Coburn had planned to lodge in a household within walking distance of her schoolhouse, but she quickly discovered that families who had any extra room were already providing accommodations to newcomers who required temporary shelter. With no alternative place as a residence, Coburn moved into the schoolhouse. Her furnishings were sparse and simple. A woodstove stood in the middle of the room and rough-hewn desks lined the walls. Moveable log benches filled the centre of the cabin around the stove, while Coburn's bed and personal items occupied one corner of the room. As soon as she had settled into her new home Coburn began a tour of the Queen's Bush to introduce herself and to announce the opening of her school. She estimated that 108 Black families resided in the community, with new settlers arriving daily. Most families lived in crude one-room log shanties without chimneys or windows, lacking the most basic necessities, such as bedding and extra clothing.[53]

As promised, by the end of February, Coburn had commenced classes and offered evening Bible lessons. She also invited community members to use the school as a meeting place. Before long her school-house became an integral part of the community. Coburn also began to acquire a "family" of children. Many were boarders who lived too far away from the schoolhouse to make the daily trip, while others were homeless orphans whom Coburn decided to raise. By 1846 she had seven children ranging in age from five to twelve living with her.[54]

The Reverend Samuel H. Brown also arrived in the Queen's Bush in February 1844 to accommodate the steadily growing AME congregation. Details of Brown's early life are unknown, but he had been born in Maryland in 1794 and even late in life he spoke with a strong southern accent. In 1828, he became an ordained minister in the AME church. At the 1840 organizational meeting of the AME Upper Canadian Conference, Bishop Morris Brown ordained him as an elder, and thereafter he regularly served in prominent positions within the church. In 1842, while residing in York County, Brown took the British oath of allegiance.[55]

After arriving in the Queen's Bush, the Reverend Samuel H. Brown selected one hundred acres on lot 16, concession 4, in Peel Township, approximately one and a half miles northwest of present-day Yatton. Brown established the Peel Township AME church on his farm, which became a centre of religious and social life for the community's Black residents. On Sundays church members assembled for Brown's religious services and, from his pulpit, he encouraged sobriety, hard work and self-reliance. Prominent men in the congregation served as trustees and lay ministers, while women organized church functions such as temperance meetings and fundraisers called missionary teas. During the warm summer months, Brown and his congregation hosted revivals and camp meetings that attracted families, both Black and white, from across the region.[56]

The AME church was not the only denomination to consider Canada West as a new opportunity for recruitment. In 1845, the New

England Wesleyan Methodist Conference sent the Reverend J.N. Mars, a Black minister, to Canada West with instructions to labour for the benefit of Black people living there. Mars travelled across the countryside, preaching and lecturing wherever he could find an audience. Wesleyan Methodist Church doctrine proclaimed itself the only true anti-slavery church because it excluded slaveholders from membership, and held the view that only non-slaveholders could achieve salvation and eternal life. The church's message delivered through Mars' enthusiastic sermons attracted many new converts in the Black communities of Norwich, Brantford, Simcoe, the Wilberforce Settlement, the British-American Institute, Chatham, Colchester and Amherstburg. Mars' popularity won the confidence and affection of those living in the Queen's Bush. On September 17, 1845, following a successful camp meeting in the community, Mars and thirty parishioners established the first Wesleyan Methodist church in Peel Township. By the following year, Mars had founded eight churches, established five large circuits ministered by itinerant preachers and had established four schools, as well as numerous temperance societies and Sabbath Schools. Province-wide the Wesleyan Methodist Church had a membership of 228.[57]

Many Wesleyan Methodists who heeded the Mars' call had formerly belonged to AME congregations. As more and more parishioners disassociated themselves from the AME church, many of its ministers felt threatened. The intense competition between the denominations often led to confrontations. Some AME ministers thought that Mars had been sent by devious American slaveholders to cajole former slaves back into slavery. Despite such claims, however, the Wesleyan Methodist church continued to enjoy remarkable success in attracting new members.[58]

During the summer of 1845, the Queen's Bush community experienced a severe drought. Most of the community's crops, especially wheat and potatoes were destroyed and the economic situation of many families further deteriorated. Nevertheless, new settlers continued to drift into the community in search of land, which strained the community's already limited resources. Fidelia Coburn remarked in a letter published in the *Liberty Standard*, that the Black residents of the Queen's Bush were in dire circumstances. Children suffered the most and she lamented that many of her students arrived at school each morning so famished that they greedily seized turnip and potato peelings that she had set aside as feed for her milch cow.[59]

To add to this burden, a land agent also arrived in Peel Township to commence the orderly sale of lots. He gave advice and information about the region, sold lots, collected sale installments or rent on leased lands, and performed inspections and services as directed by the Commissioner of Crown Lands. He explained to potential buyers that lots could be purchased on an installment plan with annual payments at ten percent interest. After ten years the balance of the sale had to be paid in full. Ironically, the improvements the Queen's Bush squatters had made to the land had raised its assessed market value up to the sum of $3.00 to $3.50 an acre. After years of privation and struggle, most families living in the Queen's Bush had achieved only a small measure of success. Most still lived on the edge of economic survival and remained cash poor. Even with an installment plan, few families could afford to purchase their farms. The time had come for the squatters to move on, and many families, Black and white, abandoned their farms.

Those families who chose to stay in the Queen's Bush had to make a down payment of $50 in order to secure title to a lot of one hundred acres. Some farmers, like John Little, who had created a successful farming operation, had the financial means to make the necessary payment. Others offered improvements such as buildings that had been erected, as security in lieu of a down payment. This arrangement could be risky because failure to pay future installments not only would lead to loss of land, but the loss of the value of the improvements, as well. Many found the decision to stay or leave difficult. Those who decided to make the transition from squatter to landholder began filing their claims at the Elora land office in the summer of 1845. The agent recorded the name of each applicant, the date the individual had arrived in the township and the location of the claim. Improvements to the property, such as buildings and the number of cleared acres, were also noted. Records show that most farmers had approximately two to ten acres cleared. Others, such as John Tillman or the Reverend Jacob Dorcey and Josephus Mallot, were more successful listing at least twenty acres under cultivation. All three men and their families lived in neat, log homes instead of the customary shanties.[60]

The year 1845 was also a desperate time for Coburn, who struggled to keep her mission and school operating. Her burden lightened, however, with the arrival of her old friends from the British-American Institute, Reverend Elias E. Kirkland and his wife Fanny. The couple settled near Coburn on the west half of lot 13 on concession 3. The next to arrive was John. S. Brooks, a cobbler from Duxbury, Massachusetts. Brooks' early background remains obscure, although it is known that he was the son of Mary W. Brooks, who lived in South Groton, Massachusetts, in 1850. Brooks had received a good education, had a strong social conscience and, although he was not an ordained minister, he had a keen interest in the ministry. Brooks had left his Massachusetts home early in the summer to conduct his own investigation into the condition of fugitive slaves living in Canada West. He decided to settle in the Queen's Bush where the Black population by that time had almost tripled to approximately three hundred families.[61] Brooks believed that in the rapidly growing Queen's Bush he "could effect the greatest good, to the greatest number."[62]

In a letter published in the May 30, 1846, *True Wesleyan*, Brooks described his initial impression of the community. He believed the condition of the inhabitants was:

> truly lamentable. Destitute of an education, their religious impressions are very incorrect, their raiment

often not sufficient to screen them from the cold, penetrating frosts of Canada, and at times lacking daily bread. The scarcity of provisions at the present times is owing in fact to the rush of new settlers coming in destitute, but more to the failure of crops by drought, last season, especially the potatoe crop.[63]

On February 3, 1846, Brooks opened the Mount Hope Mission School, approximately four miles from the Mount Pleasant Mission, on four acres of land located on the southwest corner of lot 19, concession 1.[64] Samuel White, a fugitive slave from Maryland, provided the land on a long-term loan with the stipulation that if the school ever closed the property would be returned to him. One visitor to the Queen's Bush was amazed at the size and neatness of the school and described it as "a noble school-house, which is fit for a church, or a large dwelling."[65] On opening day sixteen children arrived at Mount Hope for classes, and enrollment quickly increased to fifty-four children, with an average daily attendance of thirty-seven.[66] According to Fidelia Coburn, Brooks had an excellent relationship with his students. She noted that he had "the best tact for giving instruction to children, mental, moral or religious, of any person that I ever saw."[67] Brooks also gained the confidence of the adults living in the community. Reverend J.N. Mars praised Brooks' missionary efforts in the community and declared that he was "well liked in the Bush by all that knew him."[68]

In the fall of 1846 the teachers were encouraged by the arrival of the Reverend Melville Denslow, who had been appointed foreign missionary to Canada's Black population by the St. Lawrence Conference of the Wesleyan Methodist church in New York. Denslow had previously taught in a Black school at Norwich in Oxford County, just east of London, that had been established by the Reverend J.N. Mars. Despite the lack of textbooks and adequate facilities, attendance at his school was high. Eventually, Denslow became convinced that his services were more urgently needed in the Queen's Bush and he left Norwich at the end of the summer school term.[69]

Denslow joined John S. Brooks at Mount Hope and the two men quickly became friends. The teachers boarded with local families and later constructed a loft in the schoolhouse where, under the steeply pitched roof, they shared their meals and stored their few meager possessions. Along with their teaching duties, Brooks and Denslow also organized the first temperance society in the community. While there is no indication that alcoholism was a problem in the Queen's Bush, the establishment of the society does suggest that alcohol consumption may have been a common facet of everyday life. Frontier taverns and dances were notorious for their free-flowing liquor and drunken brawls. A drink of whisky was often part of a labourer's daily pay and it was even customary for local merchants to conclude a business transaction with a drink. Typically, temperance societies held regular meetings to discuss the evils of drinking. They also offered an opportunity for individuals to pledge their abstinence and provide support to one another. Members of the Queen's Bush Temperance society also organized so-called "cold water" picnics to supplement their meetings and attract new members.[70]

Like Brooks, Denslow was also moved by the dire straits of the Blacks living in the Queen's Bush. He reported that:

> The colored people settled here in a body, number about two thousand, and are scattered over a tract of land eight miles broad by twelve long. They are truly ignorant, degraded, debased, and poor people, and are worthy of the sympathies and untiring efforts of every philanthropic heart. Many of them are late from the South, where the early part of their lives have been spent in the vilest subserviency to the will of their inhuman masters – and though now free, they are in a measure unaccustomed to the habits

and enterprise of northern men. They come in, settle in the woods, and commence an opening, and if they manage to get through the winter, spring finds them subsisting on leeks, cow-cabbage, and wild vegetation gathered in the woods. There is a great destitution of clothing among these new settlers. Some of the children are naked – others with a shirt or pair of pantaloons, may be frequently seen. Bedding is very scarce, but the free use of wood serves in a measure as a substitute.[71]

The missionaries' letters and reports published in the anti-slavery press contain little on their methods of teaching, but most likely their one-room schoolhouses operated in the same manner as the schools they had attended in their New England towns. Typically, the school year consisted of two terms, June to August and November to March. Planting and harvest seasons were especially disruptive to school attendance, so school terms were scheduled around the agricultural season. Classes included subjects common in most public schools such as, spelling, reading, writing, arithmetic, geography and philosophy. Education was their primary goal, but the missionaries also hoped to mold their students into their idea of moral, industrious, middle-class citizens. The missionaries believed that slavery had fostered a degree of sinfulness among its victims, so they placed considerable emphasis on evangelical Protestantism's values of hard work, self-reliance, temperance and moral improvement. Each school day opened with prayers, and the children frequently used the Bible as a reading text. The missionaries influence was not restricted to just the classroom. Sundays were spent conducting Sabbath Schools for the children. Brooks once proudly noted that one of his students, an eleven-year-old girl, could recite five hundred verses from the Bible from memory. Along with memorizing Bible verses, the children were taught about the evils of drinking and gambling.

Relief assistance to needy families was intertwined with their educational and religious objectives.[72]

Without any consistent source of funding the missionaries often had to use their own resources to operate their schools. Frequently they lived on the verge of economic collapse. Moreover, like the other Queen's Bush inhabitants, the missionaries had settled illegally as squatters and laboured to make a living off the land. Between his arrival and May 1846, the Reverend Elias E. Kirkland received only six dollars in donations. To supplement their income Kirkland cultivated crops, Coburn sewed clothing, while Brooks made shoes. The results of their labour they exchanged for food and other material goods. However, during her initial months in the community, Coburn's meager diet consisted primarily of boiled peas, oatmeal and corn meal. She even gave most of her dresses to other women who were in need of warm clothing.[73]

Coburn's letters to friends and family in Maine, as well as her appeals for donations published in the *Liberty Standard* and the *True Wesleyan*, began to show results. Her reports attracted the attention of American philanthropists and female anti-slavery sewing societies, which made regular contributions. In September 1846, the Dover Ladies Anti-slavery Society Sewing Circle in Dover, New Hampshire, began corresponding with Coburn, an act that led to several donations. The following year the Anti-slavery Sewing Society of Oxford, Massachusetts, sent a box of clothing, shoes, boots and textbooks valued at one hundred dollars. Individuals, who lived in the vicinity of Coburn's hometown of Bloomfield, contributed generously to her missionary efforts. The Bloomfield Baptist Female Education Society made frequent contributions and delegates at a religious convention held in Hallowell, Maine, appointed a committee, with William R. Prescott as the treasurer, to collect and forward donations to the Mount Pleasant Mission. The editor of the Hallowell *Liberty Standard* regularly published articles about "Miss Coburn's Canada Mission" and the efforts of the committee. Nevertheless, donations were always unpredictable and never sufficient to fully support the mission. In an attempt to alleviate the problem, Coburn intensified her campaign and encouraged philanthropists to sponsor a child at a cost of ten dollars per year, plus clothing. However, despite her pleas, there is no evidence that any of Coburn's students received personal funding.[74]

Another early American organization that provided aid to the missionaries was the Wesleyan Methodist Missionary Society. During its first year of operation the Wesleyan Methodist Missionary Society raised $125 for fugitive slaves in Canada West, of which John S. Brooks received $15. On December 31, 1846, at the Society's first annual meeting held in Lowell, Massachusetts, fifty pledges of $1 each were raised to construct a new schoolhouse for Brooks.[75]

There is no indication that Canadian organizations contributed to the operation of the Queen's Bush missions. While most Canadians opposed slavery, there was no strong anti-slavery movement in Canada West in the 1840s. Most believed slavery was an American issue in which Canadians had no right to interfere. The Upper Canadian Anti-slavery Society had been formed on January 4, 1837, in Toronto, but by the end of the year it had dissolved. During the winter months of 1845-46, several meetings were held once again in Toronto, which led to the formation of another anti-slavery society, but this attempt, too, soon failed. Despite the overall indifference to the anti-slavery movement, there were many individuals who took an interest in Coburn's work. One of those, the Reverend John Roaf,[76] of the Zion Congregational Church in Toronto and agent for the Colonial Missionary Society, assisted Coburn for many years. He frequently made arrangements to have donations that arrived in Toronto forwarded to her mission.[77]

Although Coburn and the other Queen's Bush missionaries struggled financially, the Mount Pleasant and Mount Hope Missions were probably economically more stable than other missions in the province. In large part this was the result of an inheritance that

Coburn received from her father's estate after his death in January 1845. His will bequeathed $2,000 to Coburn, which she received in small annual installments. The money provided a secure, but limited means of economic support for Coburn and her missions. She used the first installment of her inheritance to enlarge her home and construct a new schoolhouse, which continued to serve as a church and meeting place for the community.[78] Moreover, the fact that Coburn was one of only a very few female missionaries in the province made her well known and her reputation virtually guaranteed her financial support. Respected by her co-workers and by members of the Black community, she was frequently described as self-denying, heroic and courageous; and often received praise from prominent American abolitionists. William P. Newman,[79] a Black Baptist minister from Ohio and a leading social activist, had little regard for the missionaries or the begging system but, in a letter to Frederick Douglass, he stated that "there is not a more worthy missionary in the world than Sister [Coburn], and but few who are useful and whose present prospects for doing good are so fair as hers."[80] When American abolitionist James G. Birney asked Silas M. Holmes, Secretary of the Detroit Liberty Association, to which Canadian missionary he should send donations, the response was that all were worthy of support but "if there is any choice between them, I think Miss Coburn and Mr. Rice [Reverend Isaac Rice at Amherstburg] should command our first aid."[81]

Alvan Stewart, president of the New York State Anti-slavery Society, was another supporter of Coburn's work. In 1846, he wrote to John Scoble, secretary-treasurer of the British and Foreign Anti-slavery Society, with the suggestion that an international society be formed to support Coburn's mission. More importantly, he proposed that if such a society could be organized its first priority should be the purchase of a tract of land for the community's Black settlers.[82] The plan never materialized.

Despite Coburn's notoriety, donations remained unpredictable and there were never enough shoes, coats, or dresses to alleviate the suffering of all the needy families. On one occasion she wrote to a benefactor, "I distributed last year four different parcels, but you would find no one nearby, that would say that they received any thing of any amount."[83] Inadequate clothing had a profound effect on the children in the community. Many children went barefoot or were thinly clad with inadequate clothing. During one particularly cold winter, Coburn temporarily closed her school because most of her students lacked warm clothes. Some children, especially younger ones, wore a shirt-like garment; similar to the one-size fits all shirts worn by enslaved children in the southern states. Embarrassed by their inability to clothe their children sufficiently, many parents frequently refused to send their children to school. To encourage regular attendance, Coburn gave these children priority when donations of clothing arrived at the missions.[84]

Amidst these varied obstacles, the missionaries struggled to carry on their missionary work in the Queen's Bush. In spite of all the hardships, they remained dedicated to their work and were determined to provide an education to the community's children. Coburn aptly summed up the feelings of the missionaries in one of her letters stating that, "many are the trials we have to encounter and were it not for the prosperity of our schools we should sink."[85] Despite all hardships, the schools did prosper and during the 1845-46 school year the two schools had their highest enrollment with a total of 225 students.[86]

CHAPTER 3

"It is times here now that tries men's souls"[1]

DESPITE THEIR BEST INTENTIONS, the efforts of the missionaries were not always received with open arms. Melville Denslow discovered that one of the hardest obstacles to overcome was the anti-white sentiment prevalent in most Black communities. With the brutality of slavery still fresh in their minds, many Blacks were suspicious of whites. Denslow explained to an American abolitionist that:

> The fact of being an Abolitionist, and coming here
> to teach among the colored people, will not give you
> favor in their eyes, because they have been abused
> from their youth up, and there is a natural jealousy
> existing against white men.[2]

Black minister, Reverend J.N. Mars, also admitted to Luther Lee, editor of the *True Wesleyan* that one of his greatest challenges was to:

> get all of their prejudice subdued that they have got
> planted against the white man. I think that prejudice
> is one of the greatest evils that we have to contend

with in this field of labor; yet at many times it seems
to be all forgotten, but the least thing brings it all up
again, and I fully believe that nothing but the grace
of God will ever remove it entirely from the heart.[3]

The missionaries were, in part, to blame for much of the anti-
white sentiment. Their paternalist and condescending attitudes were
frequently criticized by many Blacks, who were more interested in
maintaining control over their own lives. Despite such opposition,
the missionaries continued to view themselves as the guardians of
the community, often contributing much to the conflicts.

Cultural and religious differences also added to the tension
between the two groups. The missionaries were used to well-edu-
cated New England ministers who could read and expound on the
Bible, as well as other religious texts. The missionaries stressed self-
discipline and a quiet, reflective worship, and never fully appreciated
the emotional enthusiasm that Blacks felt for their own style of religion. Most Black ministers were ex-slaves and illiterate, or at best
semi-literate, and many missionaries held them in contempt for their
lack of formal religious training. They believed that most Black ministers were unsuitable religious leaders and only perpetuated superstitions acquired during slavery. John S. Brooks sent a copy of the
AME Canadian Conference proceedings to a New York philanthropist, in which he stated that his reason for enclosing the minutes was
to demonstrate the necessity of educating the Black population. His
disdain for the church leadership is obvious when he stated that:

> The individual who composed the greater amount
> of the matter contained in these minutes is and has
> been for years one of the leading members of his
> church. The Bishop is only his superior in point of
> talent and learning.
>   If their religious teachers are so ignorant what

must we necessarily conclude the condition of the
laiety (sic) to be?[4]

The missionaries were convinced that if given a chance to preach
in the Black churches they could change the ways of worship. In the
end, attempts to make Blacks conform to white standards proved
futile because most congregations simply refused to invite missionaries or white ministers into their churches. Denied access to Black
congregations, the missionaries focused their efforts on the school
children under their care. Fidelia Coburn realized that she and the
other Queen's Bush missionaries could not change the religious practices of local adults, but she never doubted her ability to accomplish
this in her students. Coburn remarked to one of her supporters that:

> The people here make their religion in outward per-
> formances and noise and we desire to bring about a
> change of habit with the children. We could not say
> a word but would set them all on fire.... We thought
> by introducing still worship it might have an
> impression and useful affect on the minds of the
> youth – endeavoring to impress their youthful
> minds with a sense of the presence of God and real
> religious heart.[5]

In frustration the missionaries claimed that Black ministers, especially those associated with the AME church, were sectarian and fostered anti-white prejudice in their congregations. Angered by the
accusations and domineering attitudes of the missionaries, Bishop
William Paul Quinn[6] and fifteen ministers addressed the issue at the
annual meeting of the AME Canadian Conference held in the
Queen's Bush on July 31, 1846. The delegates noted that the AME
church had been established because of white racism in the
Methodist Episcopal church, but it welcomed anyone regardless of

William Paul Quinn,
whose birthplace was
India, became a Bishop
in AME Church.
Taken from *A History of the*
African Methodist Episcopal
Church.

race. Nevertheless, the delegates agreed that AME ministers had the right to deny anyone access to their pulpits, especially whites who were only interested in changing the methods of worship or assuming authority over church members. The delegates also accused missionaries of misappropriating donations and declared that they were to be viewed as enemies of the fugitive slaves.[7]

Wildly exaggerated rumours about the amount of donations coming into Canada frequently circulated throughout the province, which aggravated the tensions. The charges stemmed mostly from the way in which donations were sent to Canada. While benevolent societies usually paid the shipping fees to Canada, it frequently was not enough. Moreover, they did not supply additional money for custom and storage fees or transportation costs from the border to individual communities. The missionaries seldom had the money to pay all the fees and, consequently, resorted to selling some of the donated clothing to raise the necessary money. Shipments of clothing destined for the Queen's Bush were frequently sent to Brown &

Company warehouses at the city wharf in Hamilton. As the roads into the Queen's Bush remained impassable during most of the year, the company regularly stored the barrels and boxes of clothing until freight companies could transport them to the community. By the time Coburn and the other missionaries received the donations, the storage fees alone could amount to four or five dollars. With no other option, the Queen's Bush missionaries often sold some of the clothing items to pay for the accumulated charges. As a result, many residents accused the missionaries of stealing the proceeds for their own use. In 1846, a rumour began to circulate that American philanthropists had donated $15,000 to the community's Black families to assist them with their land payments. Although the rumour proved to be unfounded, community members nevertheless, openly accused the missionaries of theft.[8]

To attract funding, missionaries frequently portrayed fugitive slaves as ignorant, degraded, helpless and objects of pity who required immediate aid. Although the intent of such reports were well-meaning, to many they appeared racist and paternalistic. American abolitionists, who toured Canada West to report on the condition of fugitive slaves for the anti-slavery press, also frequently published less than flattering descriptions. For instance, Fidelia Coburn acknowledged that S. Roys' published report about his visit to the Queen's Bush "made a great fuss here – & it was a sad misrepresentation of us & the people, for lack of knowledge & so it is with most of our transient visitors."[9] Knowing that her letters to the anti-slavery press might be published, Coburn hesitated to give negative impressions of the Black community. She explained to one benefactor that, "our views of them and their views differ very much – they think they are very wise and we think them ignorant – visa versa in every respect."[10]

While the various points of contention threatened community cohesiveness, another threat came from the rapid development in the area around the Queen's Bush. The availability of cheap, bountiful land attracted a steady influx of immigrants into Wellington and

Waterloo counties. Unlike the earlier squatters, most of the new settlers arrived with capital, agricultural equipment and livestock to
begin their farming operations. This wave of immigrants included
small-scale manufacturers and tradesmen who drastically changed
life in the community. Among these new arrivals was John Hawke, a
native of Scotland, who, in 1846, constructed a gristmill on the
Conestogo River in Wellesley Township. The mill was a welcome
relief to the farmers who previously had to haul their threshed grain
outside of the community. Shortly thereafter, Hawke's brother,
Gabriel, established a general merchandise store near the mill and
the hamlet of Hawksville quickly grew around these two enterprises.
Another early Hawksville merchant was Michael Peter Empey. Both
of these families developed associations with the Black community
by employing a number of its men.[11]

A constant stream of Black settlers also arrived in the area in the
late 1840s. These immigrants were attracted to the well-established
Black community and the belief that land in the Queen's Bush
remained affordable for even the poorest settler. One notable group
arrived in 1846 from Brantford. Reportedly, white residents had
forced them out of town because of their drunken brawls and disor-
derly conduct.[12]

In August 1846, the Peel Township Wesleyan Methodist congregation held a camp meeting in the community. Typically, camp
meetings were held outdoors and could last for several days often
well into the night with attendees sleeping in tents or wagons. From
a raised wooden platform in a shady grove of trees, the Reverend J.N.
Mars and the Reverend Elias E. Kirkland delivered emotional sermons
to an interracial audience that represented several different denominations. The Reverend Mars later remarked that, "the scared fire went
through the encampment, and there was a groaning after the perfect
love of God among the preachers and people." John S. Brooks was
among those who experienced a profound religious experience and
he joined the Wesleyan Methodist church.[13]

While the camp meeting may have inspired temporary feelings of brotherly love, the Reverend Elias E. Kirkland's relationship with local Black ministers deteriorated. Disheartened by their on-going accusations of theft and mismanagement, Kirkland and his family left Peel Township during the winter of 1846-47, and moved to New York. As spring approached, Coburn also contemplated leaving the community, but she was hesitant because by now the population of the Queen's Bush had reached 2,500, of which 1,500 were Blacks.[14] Coburn disliked the idea of abandoning her school and relief work at a time when so many families needed her services. Nevertheless, she had become frustrated with the Black community's reaction to her efforts and believed that many individuals were unnecessarily hostile. In a letter to the newly organized New York-based, American Missionary Association (AMA) Coburn lamented:

> some of them here give us much abuse (with the tongue I mean & with threats, tho we fear not) because we cannot feed & clothe them. Thinking it might do them to get the idea that we were agoing to leave, when interrogated we would say we did not know or we could stand it – we did not know but we should go.[15]

Rumours of Coburn's possible departure alarmed many parents whose children were enrolled in her school. On March 27, 1847, concerned parents assembled for a public meeting to discuss the welfare of their community and the education of their children. Wesleyan Methodist minister, the Reverend Dorsey Ambush, opened the meeting with a prayer. Born as a slave in 1814, Ambush had lived in Washington, D.C., before moving to Canada West.[16] An influential minister, Ambush had obviously been able to negotiate a positive relationship with his congregation and the missionaries. He had especially gained Coburn's respect for she described him as a:

> [p]ious man, Intelligent circuit preacher, good
> preacher, great imaginative powers. Is a sort of
> physician for a living. Unpretending. A single man at
> present. His circuit is extensive. He has great
> influence among the colored people. Is judicious.
> No tale bearer. The people under his influence behave
> well.[17]

The parents then chose Peter Edward Susand as president of the meeting. Born in 1803, Susand had lived as a slave in New Orleans. By 1837 he had escaped and lived in Oakville, Upper Canada, with his wife, Elizabeth Liticott, a native of England, and their three young children. Six years later the Susands were farming in Wellesley Township on lot 1, concession 12. Dennis Jackson, who had lived in Peel Township since 1843, served as vice-president of the meeting. James F. Elliott and Z. Dunbar Talbot acted as secretaries. Talbot remains an elusive figure, but Elliott had arrived in Peel Township in February 1844 and had settled on lot 9, concession 3. Elliott and Talbot were likely chosen secretaries of the meeting because of their writing ability.[18]

After electing officers for the meeting, the assemblage then began a discussion of the community's relationship with Fidelia Coburn and the other missionaries. Peter E. Susand delivered a prosaic speech before the large crowd, in which he used biblical imagery to encourage community support for the missionaries. He compared them to the biblical hero, Moses, who had delivered his people from slavery into the Promised Land. Susand described Canada as the Promised Land for fugitive slaves and declared that, "Moses is still with us in the form of teachers, who are instructing our children."[19] Susand concluded with a stirring demand to the assemblage to:

> Let us cherish the means of education, and thus
> show our friends that we are not unthankful for the
> benefits received. There is no lion in our midst to

claim his own rights and then usurp ours, but our rights are secured by law, and when we meet our fellows, we meet them as men. Again I say let us sustain the schools until we can build seminaries and establish schools of our own. If we were in the South we should not be permitted to meet as we do now. We could not even hold in our hands the papers now before me. We love our children. We love those who are striving to elevate them to the condition of sentient beings, and fit them for stations of usefulness.[20]

Z. Dunbar Talbot rose next, and addressed the meeting with an equally powerful speech in which he stated:

For generations past, the colored race has been controlled by the arbitary will of others. The arts and sciences have been advancing to perfection, but not by means of the cultivated intellect of the colored man. As a distinct part of mankind we have been retrograding, or at least stationary; not because we are incapable of advancement, for some of the greatest men the world ever saw have been colored men, and even at the present day we may boast of a few 'giant minds,' but as a people we have been deprived of the means of improvement, and of advancing with the age. At the present time a brighter era is dawning upon us. Public opinion is being aroused to give us our rights, and let us rejoice. The way is now opening, and means are provided for the education of our children, and the improvement of our race.[21]

After Talbot's speech, the assemblage adopted the following resolutions in support of the missionaries:

Whereas, we deem it a duty to express our views regarding ourselves, the education of our children, and also the Mighty Hand that led us from the power of relentless tyrants in the United States, to a land where our social, civil, and religious rights, are secured by law – and where we receive the treatment due to freemen, from a nation acknowledging liberty to be the birthright of the human family regardless of color and condition. And whereas we now have the means of mental culture and enjoy the blessings of the gospel unadulterated with the influences of slavery, therefore [be it]

Resolved, That we entertain sentiments of the profoundest gratitude to Almighty God our Heavenly Father, who, when we were laboring incessantly for unpaid wages and subject to the will of our task-masters, provided a way for our escape and led us through many dangers to the land of freedom.

Resolved, That we have witnessed the philanthropic labors of the several teachers now in our midst, to benefit us and our children; we cordially approve of them and we pledge our united sympathies, prayers and protection, to sustain them in their work and labors of love.

Resolved, That we entertain the deepest sense of obligation towards those of a different origin, who generously came to the aid of our suffering race.

Resolved, That from the efforts of the teachers we realize a four-fold blessing in the physical, intellectual, moral and religious training of the one hundred and ninety children under their care.

Resolved, That we hail with emotions of gratitude, the friends of suffering humanity, from whom we have received donations, and we announce to them our sincere thanks for their benevolent efforts in behalf of the sons and daughters of oppression.

Resolved, That our prayers shall ever ascend the Mount of God in behalf of those, who sympathise with us in our condition, and also for those who are still groaning under American despotism.

Resolved, that we hate the 'men-stealing, women-whipping, cradle-plundering religion of the South,' where the man who wields the blood-clothed cow-skin also fills the pulpit and claims to be a minister of the meek and lowly Jesus – he who sells our sisters for purposes of prostitution, and stands forth as the pious advocate of purity. The man who advocates the sanctity of the family relation, sunders the tie that binds husband and wife, consigns them to different parts of the country, never to be united in this world. The church and slave prison stand side by side. Jesus Christ in the person of slaves are sold to educate ministers; all for the glory of God and the good of souls. The slave-dealer gives his blood-stained gold to support the pulpit; and the pulpit in return covers his infernal business with the garb of Christianity.

Resolved, That we tender our thanks to the proprietors of the under-ground railroad, who gave us a

free passage from slavery to liberty; and that we hold
sacred in memory the name of Charles T. Torrey,
who aided many of us in our escape from bondage.

Resolved, That we hail the efforts of the Liberty
Party as an omen of good to our race, and when its
principles are carried into practice as productive of
the greatest good to the greatest number, and is the
only sure foundation of national prosperity.

Resolved, That these proceedings be published in
the Liberty Press; and other friendly papers.[22]

After the meeting adjourned, Susand and the other officers presented
the resolutions to the missionaries as a good will gesture and hoped
that they would resolve some, if not all, of the ill-feelings within the
community.

The resolutions convinced Coburn to remain in the Queen's Bush
but, in the early months of 1847, the Reverend Melville Denslow
returned to the United States. The reason for his departure remains
obscure, but correspondence from Coburn implies that Denslow's
association with the Reverend W.H. Houck had damaged his reputation to the extent that he could not find a permanent ministerial
position. Houck was a Wesleyan Methodist minister and initially
associated with the St. Lawrence Conference. He withdrew from the
church in August 1848 after charges of immoral conduct were brought
against him.[23]

With the departure of Kirkland and Denslow, Coburn and Brooks
struggled to manage the Mount Pleasant and Mount Hope schools
alone. Enrollment at the two places remained high and the combined
average daily attendance was 180 students. Even Brooks' weekly
Sabbath School attracted approximately eighty children. However,
Coburn found the responsibility of operating the Mount Pleasant

School, acting as a relief worker, as well as caring for the children under her care, exhausting. Throughout the summer and fall of 1847 she frequently complained of fatigue and sickness.[24]

Meanwhile many of the community's residents faced the challenge of having to purchase their farms. Income earned from each year's harvests determined each family's ability or inability to pay the annual installments. Farmers produced good yields of potatoes and turnips in 1847, but the yield of wheat, the predominant cash crop, remained below average for the next several years. Without this surplus cash few farmers possessed the means to pay the annual installment. Moreover, local Crown Land agents unscrupulously harassed Black squatters, especially those who were illiterate or who had little business experience. Land agents deliberately misled many individuals about the terms of payments and threatened them with eviction. Many families were so intimidated that they fled the community or sold their farms, often at below market prices.[25]

Ex-slave John Francis, described the scare tactics of the local land agents in the following manner:

> Then came a land agent, to sell and take payments. He put up public notices that the settlers who had made improvements were to come and pay the first installments, or the land would be sold from under them. The payment was to be in ten annual install- ments of 15s. 6d currency, 5s. to the dollar. It was then hard times in Canada, and many could not meet the payment. The agent, as we now know, tran- scended his powers, for some people, white and col- ored, still hold their lands, not having made payments. The agent had a percentage for collecting. His course in driving people for money, ruined a great many poor people here in the bush. Fearing that the land would be sold, and they get nothing for

their betterments, they sold out for very little and
removed to other parts. The agent himself told me
he would sell my land unless the installment was
paid. I sold my two cows and a steer, to make the
payment that I might hold the land. Others did not
do that and yet hold. One man, fearing to lose all he
had done, sold out for ten dollars, having cleared
eight or ten acres – that property is now estimated at
$15,000. Some borrowed money on mortgages, and
some paid a heavy per cent, for money to meet that
installment: which was very hard on the poor settlers who had their hands full in trying to live, and
clearing the land so that they could live. But it was
done: and it has kept many back by trying to meet
that borrowed money, and others by their moving
where they would have to begin again.[26]

Fidelia Coburn believed that the land agents had different standards for whites who defaulted on their payments. Coburn herself
had delayed paying her annual installment because Mount Pleasant's
operating costs and loans to impoverished families had depleted her
financial reserves. Nevertheless, being white she never felt threatened
that she would be evicted from her home.[27]

Many new arrivals felt that appropriating an already improved
farm was a temptation too hard to resist, and often threatened and
intimidated illiterate Black farmers. Reverend J.N. Mars lamented to
Luther Lee, editor of the *True Wesleyan*, that:

There has been some excitement in the Bush about
the land, some people here can't bear the thought
that the poor fugitive should be a man. They have
pitched their tents on the best land there is in
Canada, and many would be glad to drive them

away. Oh! where will the poor colored man find a
quiet resting place? Not this side of heaven.[28]

The large tracts of seemingly empty land on which early squatters
had been able to settle, had by now virtually all disappeared. Unable
to realize their dreams of landownership, the only recourse for the
cash-poor squatters was to sell out and move on in search of more
promising prospects. Unable to provide loans to everyone, the frustrated missionaries could only offer advice on how to legitimize land
claims and conduct business transactions. They tried to intervene
whenever whites attempted to coerce or frighten families out of the
community, but theirs proved to be a losing battle.

In 1847, ninety-one people, many whose names appear on the 1843
petition, drafted another petition to the Earl of Elgin, Governor-
General of Canada, in an attempt to save their investments. Whereas
the previous petitioners had merely requested government assistance
because they were poverty-stricken, this group claimed their right to
the land by virtue of the contributions they had made to their
adopted homeland. They reminded government officials that as loyal
subjects of Queen Victoria, they had fought in the Patriots War and
were willing to defend their homeland again if necessary. They also
insisted that their labour and sacrifices to develop the Clergy Reserve
had contributed to its transformation from an untamed wilderness
to a productive agricultural region.[29]

In a show of solidarity, Hamilton's Black community, under the
leadership of Paola Brown, Moses Crump and Peter Price, rallied
together and presented their own petition to Lord Elgin, Governor
General of Canada. The petitioners strongly objected to the situation
in the Queen's Bush and appealed to the Governor General to thor-
oughly investigate what they perceived as a violation of property
rights. Mark Kerr, Lord Elgin's aide, acknowledged receipt of the
petition and, on behalf of the Governor General, assured the petitioners that the British Constitution made no distinction between

whites and Blacks. More importantly, he promised to investigate the situation in the Queen's Bush.[30] However, government officials never offered any assistance to the Queen's Bush community.

The battle for the right to remain on the land does not appear to have led to any acts of violence, but tensions were certainly high by 1847 when Andrew Geddes, the Elora Land Agent, reported to the Commissioner of Crown Lands in Montreal, that the squatters were holding steadfast to their claims. He noted that new settlers, who tried to legally purchase land in the township had received numerous threats from the squatters. Geddes suggested that, "some pretty sharp measures must be held out in order to deter these unruly squatters."[31] It is not apparent from the document if the reference is to Black or white squatters, or both. Given that both whites and Blacks illegally occupied the land and had sent petitions to the Governor General, it seems reasonable to assume that both may have threatened violence.

The prominence of the Queen's Bush in the late 1840s as a major Black community was further substantiated when AME church officials again chose the AME church in the Township of Peel as the site for their annual meeting in 1847. The meeting, held in July, became particularly noteworthy because of the controversy created by four ministers, who were charged with rebellion. Peel Township ministers, Jacob Dorcey and Peter Curtis, who had received his license to preach in 1844, were among the group. The two men had resigned from the AME church without relinquishing their licenses and had joined the Wesleyan Methodist church. Dorcey had become the minister of the Waterloo Wesleyan Methodist church, while Curtis received an appointment to the Wellington station. The question as to how these militant ministers were to be dealt with occupied most of the conference proceedings, although the delegates found enough time to hold a revival.[32]

Just as the AME revival commenced, the Reverend J.R. Spoor, a Wesleyan Methodist minister from Williamson, Wayne County, New York, arrived in Peel Township. After learning about the Queen's

Bush, Spoor had collected four boxes of clothing and, to ensure their safe arrival, he personally delivered them to the community. In return for his generosity, the ministers invited Spoor to participate in the revival. After his return to New York, Spoor enthusiastically described his visit to the Queen's Bush in a detailed letter to the editor of the *True Wesleyan*. He reported that the majority of the Queen's Bush inhabitants were living under favourable conditions, but he noted that a number of families were still dependent on aid for survival. According to Spoor, children suffered the most because many parents were unable to properly feed or clothe them. Moreover, Spoor pointed out that some families refused to send their children to school because they lacked suitable clothing. To alter the problem, Spoor suggested that donations to the community should be aimed foremost at alleviating the needs of the children.[33]

White abolitionists were not the only ones interested in the social and economic conditions of the Black population in Canada West. American and Canadian Black leaders were similarly concerned and organized numerous meetings to discuss the topic. In August 1847, in Drummondsville, Canada West, delegates representing Blacks from across the province held a four-day convention "to take into consideration the best modes of improving the condition of the colored population in their moral, religious, and social relations."[34] The delegates adopted resolutions supporting education, but vehemently denounced the begging system. The delegates in particular attacked the begging schemes of the British-American Institute and accused Josiah Henson of mismanagement. In contrast, representatives of the Queen's Bush believed that living conditions in their community were favourable and they praised the efforts of Fidelia Coburn and John S. Brooks. They attributed the educational advancements of the community's children to the curriculum offered by the teachers at the Mount Hope and Mount Pleasant schools.[35]

Such conventions increasingly drew attention to Canada's growing Black population, prompting the American Missionary Association

Lewis Tappan of the American Missionary Association.
Used by permission, State Historical Society of Missouri, Columbia.

to expand its missionary operations into Canada West. The AMA had been established in New York City on September 3, 1846, following the unification of the Committee for West Indian Missions, the Union Missionary Society and the Western Evangelical Missionary Association. It was an independent, inter-denominational and non-ecclesiastical organization committed to anti-slavery and missionary work in the United States, as well as in foreign countries. The association's leadership and supporters included brothers Arthur[36] and Lewis Tappan,[37] Joshua Leavitt,[38] Simeon S. Jocelyn, Gerrit Smith,[39] and George Whipple,[40] all of whom were staunchly opposed to slavery. Arthur Tappan served as chairman of the AMA's executive committee from 1846 to 1857, while Lewis served as treasurer for eighteen years. A shrewd businessman, Lewis became the most influential officer in the organization and his opinions carried considerable weight in determining policies. Whipple served as the AMA's corresponding secretary and was also responsible for publishing the organization's monthly journal, *American Missionary*. As corresponding secretary,

Whipple had the most contact with the missionaries in Canada West and regularly published their letters in the *American Missionary*.[41]

AMA officials were reluctant to assume full responsibility for the fugitive slaves missions in Canada West, but they did agree to forward donations of money and clothing designated specifically for the "Canada Missions." Fidelia Coburn and the Reverend Isaac J. Rice were the first to receive this assistance. Rice, a Presbyterian minister from Trumbull County, Ohio, had been operating a fugitive slave mission in Amherstburg since 1838.[42] In return for their financial support, Coburn began a regular correspondence with AMA executives that lasted until 1849. Her letters described life in the Queen's Bush with frequent references to the schools; the achievements of the missionaries; as well as their frustrations and state of health. Over the ensuing years, a close relationship developed between AMA officials and the missionaries, who came to depend on the regular correspondence for guidance, support and even advice in very personal matters. If letters were irregular it was not uncommon for the missionaries to comment on the infrequency. In one of her first letters to the AMA, Coburn requested that any amount of money that had been designated for the Canada Missions be forwarded to her as soon as possible. Obviously in desperate financial straits, she stated "however small the amount, you will infer a great favor by forwarding it immidiatly [sic]."[43]

Cash donations, however, frequently caused problems because a variety of currencies were used throughout the province including American, French, Spanish and British coins. According to Coburn, many local merchants would not accept American currency, so she frequently had to exchange the money at banks in Toronto. After paying her travelling and lodging expenses, Coburn often lamented that very little money was actually left over to benefit her schools.[44]

In the fall of 1847, the Reverend Elias E. Kirkland and his family returned to the Queen's Bush. Kirkland had obviously been notified of the community's enthusiastic endorsement of the missionaries at the March public meeting and of the AMA's promise to forward donations earmarked for the Canada Missions. Moreover, Kirkland had been able to arrange his own financial funding from the New England Wesleyan Methodist Conference. Theodosia Lyon, a thirty-seven-year-old single teacher from Vermont, accompanied the Kirkland family to the Queen's Bush and agreed to teach at the Mount Pleasant School.[45]

On October 6, 1847, the Primitive Methodist minister, the Reverend Matthew Nichols, married Fidelia Coburn and John S. Brooks, with Charles R. Knox and James B. Knox acting as witnesses.[46] There is no indication of a long, romantic courtship between Brooks and Coburn. In their letters to the AMA there are only brief hints about their relationship. Instead, the marriage appears to have developed out of their partnership and devotion to furthering their missionary endeavours. In her October 14 letter to Lewis Tappan announcing her marriage, Fidelia Coburn Brooks stated that:

> The reason of his [Brooks] coming to labor with me
> [is] because it was so difficult to get a suitable person
> – one that was calculated for the family [children
> who boarded with her] and all the other depart-
> ments and from two years acquaintance I was
> satisfied that he would do better than [any] other
> person. The children in the family were very fond of
> him and he is very fond of children. When Brother
> Young[47] was here he and Brother Wilson adviced us
> to marry – they thought we might be more useful. In
> considering the subject we decided it was the best.[48]

According to Hiram Wilson, Coburn had endured threats and intimidation from many residents because they objected to the impropriety of a single woman living alone. He too felt that commu-nity pressure had, at least partially, prompted the marriage. In a letter to the AMA executives, he stated:

The majority of the colored people at the Bush were out against Sister Coburn in the worst way, and were at times almost upon the point of mobbing her before she married Br. John S. Brooks, & as nearly as I can recollect their marriage was the means of hushing to silence most unwarrantable & wicked reports which were being mischievously circulated.[49]

Regardless, of the reasons for their marriage, the Brooks were obviously very devoted to each other and Fidelia Coburn Brooks confided to George Whipple of the AMA that, "John will not let me expose myself to hardships that I was obliged to before he came to live with me." She went on to say:

Altho. there is such a contrast in our ages and notwithstanding the many imperfections of his wife he thinks he has got <u>one of the very best in the world</u> and her presence always chases every cloud far away whatever it may be that troubles. If John has not got a good wife, Fidelia has got a <u>good</u> husband.[50]

On November 16, Fidelia Coburn Brooks wrote a seven-page letter to the AMA, in which she described in remarkable detail her opinion of the growing division between the missionaries and the Black community. She saw the distribution of clothing as the primary cause of discord and felt that it "occasions [sic] more heart burning and difficulty, and are production of such envy to more than counterbalance the value of the things. Indeed, you can not imagine the difficulty of the distribution."[51] Although she had received forty boxes of clothing during the previous year, there had not been enough dresses, coats, pants and shirts for everyone. Fidelia thought the distribution of clothing was like:

calling together a farm flock of poultry & throw at
them a handful of wheat, not enough for a kernel to
every hen – you can not give satisfaction in any way.
They will all wish they [the clothing] had never been
sent, etc. but when they think that I am going to do
anything to stop their transportation they will be in
a rage. But few understand the materials with which
we have to labor.[52]

Disagreements on the distribution of clothing lead to the establishment of the Prudential Committee by Jacob Libertus, a Black
Wesleyan Methodist minister. Libertus and his white wife, Hannah,
both natives of Vermont, had moved to Canada West in September
1841. The couple arrived in the Queen's Bush in 1844 where Libertus
tried to make a living as a teacher. However, few parents could afford
his tuition fee, forcing Libertus to close the school after just six
months. He turned to farming to support his family, but within a
brief period of time he became an ordained minister in the Wesleyan
Methodist church and received an appointment to the Wellington
County congregation.[53]

Libertus's inspiration for the Prudential Committee was the result
of a meeting held in the Queen's Bush by members of the British
Abolition Society (BAS). Under the leadership of William P. Newman
and Mr. Dunlop, the BAS decided that it would serve as a central relief
agency for fugitive slaves throughout Canada West. Libertus and his
followers demanded that Coburn release all donations into the care
of the Prudential Committee. To coordinate local relief operations,
two sub-committees, one to determine the needs of individual
families, the other to distribute clothing, were formed. Moreover,
Prudential Committee members encouraged parents to withdraw
their children from the segregated missionary schools and enroll
them in the local common schools, to ensure their integration into
white society.[54]

While John S. Brooks had earlier praised Libertus as a dedicated community leader, whose work had advanced education and religion in the community, his relationship with Libertus now became strained.[55] In fact, Brooks and other missionaries felt threatened by both the Prudential Committee and the BAS. Fidelia Coburn Brooks, along with Reverend Isaac Rice in Amherstburg, believed that the BAS promoted hostility towards missionaries. According to Brooks, Newman and Dunlop had made malicious statements during their lecture tours, including the comment that "all the Abolitionists that were or ever had been in the Province [were] thieves, robbers, & bloodsuckers & everything else that was bad – speculating on donations by selling, enriching themselves, etc."[56] Even more damaging were claims that John and Fidelia Coburn Brooks had used donations to purchase their property and had forced Blacks to work on their farm. Fidelia Coburn Brooks adamantly denied the accusations, although she admitted that she had occasionally given farm labourers clothing in lieu of cash. She claimed the clothing had been sent by American donors with instructions that it could be used in any way that promoted her work; and since she provided food harvested from her farm to destitute families, the clothing had not been misappropriated. But she realized that Newman's and Dunlop's accusations could destroy public confidence in her missionary work, and she decided to cooperate with the Prudential Committee by giving them all the adult clothing that she had in storage. Moreover, in her report to Lewis Tappan, she recommended that the AMA should cancel future shipments of adult clothing to the Queen's Bush because the majority of the adults currently living in the settlement had sufficient clothing. Instead, she recommended that shipments of adult clothing be sent to Reverend Isaac Rice at Amherstburg, one of the main fugitive slave crossing points into Canada. She requested that only children's clothing be sent to the Queen's Bush. She hoped that providing clothing to children would boost attendance at the two mission schools to 300 students.[57]

As treasurer and the principal policymaker of the AMA, Tappan advised Brooks to retain control over all donations. Moreover, in the February 1848 *American Missionary*, he directed his readers to send donations for the Queen's Bush directly to John or Fidelia Coburn Brooks. He did act on Brooks' suggestion and recommended that only children's clothing be sent to the community.[58]

Meanwhile, Melville Denslow, who by then had moved to Buffalo, New York, learned about the formation of the Prudential Committee and saw an opportunity to regain a missionary position by offering to act as the committee's agent. He promised to solicit funds and clothing for the Queen's Bush and ship them directly to the Prudential Committee. Reverend Libertus and the Committee accepted the offer and, ultimately, Denslow sent several boxes of clothing to the settlement. The prospect of competing with Denslow was no trivial matter for the missionaries, and they viewed his association with the Prudential Committee as an attempt to gain control of the Mount Hope and Mount Pleasant missions.[59]

It is not clear how much influence Libertus and the Prudential Committee had on the community or if the Brooks' reconciled their differences with him. Nevertheless, its formation clearly indicates that public opinion had shifted since the March 1847 meeting in which residents had passed resolutions in support of the missionaries. Ultimately though, the argument was not so much about who should distribute donations, as it was an effort by the Black community to maintain control over their own lives. The Queen's Bush residents had already demonstrated their refusal to accept enslavement and discrimination in the United States. They had proven that they could survive on their own and manage their own affairs. They were not willing to give up their hard-won independence by submitting to the paternalistic control of the missionaries. Clearly, both the missionaries and the AMA had failed to appreciate the Black community's desire to preserve their independence and self-determination.

During the winter of 1847/1848, John and Fidelia Brooks travelled to New England to visit family and friends. They also met with members of the AMA's executive committee in New York City, who urged them to remain in the community and provided them with teaching supplies for their schools. The supplies valued at $90, included textbooks, alphabet cards, slates, a map, a globe and spelling cards. Dolls and candy were also included as gifts for their students, while the American Tract Society and the American Temperance Union offered publications for distribution.[60]

Encouraged and optimistic, the Brooks returned to the Queen's Bush in the spring of 1848, but they soon found themselves facing the same old problems. Their travelling expenses had cost more than they had anticipated and, by the time they crossed the border back into Canada, they were almost penniless. Without proper funds, they had stored most of their luggage and the crates of school supplies at a warehouse in Hamilton. After a long, tedious trip, the Brooks finally arrived in Peel Township only to discover that they did not have any wheat seed for the upcoming planting season. During the previous spring they had loaned most of their seed to local farmers with the promise that they would be repaid after the fall harvest. In dire need for cash the farmers, however had sold their entire wheat crop to raise money for their annual land payments and taxes. Fidelia Coburn Brooks informed the AMA of the situation and requested money as soon as possible.[61]

The Brooks financial burdens were slightly lightened by the warm welcome they received from friends and neighbours. Fidelia Coburn Brooks' students had especially missed their teacher and were eager to return to school. Thrilled by their enthusiasm, she opened the Mount Hope School earlier than usual for the spring term. On May 20 approximately seventy children enrolled for the term. In her report to the AMA, Brooks proudly noted the progress made by her students and stated that, "a large number had commenced writing – were delighted with it, & took the most pains, & succeeded the best of any children I ever saw."[62]

Nevertheless, the Brooks began to realize that they could no longer rely on the AMA or other similar organizations to sustain their mission. They had to become self-sufficient or they would forever be on the verge of economic collapse. Consequently, John S. Brooks began to devote more time to their farming operation. He did most of the work himself, but periodically hired local labourers to help build fences, harvest crops or clear additional land for cultivation. With her husband busy operating the farm, Fidelia Coburn Brooks assumed the day-to-day responsibility of managing the household and school. They both conducted Sabbath School classes and continued visiting families in the community who required assistance. The hectic schedule soon began to take its toll. Fidelia Coburn Brooks even found it difficult to maintain her regular correspondence with the AMA. When she did have an opportunity to compose a letter, she frequently complained about fatigue and health problems. On one occasion she reported that her husband had a constant nagging cough and small knots "like kernels appeared on the cords of the neck back of the ear and very soon and it was swollen quite up on the head – They have been increasing till the number is fifteen of them."[63] Overwhelmed by the rigorous schedule, Fidelia Coburn asked the AMA to hire a second teacher to assist her at the Mount Hope School.

While the Brooks were coping with the new challenges and tribulations in their lives, the Township of Peel was also undergoing changes. Although wheat remained the principal cash crop, farming had become more diversified. More importantly, fields cleared of stumps could now be plowed with horses and oxen and, instead of harvesting grain by hand, local farmers began to use mechanical reapers.[64]

Township resident, Mary Jones, noting the rapid development in a letter to a relative, commented that the:

> forest is fast disappearing. The redoubled strokes of
> the woodsman will soon lay this monster low.

Already the lofty corn [and] waving wheat have
risen as by a stroke of magic in its place. This place
has improved rapidly, every lot of land is occupied.
[And] yet scores of men are passing through here
weekly in search of land.[65]

In 1848, Archibald Kirkland, PLS, laid out a village on lots 5 and 6,
of concession 2 and 3 in the township. In the same year, George Allan,
a Scotsman, established the first store and hotel in the village. Allan
and another Scotsman, Donald Sutherland, hired Paul Willson to
build a sawmill on the banks of the Conestogo River. In the ensuing
years, Allan Village, later known as Glen Allan, grew around these
business clusters.[66] Despite the progress, another failed wheat harvest
left many farmers too poor to pay their annual installments and an
increasing number of families left the settlement. To make matters
worse, on June 8, 1848, a fire destroyed the Mount Hope Mission
School, along with over three hundred textbooks and Sabbath School
books. There had not been a fire in the schoolhouse stove for thirty-
six hours, so the teachers were convinced the incident had been the
work of an arsonist. They had no evidence, but the couple suspected
Reverend Jacob Libertus of deliberately setting the fire. In her report
to the AMA, Fidelia Coburn Brooks claimed that Libertus "has made
it his business to stir up as much prejudice, dissention & difficulty
about & with us as possible ever since he came & he is a shrewd cun-
ning man & leads many astray."[67]

If the Reverend Libertus did indeed commit arson, many in the
Black community did not condone his actions. There were many
who supported the missionaries and when gathering at the scene to
view the destruction, there was an extraordinary outpouring of grief.
In her report, Fidelia Coburn Brooks described their reaction: "It was
a melancholy time – their tears and sobs, the grief depicted on every
countenance, showing the sorrow of heart which they felt at the loss
sustained."[68] Brooks also related a conversation that she overheard

between two children when they discovered that their school had been reduced to a smoldering pile of embers:

> "Well now, I would not stay any longer, if I were they [the missionaries], and be treated so. I would go home."
>
> The other answered, "They won't do that, they love us too well; they will find a place somewhere to have a school."[69]

Such expressions of sympathy reinforced the Brooks' resolve to remain in the community. Fidelia Coburn Brooks vowed that, "if they burn all up we will not leave but he [John S. Brooks] will build underground of clay."[70]

The Brooks' were also encouraged by the support of community members, such as Lucinda Brown Mallot. After Josephus and Lucinda Mallot left the Colbornesburg Settlement, they settled briefly in the Township of Waterloo in Waterloo County, but in March 1841, the family found a permanent home on the south half of lot 18, concession 1, in Peel Township. Like many residents, Mrs. Mallot was critical of the methods in which donations were distributed in the community and suspected thee missionaries of misappropriating funds. But after a visit to the United States in 1848, she returned home a firm supporter of the missionaries. Her changed attitude seemed remarkable to Fidelia Coburn who commented in a letter to the AMA, that:

> Mrs. Malott's [sic] visit I think will be a great benefit to us. She has come back a thorough Abolitionist – she was not and was even prejudice[d] against us. I have no doubt but she will enlighten the people somewhat – she tells them that the Abolitionist friends told the same story as Mr. and Mrs. Brooks do and they should not treat them so.[71]

John and Fidelia Coburn Brooks realized that the tension in the community reinforced the need for a central organization to solicit and distribute donations for the Black population. On July 10, 1848, at the invitation of the Brooks, the leading missionaries in Canada West met in the Queen's Bush to discuss the future prospects of the missionary field in the province. The group included Hiram Wilson, his wife Hannah, Reverend Elias E. Kirkland, Theodosia Lyon, Emerson Prescott and Lorana Parker.[72] William King,[73] a Presbyterian minister with the Free Church of Scotland also attended the meeting. The presence of William P. Newman suggests that the missionaries may have tried to resolve their differences with the Prudential Committee and the British Abolition Society. The missionaries discussed the possibility of establishing a centralized organization that would provide leadership and coordinate funding for all the Canadian missions. In the end, they decided that each mission should be reorganized under the supervision of an ecclesiastical group or a missionary society. Each mission would then be independently operated and free to make decisions about relief aid, while attaining membership in an informal province-wide association. While a province-wide association failed to materialize, many individual missionaries did try to find more permanent sources of funding.[74]

PRINCIPAL LOCATIONS, NUMBERS, CHURCHES AND SCHOOLS
OF THE BLACK POPULATION IN CANADA WEST, 1848

Location	Numbers	Churches B M*			Schools
Colchester	2,000	3	1	2	1
Malden & vicinity	1,500	5	2	3	3
Gosfield	200	1			0**
Sandwich & vicinity	300	3	2	1	0

Chatham & vicinity	600	4	2	2	0
Dover & vicinity	200	0			0
Dawn & vicinity	300	2	1	1	1
London & vicinity	300	3	1	2	0
Wilberforce	250	2	1	1	0
Norwich	200	1		1	0
Brantford	100	1	1		0
Queen's Bush	1,500	4	1	3	2
Owen Sound	200	1		1	0
Oro	400	2	1	1	0
Grand River	300	2	1	1	0
Hamilton & vicinity	600	2	1	1	0**
St. Catharines & vicinity	500	2	1	1	0
Toronto & vicinity	700	3	1	1	1**
Niagara	126	2	1	1	0**
Drummonville	150	1		2	0

* B = Baptist, M = Methodist   ** Colored children in white schools

Compiled by John S. and Fidelia Coburn Brooks, Hiram and Hannah Wilson, Elias E. Kirkland, Theodosia Lyon, Emerson Prescott, Lorana Parker, William King and William P. Newman at the 10 July 1848 meeting held in the Queen's Bush. Source: *Oberlin Evangelist*, Aug. 30, 1848 and the *American Missionary* 2 (October 1848).

After the meeting, the Reverend King remained in the community for several days and held public meetings to discuss his plans for the establishment of a community of Blacks only, to be known as the Elgin Settlement in the Township of Raleigh in Kent County.[75] King invited Queen's Bush farmers to join in the new venture and several families including, the Harden family eventually moved to the Elgin Settlement.[76]

After his brief sojourn in the Queen's Bush, King submitted a report to the editor of the *Ecclesiastical and Missionary Record* describing the community. Overall, King believed that the Queen's Bush enjoyed a degree of prosperity and stated, "many of the settlers have made large improvements for the time. I visited several of them at houses, found them living comfortably, and well supplied with necessaries of life."[77] He also examined the skills of some of the students enrolled at the Mount Hope School. Despite the irregular attendance, overcrowded classroom and limited teaching supplies, King felt that most children had acquired a good education. Impressed with the school and the progress of the students, he wrote:

> Two of the more advanced pupils gave me a specimen of their composition; both the writing and style would compare favorably with white girls of the same age and opportunities. Were the school established on a permanent basis, so that the children now attending could be carried on through a regular course of mental training, some of them would make good scholars. As it is the school is depending on individual effort aided occasionally by contributions from the United States. Should the [missionaries] die, the school must cease as there is no Society responsible for its continuance.[78]

King also commented on the Brooks' weekly Sabbath School stating that:

> Mr. and Mrs. Brooks also teach a very interesting Sabbath School; the average attendance is about seventy. They usually collect the children in the morning, and keep them during the whole day, hearing them read, and recite portions of the scriptures. This

*Reverend William King,
founder of the Elgin
Settlement.*
Courtesy of Buxton National
Historic Site and Museum.

practice they have kept up regularly since they began
their labors in the bush. It is attended with many
spiritual advantages to the children; besides giving
them a knowledge of the scriptures, it keeps them
from Sabbath desecration, which is quite common
in the settlement. Some of the scholars exhibit great
strength of memory. The Sabbath on which I visited
the school, one little boy about twelve years of age,
committed one hundred and forty verses in the
Gospel of John, for the week's lesson; several other
boys and girls had committed from one hundred to
one hundred and twenty.[79]

However, King severely criticized schismatic and petty feuds between
the community's religious leaders. He believed religion was:

in a very low state, those who made any profession
were divided among themselves, each leader endeav-
oring to form a party around himself; these jealousies

had broken up all social intercourse in the settlement, and raised a complete barrier against their spiritual improvement.[80]

In conclusion, King stated that he hoped an organization could be found that would permanently fund the Mount Hope and Mount Pleasant missions to ensure their continued success.

The Brooks' wrote to the AMA and requested that the organization permanently sponsor their mission. In return for the sponsorship, the Brooks' offered to transfer all of their property, 110 acres valued at approximately $800, to the AMA. In their application to convince the AMA to sponsor their mission, the Brooks' argued that:

> when the people make a disturbance about our doings we can refer them to the Board to make known their complaints, and hope thereby to stop some of their grievances of the thousands and thousands of dollars which are begged over their heads and pocketed by us, till our eyes stand out with fatness.[81]

While waiting for a response to their request, the Brooks' forged ahead with their missionary work. Without a schoolhouse, they converted their home into a classroom. When they opened the school for the fall term, fifty students enrolled and the Brooks' quickly realized that the arrangement could not be permanent. Overworked and under considerable stress, Fidelia Coburn Brooks' health began to fail. To ease her burden, one of her more advanced students took over her teaching duties. Meanwhile, William P. Newman convinced the Brooks to rebuild the schoolhouse and promised to help the couple raise money for its construction. Encouraged by Newman, John S. Brooks made arrangements to rebuild the school. He purchased lumber, hired workmen and even established a brickyard and kiln to manufacture bricks. Brooks wrote enthusiastically to Lewis Tappan about his plans. He assured Tappan that the brickyard would become a profitable business in the future. However, all of the arrangements had been made on credit and Brooks implied that he hoped the AMA would finance the construction of the new school.[82]

Tappan sent $100, which proved to be insufficient and, in October, Fidelia Coburn Brooks reported problems with the rebuilding process. Local sawmills had refused to sell any more lumber on credit and her husband had been unable to find qualified brick makers. Consequently, John S. Brooks along with a crew of local workmen had been forced to manufacture the bricks themselves. Constructing the new schoolhouse proved too strenuous for Brooks, who became ill and confined to his bed, leaving his wife, still in poor health herself, to single-handedly manage their home, farm and school. Fidelia Coburn Brooks, exhausted by the constant worry, wrote a second letter to George Whipple. Pleading for assistance she stated, "to beg – is hard – very hard but, my dear brother, what can we do? What ought we do? The walls of our [school] house are going up rapidly and we hope will soon be completed, and bills. Bills must be paid and where is the money coming from?[83] Desperate, she also turned to Newman for help, declaring that they needed four hundred dollars to pay the workmen before January 1, 1849, or they would be forced to sell the schoolhouse. It is unclear if Newman ever contributed any money, but he did submit an article describing the dilemma to Frederick Douglass' newspaper, the *North Star*, in hopes that it would encourage American philanthropists to donate money to the Brooks' cause. In the end, the AMA paid for the construction costs and the new Mount Hope School opened in December 1848 with an enrollment of seventy-six children.[84]

In October 1848, the executive committee of the AMA decided to support the Brooks, as well as the Reverend Isaac Rice at Amherstburg. But the executive committee insisted that only money donated specifically for Canadian missions would be forwarded to them. Aware of the tensions between Blacks and the missionaries in Canada West, the AMA clearly was not optimistic about its involvement and described the missions there as "in a dark field, one that does not for the present furnish many indications of promise."[85] The AMA never considered Canada a primary field of missionary work. The organization's foreign efforts were directed to the Kaw-Mendi Mission in Sierra Leone (William Raymond's mission established for the Amistad Africans), Jamaica, Siam, Asia and the Ojibwe Indians in the northwestern territories of the United States.[86]

At the beginning of December, Mary Teall, a twenty-two-year-old teacher from Albany, New York, arrived in the Queen's Bush to teach at the Mount Hope school. Teall may have had previous teaching experience before moving to the community because acquaintances described her as well qualified for missionary work. More importantly, the Female Missionary Society of the State Street Baptist Church in Albany, New York, and the American Baptist Free Mission Society had pledged to financial support her work.[87]

With Teall's arrival, the opening of the new schoolhouse and the AMA's sponsorship, the Brooks believed that they were on the threshold of what promised to be a new beginning. In contrast, the Reverend Elias E. Kirkland was less optimistic about his future role in the community. Kirkland's clashes with local Black ministers proved to be a constant source of confrontation and, once again, he decided to leave Peel Township. In his farewell sermon held in December 1848, he sharply accused local Black ministers of promoting opposition to the missionaries simply because they were afraid of loosing their own influence in the community. He claimed that of the seven Black ministers presently in the community, only the Reverend Dorsey Ambush supported the missionaries and their work. Joined by Theodosia Lyon, Kirkland and his family left the township in February 1849 and moved to New Canaan, a newly established fugitive slave community ten miles east of Amherstburg in the Township of Colchester. Still under the sponsorship of the Wesleyan Missionary Board, Kirkland opened a school for Black pupils and ministered to local Wesleyan Methodist congregations. With the departure of both Kirkland and Lyon, Mary Teall took over the Mount Pleasant Mission School, which at the beginning of the 1848-49 school year had an enrollment of seventy-seven students.[88]

In January 1849, Fidelia Coburn Brooks reported to the AMA that a public meeting had been held in the township and community members had unanimously voted to transfer the management of the Mount Hope Mission School to the provincial government, thereby, in effect, turning it into a common school. Both John and Fidelia wholeheartedly supported the decision. The mission schools had started in the predominantly Black community to assist its residents, but the influx of white immigrants and the development of a common school system made it difficult to maintain a school solely for Black children. The Brooks realized that they had to integrate their school, so that they could provide instruction to children, Black and white. To counter any concerns that the AMA may have had about the plan, Fidelia Coburn Brooks outlined the advantages of opening the school to white children in her monthly report. Foremost, she felt that an integrated school would guarantee the continued operation of the school should they ever leave the community. Moreover, it would end any local resentment towards the "Abolition or Yankee schools." She also felt that because Mount Hope had originated as a Black school, once white students enrolled parents could not, in good conscience, deny admittance to Black children. According to Fidelia Coburn Brooks, the small number of white children already enrolled at the school felt like intruders and their parents hoped the conversion would help to unify the community. This certainly was a remarkable view in light of the fact that whites in many interracial communities across the province were attempting to segregate their local schools during this time. Surprisingly, Brooks also stated in her report, that the Mount Hope and Mount Pleasant Missions were becoming self-sufficient.[89] It is likely that her statement was an attempt to alleviate the executive committee's doubts about the prospects of the missions, for by no means were the circumstances of the missionaries improving.

However, the beginning of the new year brought an increase in the Black exodus from Peel Township. The situation became so bleak that Fidelia Coburn Brooks reported to the AMA: "It is times here now that tries men's souls – great excitement about the land – enough, with money in hand ready to buy – and those on the land struggle to make out the money."[90] Even the Brooks began to fear eviction and had to borrow money to pay their annual installment. Fidelia Coburn Brooks predicted that within a few years the Black community would no longer exist. She passionately hoped that:

> if we can keep the children drilling [in school] till then they will be better prepared to go ahead in the world. Indeed many of them will be better prepared for teachers than but few of the white teachers.[91]

With money in the AMA treasury specified for "Canada Missions," the executive committee offered to provide loans to individual Black families. While grateful for the offer, John S. Brooks felt that "the time for rendering cash assistance has passed as far as this colony is concerned"[92] Instead, he outlined a proposal to the AMA suggesting that the organization purchase a tract of land and establish an exclusively Black community similar to the Elgin Settlement or the British-American Institute. Lots would be sold to farmers based on their income. They would not be allowed to sell their property until it had been completely paid for and parents would have to agree to send their children to school. Brooks obviously realized that the executive committee would likely reject his idea, because he suggested alternatively that they at least purchase land for the community's elderly Black residents.[93] AMA executives ultimately rejected both proposals.

The progress made by the Mount Hope and Mount Pleasant students over the years had helped the Brooks cope with their countless problems. They had withstood sickness, hard labour, verbal abuse and had risked financial ruin, but now with declining enrollment of Black children at the schools, their determination to remain in the community began to waiver. Without a "flock" they felt lost. They contemplated following the displaced residents, but the migration out of the community had not been coordinated. While the majority of the residents, especially those with large families, had been attracted to the Owen Sound area, where homesteaders could receive fifty acre land grants from the government, others had moved to the Elgin Settlement. In her June report to the AMA, Fidelia Coburn Brooks lamented that:

> the inviting prospects of securing a grant of 50 acres at the "Sound" and the successful and praiseworthy labors of Fr. King in establishing a colony of colored people in the Western District have prematurely blasted our prospects.[94]

Many families had departed on their own, seeking a new beginning often in urban areas where there were more economic opportunities. Peter Edward Susand moved his family to Berlin (now Kitchener), which, in 1852, had a population of approximately seven hundred inhabitants, but with its recent appointment as the county seat, the village had begun to experience a marked increase in economic and population growth.[95] Taking advantage of the new economic opportunities, Susand opened a barbershop at a prominent location on King Street next door to the Red Lion Hotel. In the local newspaper, Susand announced that, "he does not beat 'all natur', but his lather is unrivalled and his razors (like true wit) cut deep both up and down, leave no wounds and shave clean."[96] Susand pursued other business ventures, which included operating the Meridan Coffee Salon, a confectionery shop, and a reading room where patrons could read newspapers published in a variety of different cities. Susand also

Fugitive slave, Peter E. Susand, operated a barbershop in the third building from the left, next to the Red Lion Inn. Courtesy of the Kitchener Public Library.

opened a clothes-cleaning shop. An advertisement in the *Berlin Chronicle* in 1857 announced:

> Great Economy! The Old Made New! The Subscriber has taken this method of informing the public that he is proficient in the art of renovation – color restored, and a complete lustre given to cloth and collors [sic] of coats, and cleaned of sweat and grease.[97]

William Burten moved his family from their farm on lot 11, concession 5, in the Township of Peel to Galt (now part of Cambridge) in southern Waterloo County to pursue a more stable livihood. In Galt, by then a large and prosperous commercial centre, Burten found work as a labourer to support his family.[98]

Ironically, coinciding with the exodus from the Queen's Bush was an increase in the number of fugitive slaves and free Blacks arriving in Canada West. During the winter of 1847-48, the Reverend Isaac J. Rice reported a 70 per cent increase in the number of fugitive slaves arriving in Amherstburg requesting assistance at his mission. He noted that this wave of people crossing the border included larger than normal groups of fugitives. Some clusters numbered up to sixteen individuals and included women and children.[99]

Only a few families, unable to abandon their homes remained in the Queen's Bush. These were mostly small families whose farms were scattered across Peel and Wellesley townships. Some had been able to purchase their farms, but most had used the improvements on their land in lieu of making the first payment. In her June 1849 report to the AMA, Fidelia Coburn Brooks predicted that within one year primarily white students would attend the Mount Hope School. She lamented that "to remain here without a colored school we can not."[100] The Brooks decided to emigrate to Sierra Leone and continue their missionary work at the AMA sponsored Mendi Mission. They believed their services as teachers and missionaries were now needed more urgently in Africa.[101]

It was John S. Brooks who initiated the idea of emigrating to Sierra Leone. Restless and eager to continue his missionary work, the plan consumed his thoughts for weeks until he became convinced that it was God's will for them to leave Canada West. In her application to the AMA for a transfer, Fidelia Coburn Brooks admitted that she had some trepidation about the move. She feared the ocean voyage because she suffered from seasickness and, at age forty-four, she believed that she had become too old for missionary work, especially in such a forbidding location. The "dark continent" with its tropical climate, exotic diseases and strange fevers had the notorious reputation of being the death place of many missionaries. After her rigorous life in Canada West, Fidelia Coburn Brooks doubted that she had the necessary strength to survive in such a hostile environment. Despite her misgivings, in the end her religious convictions won out over her fears. She declared to George Whipple of the AMA that, "we feel that our work is done here and that God calls us to Africa. That we could not give it up without disobeying God."[102]

Impatient to move on, John and Fidelia Coburn Brooks did not wait to settle their financial affairs or for the approval of the AMA. On July 4, 1849, they closed the Mount Hope Mission School and by mid-month they had returned to the United States to make final preparations for their journey to Sierra Leone. In August, after lengthy deliberation, Lewis Tappan accepted their request for a transfer. The AMA noted the departure of the Brooks from Peel Township in its third annual report. However, the executive committee failed to clearly describe the situation in the community, blatantly ignoring the fact that many Black families had left the township because of their inability to purchase their farms. Moreover, there was no acknowledgement of the fact that unscrupulous land agents and new immigrants had intimidated many families into abandoning their farms. Instead, the executive committee claimed that families "having opportunity to dispose of their property, and to purchase more advantageously elsewhere, had determined to remove to another district."[103]

On November 3, 1849, John and Fidelia Coburn Brooks set sail for Sierra Leone on board the brig *Lowder*. Sara Kinson (Mar-gru), one of the Amistad Africans who had been studying in the United States, accompanied them. Fidelia Coburn Brooks' fears of the ocean voyage came true, for she experienced seasickness during the entire six-week journey. Shortly after their arrival in York, Sierra Leone, both missionaries contracted a fever. Still weak from the ocean voyage, Fidelia Coburn Brooks had little strength to fight the fever and died on January 11, 1850.[104]

CHAPTER 4

"Our work here is almost done"[1]

IN THE FALL OF 1849, MARY TEALL resumed classes at the Mount Pleasant Mission School. She faced an uncertain future and admitted to one of her correspondents that she trembled with fear at the thought of managing the school on her own. Enrollment at Mount Pleasant was at an all time low, which further contributed to her anxiety. Only twenty-five Black children had enrolled for the winter term. Daily attendance had also dwindled because few of the remaining Black families lived within walking distance of the schoolhouse. The ten children who boarded with Teall were the only regular students. Little is known about the children who lived with the missionaries, but many were orphans like nine-year-old Lucinda, who had originally been taken in by Fidelia Coburn Brooks. Another child, Daniel, began boarding with Teall shortly after her arrival in the township. He performed odd jobs around the mission in return for free lodging. Both children excelled as students, but Teall had especially high expectations for Lucinda and hoped that the young girl would one day pursue a career as a teacher.[2]

It was uncertain whether or not Teall could receive funding for the Mount Pleasant Mission. She had received some money from the

American Baptist Free Mission Society, but the Female Missionary
Society of the State Street Baptist Church in Albany, New York, had
failed to sponsor her work as promised. Parents of the children who
attended her school could not provide any money either, the best
most of them could do was to supply wood to heat the schoolhouse.[3]
News of the exodus from the township had spread and it was generally believed that the Black community had disbanded altogether, so
no other missionaries ventured to the community. Even newspaper
editor Henry Bibb reported in the *Voice of the Fugitive* that "there is
not much prospect of any increase"[4] for the community. Despite her
difficulties, Teall never considered abandoning her mission, even
during the dire winter of 1849/1850 when she was forced to exchange
handmade clothing for food. Her circumstances were so perilous that
local residents James Curry and the Reverend James Sims provided
her with gifts of food.[5]

Without a strong missionary presence in the community, local
whites intensified their efforts to force Blacks out of the settlement.
After his visit to Peel Township in October 1849, H. A. Lizer, agent of
the American Baptist Free Mission Society from Elyria, Ohio,
reported to the AMA that:

> The whites in this vicinity are trying to drive the col-
> ored people away – they misrepresent, and lie about
> the colored people and also those who are laboring
> for them…. They say 'If the Abolitionists were away
> we could get rid of the colored at once.[6]

Teall pleaded for financial assistance from the AMA and requested
help in resolving a poor land deal she had made with mission property.
Before their departure, the Brooks' had given Teall fifty acres that
included the site of the Mount Pleasant School. Teall had sold forty-
six acres to a land speculator to secure money to build a new house
and barn, but had neglected to obtain the deed for the remaining

four acres. When the buyer tried to resell the property, including the Mount Pleasant School, Teall appealed to the AMA for help. She offered to resign her connection with the Female Missionary Society and the American Baptist Free Mission Society if the AMA would promise to support her and obtain a clear title to the four acres. She also proposed that the AMA enlarge her home to accommodate at least fifty student boarders. She hoped that those children whose homes were scattered across the township would live at the school, so that they could attend classes on a regular basis. Teall admitted that the addition, at a cost of $300 was expensive, but she believed the money would be well spent if the school's Black enrollment could be increased.[7]

In her letter, Teall also stated that if the children were to make any meaningful progress they had to be removed from the demoralizing influence of their superstitious and uneducated parents. She believed that parents who were former slaves were passing on the degrading behaviour acquired in slavery to their children. According to Teall, in the confines of a boarding school she would be able to transform the character, ideals and religious beliefs of the children. Teall bluntly stated:

> I see no other way but to take in orphans and those that parents will give away: for as I told you in one of my former letters it is almost useless to labour for them while they are with their parents, for the good that we can do them in school is almost all counter-acted at home![8]

The AMA execetive committee refused to build a boarding school and advised Teall to find someone locally to sort out her legal problems. Teall ultimately secured the help of Thomas Vipond, who had been a friend to the previous Queen's Bush missionaries.[9]

During this time Teall also expressed her concerns about John and Fidelia Coburn Brooks' financial affairs to the AMA. Before their departure the Brooks had granted power of attorney to Josiah B. Jackson[10] a white Quaker from Pennsylvania. The Brooks had authorized Jackson to collect their outstanding loans and use the money to pay their debts. More importantly, Jackson received instructions to sell the Brooks' property, which included land on the west half of lot 13, concession 3; east half of lot 17, concession 1; and the west half of lot 19, concession 1.[11] John Brooks had instructed Jackson to pay the local Crown Land Agent the annual installment on his holdings should he not be able to find a suitable buyer. Teall believed Jackson was unsuitable because he had a limited educational background and was, moreover, a United States citizen. According to law, only British subjects could legally buy or sell land and Teall feared that the Brooks' land would ultimately be reclaimed by the government.[12] AMA executives decided to intervene and in March 1850 the Reverend J. P. Bardwell, of Oberlin, Ohio, visited the Queen's Bush to examine the matter. However, Bardwell failed to collect all of the money owed to the Brooks. Although, he did pay their debts which amounted to eighty dollars, including the current payment on their land. With Thomas Vipond's assistance, Bardwell compiled a list of Brooks' debtors, each person's race and ability to repay the loan. The list clearly indicates that Brooks' financial dealings involved both white and Black members of the community. Based on information he had received from Bardwell, Vipond, and Jackson, Lewis Tappan asked Vipond to administer the Brooks' financial affairs and to obtain the title to the Mount Pleasant Mission.[13]

Meanwhile Black families, who had remained in the township, struggled to maintain their tenacious hold on their land. With the ever-growing number of immigrants streaming into the region, real estate values had increased as the demand for land intensified. With land prices at $4 to $5 per acre, poor families found it virtually impossible to purchase their farms and, in July 1850, ten Black petitioners made one final attempt to gain government assistance. In their petition they stated:

That there was a proclamation issued in the year
1840 to the effect that every man of colour assisting
in putting down the Rebellion of the years 1837 &
1838, by going to the Queen's Bush was to get a deed
of 50 acres of land with the privilege of purchasing
50 acres more of the lot if able to do so.

That your petitioners in consequence removed
with their families to the aforesaid Queen's Bush
and located in it. That after nine years privations &
hard labour, your petitioners succeeded in clearing
on an average 20 acres of Land with corresponding
improvements.

That your petitioners are now informed by Mr.
Gayters Crown Land Agent in Elora that their farms
and improvements are in the market.

Your petitioners therefore humbly entreat you
will take their case into your humane consideration...[14]

Perhaps realizing the futility of yet another request for government
intervention, the majority of the Queen's Bush residents did not sign
the petition.

In the summer of 1850, the AMA executive committee contemplated sponsoring Mary Teall, but wanted to make sure Teall did not
harbour any sectarian views. On September 18, Teall drafted a long
reply to the committee, in which she adamantly stated:

I cherish nothing of the kind. I could as cheerfully &
as freely labour with one that called themselves
Methodist or Presbyterians or any other name. If I
was convinced that they were a child of God as I
could with a baptist.... I believe it to be utterly
impossible for any one to labour efficiently in the

cause of Christ, & at the same time retain sectarian
prejudices.[15]

Aside from concerns about the executive committee's questioning of
her religious convictions, Teall was also worried that the high
number of white children enrolled in her school would have a negative influence on their decision to subsidize her. Of the eighty students enrolled, only thirty were Black, and Teall feared that the
committee would refuse to sponsor her if they doubted that her
school benefited primarily Black children. To counter any criticism
she stressed that, "some of them are as needy as any of the colored
children; and surely their souls are just as precious. I can not in conscience keep the word of God from those that seek after it."[16]

Mary Teall was not the only missionary in trouble by the end of
1850. The British-American Institute had successfully attracted a
large number of Black families and, in time, the population of Dawn
had increased to approximately five hundred. Despite numerous
contributions from philanthropists and benevolent organizations
the Institute's debt had risen to nearly $5,000, mainly as a result of
poor leadership and improper management. Co-founders, Josiah
Henson and Hiram Wilson were reformers whose ideals and goals
were well intentioned, but both lacked the necessary leadership qual-
ities. Moreover, the community had ambitious plans that were
beyond its financial capabilities and ultimately kept it dependent on
white philanthropy. In 1850, Wilson left the Institute and moved to St.
Catharines, where he opened another school. During the same year,
the AMA severed its connections with the Reverend Isaac Rice in
Amherstburg, amidst rumours of adultery, drunkenness, debt and
theft. Since its founding, the Elgin Settlement had encountered per-
sistent opposition from local whites who wanted to restrict Black
immigration into their community. Edwin Larwill led the opposition
movement and claimed that the Elgin Settlement would lower local
property values, encourage miscegenation, lead to a war with the

United States, create social chaos and discourage European immigration. While Larwill and other opponents of the Elgin Settlement had failed to prevent Blacks from settling in the community, their racist attacks were a constant source of agitation.[17]

Meanwhile, in September 1850, United States President Millard Fillmore signed into law the Fugitive Slave Bill, which empowered judges to grant certificates to claimants of fugitive slaves to return them to their owners. To obtain the certificate, claimants only had to provide a written or oral affidavit stating that the individual was a fugitive from slavery. The alleged fugitive, in contrast, could not testify on his own behalf and had no recourse to a trial. The law also stipulated that anyone caught assisting fugitive slaves could be fined up to $1000 and be imprisoned for six months. As a consequence, many slave catchers not only arrested fugitive slaves, but free Blacks as well, falsely accusing them of being runaway slaves.[18]

With the enactment of the Fugitive Slave Law, every Black person became immediately vulnerable to being forced into slavery, and a wave of terror swept through many American Black communities. Outraged by the law, Black and white citizen groups formed vigilance associations vowing to use force if necessary to thwart the efforts of slave catchers. Not surprisingly, passage of the law promptly resulted in another wave of Black immigration into Canada West. Contemporary northern American newspapers provide abundant references to fleeing Blacks and in many locations this resulted in significant reductions in local Black populations. In Columbia, Pennsylvania, the Black population declined from 943 to 487, while in Rochester, New York, all but two of the 114 members of the congregation of the Negro Baptist Church fled. In December 1850, Hiram Wilson estimated that in the three months since the enactment of the law 3,000 individuals had immigrated to Canada West. Henry Bibb in the *Voice of the Fugitive*, stated that a steady stream of immigrants was arriving in the province through Windsor and Amherstburg. Most observers agreed that the hardships experienced by these refugees were quite minimal compared to the plight of earlier fugitive slaves. Most families who left the United States because of the new law had money, trade skills and personal property, and were often able to find suitable lodging and employment. Black social activist, Samuel Ringgold Ward commended this wave of immigrants describing them as equal in all respects to newly arriving European immigrants.[19]

Canadian ambivalence to the anti-slavery movement changed after the passage of the Fugitive Slave Law. As the Black migration into Canada West increased, public opinion could no longer ignore the issue and many Canadians, Black and white, publicly condemned the law. In Toronto, on February 26. 1851, abolitionists founded the Anti-slavery Society of Canada (ASC), whose aim was the abolition of slavery worldwide. The ASC endorsed Black-organized communities and opposed colonization schemes, as well as, the extradition of fugitive slaves from Canada. To convey its message the ASC hired anti-slavery lecturers to tour the province. Many were well-known American Black abolitionists such as Frederick Douglass, Jermain W. Loguen and Samuel Ringgold Ward, who provided vivid descriptions of the brutality of slavery and urged the immediate emancipation of all slaves. Toronto women formed an auxiliary society known as the Toronto Ladies' Association for the Relief of Destitute Coloured Refugees. Within the first year of its existence the organization raised over nine hundred dollars and distributed clothing, bedding, and money to countless families.[20]

The passage of the Fugitive Slave Law, and the resulting increase in donations that amounted to $1,144.47 designated specifically for Canadian missions, encouraged the AMA to direct more money to Canada West. By the end of the year the executive committee agreed to sponsor Mary Teall, as well as Hiram Wilson's missionary operation in St. Catharines and appointed the Reverend David Hotchkiss,[21] a Wesleyan minister, to replace Isaac Rice in Amherstburg.[22] The committee also hired Teall's sister, Susan, to teach at the Mount Pleasant School. As soon as Mary Teall received notification of the decision, she immediately sent off a letter thanking the executive committee and, in desperate need of supplies, she requested:

> two shawls, two pairs of gaiter boots, size 3 1/2 or 4, one small pocket bible red morocco cover, one volume of Bunyan's Pilgrim Progress and six small volumes of your own choosing for prizes, besides a little missionary box such as are used in sab.sch's [Sabbath Schools] at home.[23]

She also asked that only children's clothing be sent to her mission, emphasizing that, such gifts guaranteed school attendance. Teall stated that, "the parents will not encourage the children to come unless I pay them something, and clothing seems to be the most suitable and in some cases very much needed. Books and shoes are more necessary if they can be had, as they are very costly here."[24]

During the winter of 1850-1851, Mary Teall travelled to New York City to speak with AMA executives about her missionary operation. She hoped that a personal interview with the association's executives would increase their support of the Mount Pleasant Mission. Meanwhile, twenty-five-year-old Susan Teall made preparations for her journey from her home in Knoxville, Pennsylvania, to Canada West. Accompanied by her father, she travelled to Niagara Falls where they met Thomas Vipond, who escorted them from the border to the Queen's Bush settlement. After a lengthy and tiring journey, Vipond and the Tealls arrived at the Mount Pleasant Mission on January 6, 1851.[25]

On February 22, Mary Teall returned from her trip to New York City. Overall, her meeting with AMA officials had been positive and she resumed her teaching duties with renewed enthusiasm. Moreover, with her sister at her side, Teall felt more confident in her role as a missionary. This sense of security, however, would be short-lived.[26]

At the end of February, Matthew Swan, a Wesleyan Methodist minister moved to Peel Township with his wife, Eliza R., and their two-year-old daughter, Anna. With Mary Teall's permission, Swan held afternoon and evening worship services at the Mount Pleasant schoolhouse. Community members responded enthusiastically to his sermons and asked Swan to hold a protracted revival. Swan's passionate sermonizing continued every night for several weeks and created a surge of excitement in the community. Thirty people were converted to the Wesleyan Methodist Church, many of whom were Teall's students who had been influenced by the intense emotional energy of the revival. Lucinda, the young orphan girl, who boarded with the Tealls, was among the newly baptized. Although Lucinda did not have any parents, her grandmother had remained her legal guardian and Teall had neglected to seek her consent for the baptism. Outraged by her granddaughter's association with the Wesleyan Methodist Church, she removed the child from the Teall's home. As news of the incident spread through the community, other parents also began to withdraw their children from the school and enrollment plummeted to only fifteen children. In her subsequent reports to the AMA, Mary Teall admitted that she had made a serious mistake by endorsing Swan's revival. Nevertheless, she refused to close the school and continued to conduct her weekly Sabbath School. In fact, she reported that despite the low enrollment her Sabbath School students had organized a fundraising campaign to purchase new books. The children had collected almost two dollars and hoped to have a total of five dollars by the end of the summer.[27]

During this same time period, questions about Mary Teall's moral character began to surface in the community. Teall had hired Thomas Vipond to repair and enlarge her home, and while working on the house he became ill. Although his own home was only a mile away in Wellesley Township, he decided to convalesce with the Teall sisters. The arrangement strained the limits of what was considered to be acceptable behaviour and many residents began to realize that Mary Teall and Vipond, a married man with five children, were having an affair. Mrs. Curry, wife of fugitive slave James Curry, spoke privately with Teall and tried to persuade her to end the relationship. Increasingly, community members began to confront her publicly, telling her at one point "that she had better never come to Canada than to separate man and wife."[28] However, social pressure had no affect on Teall or Vipond and despite repeated threats they continued their liaison. Concerned for her safety, James Curry reported the incident to Lewis Tappan, of the AMA, in April 1851 stating that, "indeed so odious is their conduct become that Tar and Feathers has been threatened."[29] Tappan, however, doubted Curry's allegations and requested more details. He also sought Hiram Wilson's opinion and in his response, Wilson described Teall as "a faithful, good woman, and is doing all the good she can." Moreover, he was certain that the accusations were a consequence of her work "among a rebellious, ungrateful people, where party spirit, and where jealousies are as fruitful as flies in midsummer."[30]

In August, Curry submitted a second letter to Tappan that once again described the couple's on-going affair. Curry claimed that Teall's impropriety had adversely affected her usefulness as a teacher because most parents had withdrawn their children from the Mount Pleasant School and enrolled them in the local common schools. According to Curry, only twelve children attended classes at Mount Pleasant and of that number only three were Black. To lend credibility to Curry's statements, Dennis Jackson, William Johnson, Mary Norris, Nancy Prater, Daniel Youbanks, Benjamin Wilson and the Reverend Samuel H. Brown added their signatures to the letter. Likewise, white community members John Roos, Lewis Robinson, Reverend James Sims and Peter Sims, a deacon in the Baptist church, also signed the document.[31] The executive committee did not immediately act on the charges, but curtailed all correspondence to her over the next several months.

During the summer of 1851 the Queen's Bush AME minister, Samuel H. Brown, also became embroiled in a scandal. Without the authority of the Bishop of Canada, Daniel A. Payne,[32] Canadian ministers

*Born in South Carolina
in 1811, Daniel Alexander
Payne was elected Bishop
of the African Methodist
Episcopal Church in
1852.*
From Payne, Daniel A.,
*Recollections of Seventy
Years,* published in
Nashville, Tennessee in
1888.

had elected Brown to the position of General Superintendent of the
Canadian Conference. Angered by the threat to the leadership of the
denomination, Payne impeached all the ministers at the annual
meeting of the Canadian Conference. Brown pleaded guilty, but
claimed the Canadian ministers had acted on the advice of the
Reverend Edmund Crosby, former AME missionary to Upper
Canada. Crosby had supported the action because, in his opinion,
American church leaders had neglected the Canadian churches.
Brown asked for forgiveness on behalf of all the ministers and relin-
quished his position as General Superintendent, prompting Payne to
forgive him and all the other ministers.[33]

In his 1891 published history of the AME church, Bishop Payne
commended the Reverend Brown's actions stating that:

> Rev. Samuel H. Brown cannot be too highly praised
> for his ready compliance with what the Disicipline of

the AME Church required, because it was evidently in his power to do the Connection in Canada great harm, even if he did not succeed in its entire over-throw. Had he been as turbulent, ungovernable and ambitious as he was talented and shrewd, all the power of the Church in the United States would have been insufficient to subdue him, or prevent the mischief which he could have accomplished.[34]

During the annual meeting of the AME Canadian Conference, a number of new ministers were ordained including Henry L. Dawson, who had emigrated to Canada West in the 1840s. His first assignment was to the Hamilton Circuit, an extensive circuit that included the Peel Township AME church and stretched as far north as Owen Sound in Grey County.[35] During the conference, Dawson and three other delegates drafted a series of resolutions, which outlined the denomination's views on American slavery. Conference delegates unanimously adopted the resolutions, which read in part:

Whereas, Slavery is a most gross outrage against humanity, and a positive violation of every one of the ten commandments of God, and destructive of all political, moral and religious rights; and

Whereas, Slavery is in itself theft, murder, rob-bery, licentiousness, concubinage, adultery, and everything else that is sinful and devilish between heaven and earth; therefore,

Resolved, 1st. That it is the bounden duty of all our ministers most faithfully to lift up their voices against the monstrous iniquity, and more especially American slavery, for reasons too obvious to be named, it being the vilest upon which the sun ever shone, and in defiance of the laws of God, the claims of humanity, and the rights of our poor, outcast, downtrodden brethren.

Resolved, 2nd. That we will not open the doors of our houses of worship to any slaveholding preacher or lecturer, or their aiders and abettors, under any circumstances whatsoever, where we have a knowledge of the same.

Resolve, 3rd. That the African Methodist Episcopal Church has been, theoretically and practically, anti-slavery from its commencement until the present, and was never otherwise known to be – empty and vain assertions to the contrary, notwithstanding.

Resolved, 4th. That on account of slavery, oppression, and a desire peaceably to worship God according to the dictates of their own consciences, and to secure these blessings to their children after them, were the causes that impelled our fathers to found and establish, by the grace of the God, this, our beloved Zion.[36]

Based on the census taken by Timothy O'Callaphan of Peel Township in 1851, the Black population numbered 154. At first glance this figure seems to confirm the massive exodus of Blacks described by the missionaries. However, after cross-referencing the census with other sources, it became apparent that O'Callaphan had not always filled in the designation of colour column when enumerating Black families. After combining all the available sources making reference to members of the Black community, it is more likely that at least 192 Blacks lived in Peel Township. In contrast, Michael Peter Empey's enumeration of the Black families in Wellesley Township for the 1851 census appears to be more reliable. He reported that forty-five Blacks lived in Wellesley Township, bringing the total Black population of the two townships to 237.[37]

The census provides valuable insights into the demographics of the Queen's Bush Black community. While families of African descent were scattered across the two townships, the majority lived in southern Peel Township between concession 1 and 5. Although the census does not list them as consecutive households, John Little, Samuel White, Josephus Mallot and Thomas Gibbs all lived on concession 1. A similar cluster of families that included John Goins, Dennis Jackson, Henry Smith, Jacob Stewart, and David Osborn lived on concession 2. The majority of the community's residents, who were over age eighteen, stated that they were natives of Canada. Those who were over age eighteen, but who had been born in the southern United States were from the slave states of Maryland, Virginia, North Carolina, Kentucky and Tennessee. Only three children out of a total of 133 had been born in a slave state, while 114 children were natives of Canada. One hundred thirty-seven individuals reported that they were members of the Wesleyan Methodist Church, while twenty-six were associated with the African Methodist Episcopal or Methodist Episcopal churches. Other religious affiliations included the Baptist Church and Church of England, Church of Scotland, Christian and Catholic churches. One Peel Township farmer, Charles Smith, did not report any religious association, but simply stated that he believed in the "equality of rights" for all.[38]

Interestingly, race was not an obstacle to marriage, for at least five interracial families resided in the community. In each case, a Black man had married a white woman. Peter E. Susand's, wife, Elizabeth, had been born in England, so had Levi Jones' wife, Elizabeth. William Gordon's wife, Margaret, was a native of Ireland. Thomas Armstrong's wife, Martha, had been born in Canada and the Reverend Jacob Libertus' wife, Hannah, was a native of Vermont.[39]

The names of Queen's Bush residents, Major Mingo, Major Harding and Patsey Douglass all suggest a slave past, although African names frequently used by slaves in the Deep South, such as Cuff, Juba and Minta, were not found among Queen's Bush families.

Most parents chose Anglo-Canadian names for their children and
frequently used the names of family matriarchs and patriarchs. Three
successive generations of the Palmer family were named William;
Joseph was a favourite name in the Mallot family. Vincent Douglass,
James Dunn, Ben Eady, John Francis, John Goins, Alfred Moodie,
and Solomon Tibbs were all named after their fathers. Females were
often named after their mothers, although the practice was not as
common as naming sons after their fathers. Ben and Margaret Eady
named their third daughter Margaret. Jeremiah and Mary Ann
Powell also named one of their daughters Mary Ann. Children were
also occasionally named after Black or white community members
indicating that friendships existed between both races. In honor of
the missionaries, George and Sophia Harper named their children,
Fidelia, Jonathan, and Mary A.

The Black population of Wellesley Township was not only smaller
than that of Peel Township, but it also differed in its economic status.
While all of the adult men in Peel Township were reported to be
farmers, only five families in Wellesley Township made a living by
farming. Men who were the heads of households in four other families worked as labourers, while Thomas Armstrong operated a
wheelwright shop and was the only Black businessman listed in the
community. Fourteen-year-old Abner Posey, worked at whatever job
he could find as a labourer or as a servant and fifteen-year-old,
Daniel Brown attended school, but worked part-time as a domestic
servant in the home of Michael Peter Empey, who owned a general
merchandise store in Hawksville.[40]

In a letter dated September 23, 1851, to the AMA, a melancholy
Mary Teall summed up the previous year admitting that it had been
a difficult time for her. She lamented:

> The past year has been one of unusual care, toil, &
> suffering, both mental, & physical. Our work for the
> colored people here is almost done as they have

nearly all moved away; there will not be over 20
scholars for the coming winter.[41]

The next day Teall drafted another letter to the AMA requesting supplies for the mission for the upcoming winter. She warned George
Whipple that, "I have dealt out <u>my</u> bedding, clothes to the extent this
summer, that we shall <u>suffer</u> ourselves unless we have a new recruit
before winter sets in."[42]

By the end of 1851, Thomas Vipond, whom the AMA had hired to
untangle John Brooks' financial affairs, was also frustrated. After
wrangling for several months with Brooks' debtors, he had collected
only $120. Vipond relinquished the job complaining that it was
"tedious and troublesome."[43] He turned the money over to Mary Teall,
who divided it among several families "that were about to be stript
[sic] of their all."[44] In his final report to the AMA, Vipond included a
lengthy list of individuals who still owed money to John S. Brooks. Of
great interest are the additional notes concerning the ability of the
debtors to repay their loans. Josephus Mallot, wanted to clear his
debt, but his economic circumstances were so poor that he could not
pay in cash, so he offered to work for Mary Teall. Vipond encouraged
the arrangement and reported to the AMA that, "it would be a pity to
distress him as he is an honest colored man and industrous [sic]."[45]

In November, Mary Teall confided to a correspondent that the
demise of her school had become inevitable and that she would probably close it in the spring. The deteriorating financial situation of the
two sisters had become so critical that for several months they had
not known "where the next mouthful of food was coming from."[46]
Their situation hardened Teall's attitude towards the missionary
system and she bitterly criticized it as ineffectual, stating:

> I feel assured that our friends at home that sit down
> at their ease, & never have entered such a field as this,
> know but little of it hardships, & toils. I am more &

more convinced that this is not the right system to
benefit the colored people, or to do them any <u>perma-
nent</u> good, for my part I am not satisfied; my conscience is not at rest, our labour is nearly all lost, it is
to much like water spilt upon the ground which of
course cannot be gathered up again, nearly all we can
do for the children is counteracted at home by their
vicious parents. What shall be done? It was to solve
this query that I went all the way to N. Y. last winter,
& came back as wise as I went. But something <u>must</u>
<u>be</u> <u>done</u> if you wish to do them any lasting good. My
proposal is an orphan home for females only.[47]

Although in a letter written to the AMA a month later she optimisti-
cally reported:

There are still remaining some 10 or 12 families of
colored people within reach of the school & they
have said that they were going to send [their children to school]. But after all the opposition & persecutions there is a bright side: some good has been
done & can still be done.[48]

Disturbing rumours about Teall's illicit affair with Thomas Vipond
continued and eventually reached the Reverend Elias E. Kirkland in
New Canaan. Unable to ignore the gossip any longer, George
Whipple finally broached the subject. In her reply to inquiries, Teall
explained that the accusations against her character had begun as a
result of the baptisms performed at the Reverend Swan's protracted
revival. She assured Whipple that the accusations were:

a heavy blow. I never knew till then that a good
<u>name</u> was more to me than life itself. I must confess

that I was anxious to know whether you had heard of the persecutions & whether it had affected you or not. I thought it had, & perhaps not without grounds for I wrote three or four times after my return [from New York]; & received no answer, nor did I receive any communication from the board after till in the fall, hence the conclusion that you had heard, & believed the reports.[49]

Anxious to make light of the rumours and to prove that she had made substantial contributions to the community, Teall drafted a summary of her accomplishments. While lengthy, it does provide a glimpse at the varied services that she offered to the community. Teall proudly reflected that since her arrival she had taught approximately two hundred children how to read and write. The students who had attended her school:

Up to this time [winter of 1850] they were all colored children, with two or three exceptions, but as the colored people began to move away, their number has been on the decrease ever since; & in their place we have white settlers, whose children are as needy as they. There are however, some 10 or 12 families of colored people still within reach of the school, that will most likely remain in the neighborhood. The winter of 1851 my school numbered 80 scholars 30 of them colored children – & last summer 42 – 11 colored. This last winter its number was 43 – 17 of whom were colored. In connecion (sic) with the school, I commenced a sabbath school in February 1849, & have continued it ever since both summer and winter. Sometimes it has numbered between one & two hundred – in the winter, generally about

60 – sometimes more. We also have a female prayer meeting once a week.[50]

Not only had she provided assistance to Queen's Bush residents, but she had helped families who had relocated to Grey County, as well.[51] Whenever possible she sent them books and clothing, yet as Teall related to the AMA:

> some children whose parents have removed to a great distance, in the interior, have traversed the distance of a hundred miles back to me through the forest, to get books, clothes. In some cases I have been under the painful necessity of sending them empty away – having nothing to give.[52]

Teall obviously hoped her letter would renew the AMA's confidence in her role as a missionary teacher and reaffirm its commitment to financial aid.

In her report to the AMA dated February 1852, a worried Teall expressed her concern for the plight of the dwindling Black community. The previous year's harvest had been poor and the price of wheat had dropped. Life for many families had become an incessant struggle as they clung tenaciously onto their land.

> The taxes are very heavy on the people here, that together with their Installments often tear poor industrious families to pieces, & causes great suffering. It is almost impossible to get a dollar in money here, you can judge from the price of wheat which has been only 3 shillings of our money, or as it is called here York money, a bushel this winter.[53]

To further illustrate the bleak situation, she described the on-going struggle of one of her neighbours, a:

> poor, pious, industrious, colored family. Quite an exception to most here, who borrowed about two years ago nearly two hundred dollars to secure 50 acres of land, & to pay it the husband, & father has been absent whenever he could leave his family in towns below & twice has gone over to the states to collect the money, & when he had got all payed but $30 a few weeks ago his oxen & three cows were seized, & taken from him, & they were his only dependence: the oxen to work his land, & the cows to support his family, to keep them in groceries etc with the butter made from them, & by the by the old lady had raised them all herself from one old cow. The same inhuman man seized them once before, has caused so much cost that the whole [debt] now is nearly $50.[54]

Teall gave the family twenty dollars, although she could barely afford to donate the money. She further lamented that she had received very few donations since the departure of John and Fidelia Coburn Brooks. The only substantial contribution made to the mission during the year had been thirty dollars from the AMA. Teall's only other source of income had been the modest $2 a week fee that she received from the occasional student boarder. Desperate for help, Teall stated, "there are here some wicked evil designing men who are doing all they can to root out, & send away every colored family in the place, & as far as it is my power I am determined to frustrate their design. Will you help me?"[55] The AMA continued to send money sporadically to Teall, but it did not sufficiently meet all of her needs.

The course of Teall's life dramatically changed in April 1852 when she became pregnant. Under the pretense of being ill she informed her sister, Susan, that she needed a rest from the trials and tribulations of administering the school. The unexpected news surprised Susan Teall, but she agreed that a vacation would improve Mary's health. After receiving money from Thomas Vipond for her travelling expenses, Mary Teall packed her baggage and left for the United States without revealing her destination. Fearful that her absence would alarm AMA executives, Teall warned her sister not to notify them of her departure. Susan Teall heeded her sister's warning and did not correspond with the AMA for the remainder of the summer. However, ensuing correspondence from Mary Teall to her sister and to the AMA indicates that she visited relatives in New York, including her uncle, Dr. Samuel T. Teall, of Lockport. By July, Teall had moved to Wellsborough, in Tioga County, Pennsylvania, where she lived with her father and sisters.[56]

At the end of June, ASC agent, Reverend Samuel Ringgold Ward arrived in nearby Elora to present a lecture. Ward had become one of the Society's most active agents and had gained a reputation as an electrifying orator. In addition to his successful public lectures, Ward played a valuable role in organizing auxiliary anti-slavery societies in Kingston, Hamilton, London, Windsor and Grey County. Ward's whirlwind schedule prevented him from touring Peel Township, but it is likely that many community members attended his lecture held at the Elora Methodist Church. Typically, Ward's lectures focused on the accomplishments made by Blacks despite slavery and racial discrimination. He emphasized that their progress as freemen dispelled pro-slavery myths that Blacks were intellectually inferior to whites and were a dependent race. As a result of travels across the province, Ward concluded that overall Canadians condemned slavery and generally sympathized with the plight of fugitive slaves. However, he felt that Canadians were too often imbued with the same racist sentiments as Americans. Ward noted that Blacks in Canada West were often the victims of racially motivated abuse and were frequently refused accommodations in taverns and hotels, on omnibuses and steamboats. He also criticized school boards that excluded Black students from local schools. Ward reminded his audiences that under British law there was no distinction between whites and Blacks, and he encouraged Blacks to use the law to protect their civil liberties. He also urged his audiences to avoid living in segregated communities and to settle throughout the province to facilitate integration into Canadian society.[57]

Despite the efforts of the ASC and agents, such as Ward, the Canadian anti-slavery movement did not lead to any fundamental improvements in the social and economic conditions of the Black population. Incidents of racism remained prevalent in the province and, by 1857, the ASC was merely a relief operation for fugitive slaves who arrived in Toronto.[58]

In early 1852, after a trying year and a half in Sierra Leone, John S. Brooks returned to his Massachusetts home. In a solemn letter to George Whipple, Brooks complained that he was in extremely poor health, plagued by constant fatigued, swollen feet and aching joints. Worst of all, ulcerated sores that would not heal covered his legs. Brooks confided to Whipple that he was so debilitated that he felt like "a broken down man" and he feared that he might be dying.[59]

Brooks' health slowly improved and in June he travelled to Peel Township to sort out his complicated financial affairs. Upon his arrival, Brooks discovered that the township had drastically changed. Most of the Black families, whom he had previously known, had moved away. Although many families still lived in shanties, carefully constructed log cabins, fenced fields and orchards dotted the landscape. New hamlets such as Winfield on the sixth concession had sprung up while Allan Village overlooking the Conestogo River had grown into a sizable settlement. The village boasted two blacksmith shops, three shoemakers, a cooperage, two potash manufacturers, a tanner and two taverns. George Allen had become one of the most successful businessmen in Peel Township. Employees at his sawmill were cutting approximately sixty thousand feet of lumber per year and, in 1849, Allen had commissioned Paul Willson to construct a gristmill to add to his growing number of business ventures. The local post office known as Peel operated in Allen's store and had become one of the community's social centres. Farmers gathered at the store to collect their mail, discuss politics, local land sales, the weather, crops and just to gossip. Migration into the township had continued to increase partly because of road improvements. In 1849, Sam Wissler, the Peel Township representative to the District Council of Wellington had promoted the passage of a bylaw that called for the creation of a road between Salem and Alma. The road had opened up the northern half of the township to a new influx of settlers. The road between Guelph and Arthur, which had once been almost impassable during most of the year had also been greatly improved. Nearby towns, including Waterloo and Berlin, were developing into prominent centres of trade and industry making access to goods and services easier for the Queen's Bush residents.[60]

While delighted to renew old friendships, Brooks' visit was a time of personal despair and uncertainty. His earlier correspondence to the AMA had illustrated a confident, energetic young man with a strong devotion to missionary life. However, his correspondence to the AMA during his stay in Peel Township reveals a brooding, melancholy man uncertain about his future and still grieving for his wife. Grappling with his personal problems, Brooks tried to concentrate on locating a buyer for his property holdings despite the fact that ownership had been transferred to the AMA. A farmer named Knox[61] had been living on the Mount Hope Mission property and had paid one of the installments, but failed to make any additional payments. The situation was further complicated by the fact that Knox had removed lumber, bricks and approximately fifty fruit trees from the property without permission or reimbursement. A prospective buyer offered nine hundred dollars for the farm, but Brooks refused to sell, confident that it was worth at least $1,200. Unwilling to sell the land below market value, but unsure of how to resolve his financial problems, Brooks considered moving permanently back to Peel Township. While contemplating the idea, Brooks thought it prudent to take the oath of allegiance, to ensure that he could legally purchase or sell land. He also intensified his efforts to collect his outstanding loans, but the fall harvest was still several months away and few farmers had any money. Those who did were saving it for their annual land payment and taxes. By early August, Brooks had collected only $14, but his health had improved and with it had come a renewed enthusiasm for his missionary work in Africa. When Thomas Vipond offered to buy the property on the east half of lot 12, concession 3, at a fair price, Brooks gladly accepted. With cash in hand and the realization that he would never collect all of the money owed to him, he left the township and returned to the Kaw-Mendi Mission in Sierra Leone. He would never return to Peel Township.[62]

Shortly after Brooks' departure, Susan Teall finally drafted a letter to the AMA. She reported that she had conducted a large summer school with an enrollment of eighty students. Almost all of the children were under age sixteen and the daily average attendance had been between fifty and sixty students. However, only thirty-five students had enrolled for the winter term and on average the daily attendance ranged from fifteen to twenty students. Of the thirty-five enrolled students only ten were Black. The majority of the community's chil dren, Black and white, had enrolled in the township's common schools. During the ensuing months Teall did not correspond further with the AMA and managed the Mount Pleasant school alone without any apparent financial assistance.[63]

By 1852 the official membership of the Peel Township AME church had dwindled to forty-nine. To halt the decline in membership, the Reverend Samuel H. Brown proposed at the annual Canadian Conference meeting in St. Catharines, that the church be removed from the Hamilton Circuit. He suggested that the Peel Township church should be combined with the Owen Sound church to form a smaller circuit that would be more manageable for the Reverend

Henry Dawson. Conference delegates agreed and called the new circuit the Queen's Bush Circuit.[64]

At the end of the year, Mary Teall, who in the meantime had
moved to New York City, gave birth to a daughter. Unable to remain
silent any longer, she notified the AMA of her circumstances, begged
for forgiveness and requested a loan to enable her father and herself
to homestead in the western United States. As an unwed mother she
was deeply worried about her future and asked George Whipple for
guidance. She explained that she felt "utterly incapable of deciding. I
wish to do right and must look to others for direction. My brain reels,
and I am lost in a thick dark image. Pray for me."[65]

AMA officials were shocked by Teall's revelations. In search of an
explanation, George Whipple wrote to the Reverend Elias E. Kirkland
at New Canaan, who personally knew both Vipond and Teall.
Kirkland responded:

> O how can we tell who to trust. I am more surprised
> at Thomas Vipond than his victim. He a professed
> minister of Jesus Christ – a friend of the missionary
> & colored man & who has an unblemished charac-
> ter while I lived in that vicinity for more than three
> years.[66]

Whipple also questioned Susan Teall accusing her of aiding and pro-
tecting her sister. Susan adamantly denied any knowledge of the
illicit affair, but she defended her and her sister's relationship with
Vipond describing him as:

> the firm friend of the teachers, & of the colored
> people. When we have had any work to do, we have
> generally engaged him to do it. He has also assisted
> us in doing business, obtaining provisions, etc., so
> that he has frequently been here, but I had never

doubted the character which he bears for sterling integrity.[67]

Whipple also corresponded with Vipond and demanded to know his intentions concerning Mary Teall's future. Vipond promised to support Teall and his child, but he admitted that he could not send any money before the fall harvest. He had given his entire savings, $250, to relatives in England to finance their emigration to Canada and he had nothing else to offer. Vipond begged Whipple not to reveal the child's birth to his eighty-two-year-old mother, but he demanded to know Mary's whereabouts. In desperation he stated, "I can think on any other subject but this. I will find her if I have to traverse the burning sands in the search, hide her you can not from my eyes."[68]

On February 28, 1853, Susan Teall sent a letter to George Whipple recommending that the Mount Pleasant Mission School be closed. She feared that the reputation and accomplishments of all the previous missionaries would be jeopardized if the community were to learn about her sister's illegitimate child. The executive committee agreed with her decision. Teall finished the term and closed the school in early April. In one of her last letters from Peel Township to the AMA, she confided to Whipple:

> It has been a trial for me to leave this field, yet I feel that it is best & when duty calls tis mine to obey. I hope still to be useful in whatever sphere I am placed by the will of Divine Providence: tho my sympathies are with the cherished & downtroden children of Africa. The only thing I have to regret in leaving, is that my duties have not been more faithfully performed.[69]

Teall returned to her home in Knoxville, Pennsylvania, where she took up a teaching position in one of the local schools.[70]

"Most of the colored people living here are doing as well, if not better, than one could reasonably expect"[1]

SUSAN TEALL'S FINAL LETTER to the AMA ends nine years of richly detailed correspondence about the Queen's Bush. The AMA's records do not provide any additional information about the community and it is, therefore, not known how the missionaries' departure affected the community. One resident, John Francis, complained that the teachers who taught in the township's common schools did not discuss slavery in their classrooms. Francis planned to teach his own children "about slavery, and get books to show them what we have been through, and fit them for a good example."[2]

In July 1853, the seventy-member Peel township AME congregation once again hosted the annual meeting of the Canadian Conference. Province-wide, the denomination had reached a membership of 1,069 and the fourteen ministers who attended the meeting represented a total of twenty churches. The Reverend William Paul Quinn, Bishop of the Indiana and Canadian Conferences, presided over the meeting along with Reverend Willis Nazrey,[3] who served as Bishop of the Baltimore and New York Conferences. Although discussions revolved mostly around church matters, the delegation also drafted resolutions recognizing Canada as a safe haven for fugitive slaves and urged parishioners to take the oath of allegiance to become British citizens. Several ministers including, Samuel H. Brown, Alexander Hemsley, William H. Edwards and Peter O'Banyon did pledge their allegiance to the British government. The delegates also engaged in a lengthy discussion about the observance of Emancipation Day, which they felt had evolved into a celebration devoted to parades, sporting events and dancing. Concerned that the significance of the day was not being observed, the ministers agreed to conduct thanksgiving prayer services in their communities as part of the day's festivities.[4]

The disciplinary trial of the Reverend Henry Dawson, minister of the Queen's Bush Circuit, constituted another major part of the meeting. Although the Queen's Bush Circuit had been organized the previous year out of the larger Hamilton Circuit, Dawson still had trouble attending to both the Peel Township and Owen Sound congregations. Dawson's peers accused him of neglecting his duties and Bishop Quinn discharged him from the circuit. Thomas Pearce, a newly ordained deacon, became Dawson's successor.[5]

On July 15, the ministers ended their four-day meeting with a special memorial service for Reverend Samuel H. Brown's wife, Priscilla, who had died on April 23, at the age of 67. Brown's long-time friend and associate, Reverend Alexander Hemsley delivered the eulogy and Reverend Richard Warren,[6] of the Sandwich AME church, offered the closing prayer. The following morning the ministers thanked the community for its hospitality and officially adjourned the meeting.[7] It would be the last AME Canadian Conference annual meeting to be held in the community.

As the influx of Black immigrants to Canada West increased in the 1850s, many of them found it difficult to find employment and white public opinion increasingly demanded segregated schools.[8] Racial sentiments such as those of Thomas Connon, who lived near the Queen's Bush in Elora, were not uncommon. In a letter written in 1853 to his aunt in Scotland, Connon complained that the number of

Blacks immigrating to Canada West was on the rise. He hoped that the local Black population would not increase because he thought Blacks were "great thieves in parts of the country where they are the inhabitants."[9]

Many reports by abolitionists anxious to solicit aid for fugitive slaves also painted a gloomy picture of the Black community in Canada West. They contended that most Blacks were destitute and required a great deal of assistance. In 1855, Benjamin Drew, a Boston journalist and abolitionist, travelled through Canada West and talked to over one hundred individuals from fourteen different communities. He subsequently published 114 of those the interviews in his book, *The Refugee: Or the Narratives of Fugitive Slaves in Canada*. Drew hoped that by allowing Blacks to speak for themselves the American public would learn their true economic and social conditions.[10]

While visiting the Queen's Bush area, Drew interviewed Thomas Elwood Knox, Sophia Burthen Pooley, John Francis, William Jackson, John Little and his wife, Eliza. Despite the earlier problems that had beset the community, they all agreed however, that the community enjoyed a more peaceful existence. Thomas Elwood Knox believed that most families were "doing as well, if not better, than one could reasonably expect."[11] Moreover, he insisted that Blacks and whites lived amicably together in the Queen's Bush and declared, "all are equal here: I have been about here a great deal, but have seen no prejudice at all."[12] Eliza Little reported that, "the best of the merchants and clerks pay me as much attention as though I were a white woman: I am as politely accosted as any woman would wish to be."[13]

William Jackson thought that the actions of newly arrived fugitive slaves often provoked some of the racial attacks because they did not realize the accepted limits of freedom. He believed that they "feel so free, that they go beyond good limits, and have not courtesy enough. But I find that they get over this after awhile."[14] Jackson claimed that he had never encountered any prejudice in the Queen's Bush himself stating that, "I have heard white people who lived at Queen's Bush say, that they never lived amongst a set of people that they had rather live with as to their habits of industry and general good conduct."[15]

Life in the community had been similarly good for John and Eliza Little. The couple had nearly one hundred acres under cultivation and their previous year's harvest had included, 700 bushels of wheat, 200 bushels of potatoes, 100 bushels of peas, 250 bushels of oats, and 10 tons of hay. Impressed with Little's farm, Drew described it as "one of the best, and among the best managed" in Peel Township.[16]

Little took great pride in his accomplishments stating that:

> I thank God that I am respected in this neighbor-
> hood by the best men the country can afford – can
> lend or borrow two thousand dollars any time I am
> asked, or choose to ask for it. I don't say this for the
> sake of boasting – I say it to show that colored men
> can take care of themselves, – and to answer any
> who deny that Canada is a good country.[17]

In contrast, John Francis had not been quite as successful as Little, ascribing many of the failures of Blacks to their lack of education. He told Benjamin Drew that "the colored people in the Queen's Bush, are doing pretty well – they have many drawbacks: as they can keep no books nor accounts, they are liable to be overreached – and are overreached sometimes."[18]

Given the existence of discrimination in other bi-racial communities, it is probable that racial incidents did occur in the Queen's Bush. Although much of the available evidence suggests that the relationship between Blacks and whites was mostly harmonious. This may have been due, at least in part, to the integrated nature of the community. Black families were not segregated to any particular section of the community and many individuals interacted socially with whites by attending the local schools and community events. According to the marriage records of the period 1840 to 1869, Blacks and whites did occasionally intermarry. In 1858, Jacob Dever, a young Black man, obviously did not fear any reprisals when he placed an ad in the Fergus *British Constitution and Fergus Freeholder* looking for a wife. The twenty-three-year-old bachelor stated that he had no objection to her being English, Irish or Scottish, as long as she had an education, could speak different languages and play the piano.[19]

Many of the Queen's Bush residents interviewed by Drew appreciated the symbolism of their experience in Canada, realizing that their success would lend credibility to the American anti-slavery movement. John Little relished the power of his achievements to disprove pro-slavery claims that Blacks would become sickly and die if they were emancipated:

> I thank God that freedom has never overweighted us: some it has, but I have worked to support it, and not to discourage it. I thought I ought to take hold and work and go ahead, to show to others that there is a chance for the colored man in Canada; to show the spirit of a man, and a desire to improve his condition. As it is so often said by slaveholders, that if the 'niggers' were free, and put in a place where they would be together they would starve to death, I wanted to show to the contrary.[20]

Little also had a message for his former owner:

> I would like to show this [farm] to that everlasting scoundrel, E-, my former master, and tell him, 'All this I would have done for you cheerfully, and thought myself at home and felt happy in doing it, if you would have let me: but I am glad that you scarred and abused me, as it has given to myself and my family the fruits of my own labor.'[21]

For those Blacks struggling in urban areas, Little offered his own success as a model of self-improvement:

> I would like to show it to those stout, able men, who, while they might be independent here, remain in towns as waiters, blacking boots, cleaning houses, and driving coaches for men, who scarcely allow them enough for a living. To them I say, go into the backwoods of Queen Victoria's dominions, and you can secure an independent support. I am the man who has proved it; never man came into an unsettled country with lesser means to begin with. Some say, you cannot live in the woods without a year's provisions, – but this is not so: I have come here and proved to the contrary. I have hired myself out two days to get things to work on at home one. If there is a man in the free States who says the colored people cannot take care of themselves, I want him to come here and see John Little.[22]

In July 1855, the sixteenth annual meeting of the AME Canadian Conference convened in Chatham. Once again the Queen's Bush Circuit became a topic of discussion when charges of improper conduct were brought against Reverend Thomas Pearce. In his defense, Pearce called on Robert Johnson, the local preacher for the Peel Township church, and Augustus Carr, the circuit steward. The delegates concluded that the charges against Pearce could not be proven. Nevertheless, he was reassigned to the Brantford church and the Reverend Samuel H. Brown returned to the Queen's Bush Circuit. Controversy followed Pearce and, in 1860, church leaders expelled him from the church.[23]

Aside from Pearce's trial there was a much larger issue at stake. By 1855, the AME Canadian Conference had a membership of 2,090 and for seventeen years it had essentially been administered as an American denomination. Canadian AME church members felt it was time to sever these ties and resolved to form a distinctly Canadian church that would confirm their allegiance to their newly adopted homeland. On July 25, Canadian delegates unanimously requested that the Canadian Conference be dissolved, so that a new church could be organized. The request "fell upon the ears of the Conference like a clap of thunder in a clear sky."[24] When the American clergymen recovered from the shock, they acknowledged that it was a reasonable proposal and promised to consider the matter. Church leaders discussed the matter at the General Congress held in Cincinnati, Ohio, in May 1856 and agreed that a separate church should be established to meet the specific needs of the Canadian congregations. In accordance with the decision, thirty-one Canadian and American bishops, elders, itinerant ministers, local preachers and lay delegates assembled in Chatham the following September for the last meeting of the Canadian Conference. It was the largest group of clergymen ever assembled at a Canadian Conference with the Reverend Samuel H. Brown acting as its president. During the afternoon session of the second day, the Reverend William H. Jones,[25] rose before the assembly and read a resolution requesting that the Canadian Conference be granted permission to secede from the mother church. The delegates adopted the resolution and on September 29, Bishop Daniel Payne officially announced the end of the AME church in Canada.[26]

Organizing the newly established church dominated the remainder of the meeting. Delegates patterned the structure after the AME church, the most significant difference being the resolution that acknowledged Queen Victoria as the rightful sovereign. In loyalty to the British government, the delegates adopted the name British Methodist Episcopal (BME) and elected AME Bishop Willis Nazrey as their new bishop.[27]

During the course of the meeting, the Queen's Bush Circuit was renamed the Peel Circuit. The circuit administered by the Reverend

Bishop Willis Nazrey, first Bishop of the British Methodist Episcopal Church.[28]
From Wright, Richard, *Encyclopaedia of the African Methodist Episcopal Church: Containing Principally the Biographies of the Men and Women, Both Ministers and Laymen, Whose Labors During a Hundred and Sixty Years Helped Make the AME Church What It Is,* published in Philadelphia, by the Book Concern at the AME Church in 1947.

Samuel H. Brown included the Peel Township church, the Owen Sound church and a church in Artemesia Township in Grey County. Searches of AME and BME records have failed to provide the exact location of the Artemesia Township church, however the earliest Black settlement in the township was along the Durham Road near present-day Priceville. Therefore, it seems reasonable to conclude that the Artemesia Township church may have been located in this same area. Nevertheless, according to the published minutes of the meeting, the church had thirty-seven members.[29]

In September 1857, Richard Randolph Disney, a young minister from Maryland, travelled to St. Catharines to attend the second annual conference of the BME church. Disney was the freeborn son of Henry and Rebecca Disney of North East, Maryland. At a young age, he moved to Baltimore where he found employment with Solomon McCabe, a barber and prominent member of the city's free Black community. Disney received an education in the local Black school and attended the Bethel AME church with the McCabe family. He developed an interest in the ministry and, in 1851, he enrolled in the Osgood Seminary, a Congregationalist seminary, in Springfield,

Reverend Richard Randolph Disney, minister of the Peel Township BME Church from 1857 to 1859.

From Wright, Richard, *Encyclopaedia of the African Methodist Episcopal Church: Containing Principally the Biographies of the Men and Women, Both Ministers and Laymen, Whose Labors During a Hundred and Sixty Years Helped Make the AME Church What It Is,* published in Philadelphia, by the Book Concern at the AME Church in 1947.

Massachusetts. In 1856, he received a license to preach in the AME church and moved to Canada West.[30]

Disney's formal religious training impressed the delegates at the BME annual meeting and they admitted him to the church on a trial basis. For his first assignment Disney accepted the pastorate of the Peel Circuit under the guidance of Reverend Samuel H. Brown. In recognition of his devotion to his ministerial duties, Bishop Nazrey ordained Disney as a deacon in 1858 at the third annual conference of the BME church. Most likely as the result of a recommendation by Disney and Brown, delegates at the meeting reorganized the Peel Circuit. The Owen Sound and Artemesia Township churches were removed from the Peel Circuit and reassigned to the Oro Circuit, which included churches at Barrie and Collingwood.[31]

In August 1859, the Reverend Disney, along with fourteen other ministers, assembled in Chatham for the fourth annual BME church meeting. They drafted strongly worded resolutions condemning slavery and the American Colonization Society (ACS), which had been established in 1817 by Americans who believed that whites and free Blacks could not live together. Supporters of the ACS viewed free

Blacks as a threat to society, while slaveholders felt that their presence would undermine the institution of slavery. ACS members favoured emigration of free Blacks and, between 1820 and 1861, approximately ten thousand free Blacks and newly manumitted slaves were sent to Liberia under the sponsorship of the colonization society. BME ministers opposed the white-controlled ACS declaring that its primary goal was to "rid the country of the free colored population, that the slaves may be held more secure."[32] Conference delegates also condemned the Reverend William P. Newman for falsely claiming that Blacks in Canada West, especially Methodists, were starving in order to attract donations from American philanthropists. The delegates denounced his statements as "disgraceful to himself and to the inhabitants of Canada."[33] More importantly, they ordered all BME ministers to determine if any of their parishioners had received aid from Newman, and if so, to report the amount to the Church treasurer, who had instructions to refund the money. The ministers also adopted a resolution that forbid BME members from:

> participating in any way whatever in these disgraceful and unmanly appeals to the United States for food and raiment; we would instruct them in all cases of suffering to apply to their pastor, and if he cannot render the necessary assistance from the poor fund of his charge, let application be made to the authorities of the Church, at Chatham.[34]

In reaction to Newman's slanderous statements, the members of the Committee on Education, under the direction of the Reverend William H. Jones, issued a report on the condition of the Black population in Canada West, which stated:

> That the colored people of Canada are making manifest progress in civilization and refinement, and in

several settlements they contribute their full share
to the wealth, industry, and intelligence of the community.

That we rejoice that we are able to record, that provisions are made by law for the education of our
children in common with others, and that our people
generally appreciate this privilege, and hundreds of
colored children in Canada are to be found daily in
School, making rapid progress in the acquisition of
knowledge. We are also happy to report that in every
Circuit and Station of the British Methodist Episcopal
Church, sabbath schools have been organized, and
they are in most cases well attended. There are several literary societies within the bounds of the
Conference doing much to elevate the literary character of the Church, and we earnestly recommend
that every minister in charge, form literary societies
in their respective fields of labor, for the advancement of our people in useful knowledge.[35]

By 1859 the Peel Township BME church under the guidance of the
Reverend Disney and the Reverend Brown had eighty-eight members. The ministers had also encouraged the community's youth to
be active in the church and seventy children attended his Sabbath
School. Four male and three female teachers, who had acquired
eighty-five religious books for the church library, taught the students. But by now, Disney's two-year tenure had ended and church
officials reassigned him to the BME church in Buxton.[36]

With the departure of Disney, came the Reverend George W.
Clark, who had been born in 1811 in the United States and who had
previously served as a local preacher in London, Canada West. Clark's
services to the Peel Township congregation eventually would gain the
approval of the BME leadership and, in 1860, Bishop Nazrey ordained

him as an elder. During the ensuing years Clark served on several BME committees, including the three-member Temperance Committee, where he helped draft resolutions requiring ministers to establish temperance societies and the Committee of Missions, which oversaw fund raising for missions in Central America.[37]

In August 1860, BME ministers met again in St. Catharines. By now, the church had a membership of 2,008 and included: six stations, five circuits and missions, twenty-one churches, fifteen preaching places, three parsonages (one in Peel Township), eighteen itinerant ministers, four deacons, two licentiates, four local deacons, sixteen local preachers and 167 teachers, who instructed 1,189 children at twenty-two Sabbath Schools. The increase in church membership along with a demand for preachers had been so great during the past year, that Bishop Nazrey felt compelled to appoint three local preachers as itinerant ministers on his own authority without waiting for the approval of the annual conference.[38]

Faced with the challenge of administering the rapidly growing denomination, Bishop Nazrey requested that an assistant be elected to help him draft letters, compile reports and perform a countless other church related duties. Conference delegates elected the Reverend William H. Jones of Chatham to serve as Nazrey's assistant, but he declined the position. Delegates held a second ballot and elected the Reverend Samuel H. Brown. A popular minister, Brown had gained the respect of his peers because of his vast experience and knowledge of the Church Discipline. Perhaps not their first choice, his appointment nevertheless was an honour.[39]

While BME churches were enjoying a period of prosperity, the Peel Colored Baptist Church in Glen Allan struggled to survive. In 1857, the church had a small congregation of twelve members, but no permanent minister. Two years later, John Lawson served as the congregation's minister and under his leadership membership had increased to twenty. In 1860, the *Canadian Baptist Register* reported that during the preceding year Lawson had baptized seven people, supervised a

Sunday School with twenty-six students, and had preached at two stations. Officials of the Baptist Missionary Convention were so impressed with Lawson's efforts that they encouraged him to extend his labours to Normanby.[40]

But Lawson received little payment for his ministerial services and was forced to devote more time to farming to supplement his income. By 1861 church membership had declined, and the editors of the *Canadian Baptist Register* chided Lawson for neglecting to spread the gospel, stating:

> This colored brother preaches to the colored people, in Peel, and as many of the white population as come to hear him [sic]. The result of his labors have been by no means satisfactory as we could have wished. There has been no baptisms or conversions reported during the year, and the number of Church members is smaller this year than last, two having died and one only added by letter. Bro. L. seems to have *visited* but little, having reported during the year only 67 visits, while other missionaries report from 100 to 261. It is a noticeable fact, as may be seen from an examination of the statistics, that those of our brethren who do least in the way of pastoral visitations, are the least successful; while he who visits most, is most successful. A glance at the tabulated statement will prove this. Our fear is, in regard to Bro. Lawson's case, that he divides his time between pastoral engagements and secular work – his income being inadequate to the support of his family. All the remarks he makes in his last report are these: 'Brethren, I have nothing new to tell you, but through many difficulties I am striving to preach the gospel.'[41]

Lawson continued to minister to his small congregation until at least 1877, which is the last time the Peel Colored Baptist Church appears in the *Canadian Baptist Register* or the *Baptist Year Book*.[42]

On November 6, 1860, Republican candidate, Abraham Lincoln, became the sixteenth president of the United States. Within days of his election Southern pro-slavery leaders began to contemplate secession and in an effort to formulate a compromise, the United States Congress convened. Senator John J. Crittenden of Kentucky, introduced a series of proposals on December 18, but they were ineffectual and, two days later, South Carolina's state legislature voted to secede from the Union. At his home in Springfield, Illinois, President-elect Lincoln promised to hold the Union together, but he remained adamant that he would not compromise on the issue of the extension of slavery into the western territories. By March 4, 1861, when Lincoln was sworn into office, seven southern states had seceded from the Union and formed the Confederate States of America. They elected Mississippi Senator Jefferson Davis as President and adopted a constitution similar to that of the United States, but one that clearly protected states rights and the institution of slavery. On April 12, 1861, the Civil War began when South Carolina forces fired on Fort Sumter located in Charleston's harbor. Three days later President Lincoln declared a state of insurrection and called for 75,000 volunteers for three months military service. Canadians, Black and white, watched the events closely, for the war raised questions about the future of the Black population in Canada West. Many Canadians feared that the U.S. federal government would attempt to annex the Canadas if victorious in defeating the Confederates. There were even fears and speculation that a Southern victory would result in the re-enslavement of free Blacks and the enslavement of those who had been born free. Despite Queen Victoria's proclamation of neutrality on May 13, 1861, many white Canadians enlisted in the United States Army in search of adventure, bounty money, or because of their anti-slavery views. Those of

African descent, both Canadian and American, were similarly eager
to join the Union Army. They believed that if they demonstrated
their patriotism by serving in the military, the government would be
forced to abolish slavery and grant all Blacks equal rights and citizenship. But their offers to serve in the military were rejected. The
Lincoln administration claimed that the aim of the war was the
restoration of the Union and not the abolition of slavery. Others
argued that Blacks would not make good soldiers or simply refused
to contemplate the idea of Black and white soldiers fighting side by
side in what they essentially perceived as a white man's war. Forced to
sit by idly and watch the war unfold, Blacks on both sides of the
border feared for the safety of friends and relatives who remained in
slavery in the Confederate states.[43]

Based on the 1861 census, at the outbreak of the Civil War, the
Black population of Wellesley and Peel townships numbered 323, an
increase of 36 per cent since 1851. As with the 1851 census, the accuracy
of the 1861 census is questionable and should be viewed with caution.
Nevertheless, according to the census, the Black population of
Wellesley Township consisted of six households with forty-two
individuals; while 281 Blacks lived in fifty-eight households in Peel
Township. Only thirty families residing in the area in 1851 were
listed in the 1861 census. Most Black households consisted of married
couples with children, but four households included more than one
family. For instance, Vincent Douglass' home in Wellesley Township
included his wife and children, and George Brown, his wife and
infant son, as well as eighteen-year-old Angeline Banks. At least
eleven households included children under age twenty with a
different surname, which may indicate that they were orphans or
"working out," as was customary among the surrounding population. Two households had visitors from other communities. James
Thomas, a twenty-six-year-old bachelor from Hamilton was listed
with Mark Harris; while Julia and Catherine Johnson, of Simcoe,
were visitors in Robert Johnson's home.[44]

By 1861 only a small minority of twenty-six families reported that they were independent farmers. The vast majority of Blacks in the community earned their living as labourers. Typically, employment as a labourer in a rural area such as Peel or Wellesley Township, would have been part-time, or at best seasonal, and have included planting and harvesting crops, clearing land and chopping wood. Literacy was not common among most of the adults, especially those who were ex-slaves. The second generation of Black residents were more literate than their parents had been, which clearly indicates that families valued education and took advantage of the local schools.[45]

DISTRIBUTION OF THE BLACK POPULATION
OF THE QUEEN'S BUSH BY BIRTHPLACE, 1861

	Age	
Birthplace	<18	18+
Canada West	141	30
Nova Scotia	2	2
United States	34	112
Unknown		2
Total	177	146

Source: 1861 Canadian Census, Canada West, Waterloo County, Wellesley Township and 1861 Canadian Census, Canada West, Wellington County, Peel Township.

Of the total Black population, 171 individuals reported Canada as their place of birth. One hundred forty-six named the United States, and five members of the Cromwell family were from Nova Scotia, while two individuals did not report a place of birth. A total of 204 individuals reported membership in the BME, Episcopal Methodist or Colored Methodist churches; ninety-nine residents were Baptists and five were members of the Free Presbyterian Church. Henrietta Still and her children, Charles and Sophia, were Quakers. Although, in 1851, the Wesleyan Methodist church had been the most popular church with a membership of 137, in 1861 only one resident reported affiliation with that denomination.[46]

As the census suggests, the BME Church had attracted a large following throughout the province. In 1861 alone, 500 individuals joined the denomination. With an increase in membership, many congregations were forced to construct larger churches. The Chatham congregation, with its two hundred members embarked on one of the most ambitious projects. The congregation's minister, William H. Jones, designed the brick edifice and then toured the northern United States to raise money for its construction. When completed in 1861, at a cost of $5,000, the new church had a seating capacity of 1,500.[47]

In 1862, the Peel Township congregation, which had 165 members with a Sabbath School enrolment of sixty children, was also in need of a new sanctuary. Local carpenters and labourers worked throughout the summer months to complete the simple frame structure, which they built on the Reverend Brown's farm, probably near or on the site of the original church. The financially solvent congregation paid $400 for the new church, which included 4,500 feet of lumber, 600 feet of timber and 9,000 shingles. At the dedication ceremony, church members celebrated the completion of their new sanctuary, and the Reverend George W. Clark boasted that a hundred dollars still remained in the church treasury.[48]

In June the Reverend Samuel H. Brown and the Reverend George W. Clark left their Peel Township homes to attend the annual meeting of the BME church in London. Bishop Willis Nazrey was unable to take part, so Brown presided over the seven-day conference. One of the most pressing points on the agenda was a disciplinary hearing into the dealings of a group of ministers who had challenged Nazrey's position by proclaiming Reverend Augustus R. Green as Bishop of the BME church. The ministers who supported Green included Charles H. Pearce,[49] George W. Broadie,[50] Henry J. Young,[51] William Douglass[52] and Edward Brook.[53] As a result of the trial, all six ministers were charged with insubordination and expelled from the church. In response, they established their own denomination, calling it the Independent Methodist Episcopal Church and elected Green as the Bishop.[54]

The Reverend George W. Clark, minister of the Peel Circuit, although only peripherally associated with the dissident ministers, was also accused of supporting the faction. Clark acknowledged his part and asked for forgiveness. The delegates, moved by his apology, voted not to expel him from the church. Clark nevertheless resigned his position as minister of the Peel Circuit and joined the AME Ohio Conference. James Baker, formerly a deacon in the Zion Wesleyan church, replaced Clark. When Baker died the following year, local preacher Robert Johnson assumed the pastorate.[55]

In September 1862, President Lincoln issued his Emancipation Proclamation, which took effect the following the first day of January. The proclamation freed slaves in the Confederate States, but it excluded several slave states that bordered the Confederacy because Lincoln needed their political support. It also did not apply to those slaves in areas of the south under Federal military occupation. In reality, the proclamation only freed slaves in the states which were in open rebellion against the federal government and in any case, beyond Lincoln's jurisdiction. Although some states had already begun to raise exclusively Black troops, a clause in the proclamation officially allowed Black men to serve in the Union Army. In May 1863, the War Department established the Bureau of Colored Troops to recruit and oversee the management of Black units. Many of the Black regiments previously organized by state governments were redesignated as United States Colored Troops.[56]

Many young Black men in Canada West, eager to join the war

effort, enlisted in the newly created Black regiments. As a result, many Black communities, such as the Elgin Settlement, witnessed drastic reductions in their populations. Between 1863 and 1865 over two-thirds of Elgin Settlement's young men left Buxton. Community leaders including Mary Ann Shadd and Josiah Henson joined the war effort by serving as recruiting agents.[57] BME clergymen continued to profess their loyalty to the British government, but admitted that "we nevertheless feel for the unhappy bondman as if in bonds with him, and we are therefore deeply interested in the terrible civil war now raging in the neighbouring Republic, arising from the unholy demands of a system of slavery which is not only an outrage upon man, but an insult to every attribute of God."[58] In June 1863, BME ministers adopted a resolution stating that:

> We are in favour of colored men, in compliance with the request of the Federal Government, shouldering arms and marching to the battle-field to put down the ungodly man-stealers, who, in this war, have no right which coloured men are bound to respect.[59]

Although allowed to enlist, Blacks did not enjoy the same rights as white soldiers. They were forced to serve in segregated units under primarily white commissioned officers. Racist apprehensions about the quality of Black soldiers meant they did not receive the same pay as their white counterparts. Black soldiers received $7 per month, plus $3 for clothing, while whites were paid $13 and $3.50 respectively. Black soldiers challenged the discriminatory treatment and soldiers in the renowned 54th Massachusetts Regiment went so far as to serve without pay as protest against the unfair practice. Unable to ignore the issue, Congress finally passed a bill on June 15, 1864 equalizing the pay between Black and white soldiers. Despite the discriminatory treatment, Black soldiers made significant contributions to the war effort. Before the war ended over 186,000 Blacks, Canadian and

American, served in the Union Army; of that number approximately 38,000 lost their lives. Most deaths were attributed to poor medical care, unsanitary living conditions and overwork.[60]

As the war continued in the United States, the Black inhabitants of Peel and Wellesley townships sponsored an Emancipation Day celebration in the village of Hawksville on Saturday, August 1, 1863. The day commemorated the abolition of slavery throughout the British Empire, but most likely those who attended the event discussed the war and the ramifications of the Emancipation Proclamation. By 11 a.m. approximately 2,500 people had converged on the village and the Berlin Band opened the day's festivities by leading the procession to the Town Hall where the Reverend Milner preached a sermon. The gathering then proceeded to Temperance Island where a cadre of cooks and waiters served dinner and the afternoon orations were provided by the Reverends Downey, Milner, Lawson and Miller.[61]

In the summer of 1863, Dr. Samuel Gridley Howe and Mr. J. M. W. Yerrington visited Canada West on behalf of the American Freedmen's Inquiry Commission. The two men had been instructed to investigate the economic and social condition of the Black population in order to formulate recommendations for the impending emancipation of approximately four million slaves in the South. Howe's published report, *The Refugees from Slavery in Canada West*, was based on observations made during his tour, as well as conversations with both white and Black community leaders in St. Catharines, Hamilton, London, Toronto, Chatham, Buxton, Windsor, Malden and Colchester. Some of the conclusions expressed by Howe in his report have been proven to be erroneous and most likely reflect the prejudices of his time:

> the negroes of Canada, being for the most part hybrids, are not of robust stock, and are unfavorably affected by the climate; that they are infertile, and their infertility is increased by intermarriage with each other; and therefore, unless their number is

kept up by immigrants from the United States, or by
some artificial encouragement, they will decrease
and disappear in a few generations.[62]

On a more positive note Howe stated that Blacks, due to their hard
work and thrift, had promoted the industrial and material interests
of Canada West, and thereby had become valuable citizens. However,
similar to the conclusions reached by Benjamin Drew ten years earlier, Howe found that racial animosity was just as prevalent in
Canada West as in the United States. He noted that racism tended to
be rampant in urban areas with large Black populations, but those
cities with a low ratio of Blacks to whites appeared more tolerant.
Consequently, Howe thought that Blacks should disperse throughout
the province to avoid racial hostility and prejudice.[63]

Although it is unknown whether Howe visited Peel Township, he
did remark that Black families who worked as farmers, in general,
enjoyed a comfortable standard of living. Nevertheless, he felt that
their isolation hindered their intellectual development in compari-
son to individuals living in urban centres who had access to better
schools, literary societies and mutual aid societies.[64]

In summing up his observations, Howe concluded that the Black
population of Canada West, which he estimated to be twenty thousand, had proven beyond a doubt, that free Blacks were capable of
self-guidance and were loyal supporters of any government that
ensured their freedom and equal rights. He firmly believed that the
Black experience in Canada West confirmed the notion that the:

> negro does best when let alone, and that we must
> beware of all attempts to prolong his servitude, even
> under pretext of taking care of him. The white man
> has tried taking care of the negro, by slavery, by
> apprenticeship, by colonization, and has failed dis-
> astrously in all; now let the negro try to take care of

himself. For, as all the blood and tears of our people
in this revolutionary struggle will be held cheap, if
they re-establish our Union in universal freedom, so
all the suffering and misery which his people may
suffer in their efforts for self-guidance and support
will he held cheap, if they bring about emancipation
from the control of whites.[65]

In 1852, at the height of its involvement in the Canadian missionary movement, the AMA had sent $1,441.14 to Canada West and had
sponsored ten missionaries at five different missions or schools. The
missionaries were: Mary and Susan Teall; Elias E. Kirkland and his
wife; Theodosia Lyon; Hiram Wilson and his second wife; David
Hotchkiss and his wife; and Mary Ann Shadd. Just twelve years later,
in 1864, the AMA suspended all aid to Canada West. The withdrawal
of seven missionaries between 1853 and 1854 and a continuous decline
in donations contributed to the AMA's decision to end its support.[66]

The resignations of Mary and Susan Teall have already been
explored, but a brief examination of the other missionaries is offered
here to illustrate the decline of the missionary movement in Canada
West. After eight years in Canada West, under the sponsorship of the
Wesleyan Missionary Board and then the AMA, the Reverend Elias E.
Kirkland had become disillusioned with missionary life. In New
Canaan, as in the Queen's Bush, he became embroiled in disputes
with Black ministers. Kirkland believed the ministers opposed his
missionary endeavors because they were afraid of losing their
influence over the Black community. He also found it frustrating that
no central benevolent organization had ever been established to
coordinate the work of the missionaries in Canada West. In a letter
dated December 27, 1850 to the AMA, Kirkland candidly stated:

There has been some efficient laborers among this
slavery-cursed people, and some who would have

accomplished more had they been properly sustained. Want of a system and a perfect understanding between laborers has tended to cripple our efforts.[67]

He sharply criticized the administrators of the Wesleyan Methodist Missionary Board and the AMA for their lack of leadership by stating that he could have accomplished more as a missionary if he had had, "the council, prayers and guidance of faithful and experienced men." Moreover, he felt:

> There is work enough to be done but in order to accomplish the greatest amount of good there should be no separate interest. The Wesleyan Board and the A. M. Board ought to be identified in their work here. If there is not a perfect understanding between them our work may clash.[68]

In 1853, Kirkland notified the AMA of his resignation complaining that, "the amount of good that I am doing does not pay for the expense of keeping us here with the sacrifice of feeling etc. that we have to make by remaining."[69] Not wanting to assume responsibility for Kirkland's dissatisfaction with missionary work, the AMA refused to disclose all of his reasons for leaving Canada West. The official statement in the 1853 AMA annual report indicates that Kirkland had resigned because:

> opposition to white missionaries manifested by the colored people of Canada had been so greatly increased by the interested misrepresentations of ignorant colored men, pretending to be ministers of the gospel, that he thought his own and his wife's labors, and the funds of the Association, could be better employed elsewhere.[70]

Although the AMA sympathized with the Black community's desire to have teachers and missionaries of their own colour, it was not until 1851 that the organization finally hired its first Black teacher. An experienced teacher, Mary Ann Shadd opened a school in Windsor in 1851 under the sponsorship of the AMA. Just two years later the AMA suspended its aid, claiming that Shadd was not an Evangelical Christian. Shadd had been a Roman Catholic, but later converted to the AME church. In Canada West she had opposed the denomination's segregationist views and had joined the Methodist church. Because she had previously disclosed her religious convictions, Shadd felt that her sharp criticism of Henry Bibb and the Windsor-based Refugee Home Society was the real reason behind the AMA's withdrawal of support.[71]

In 1854, Hiram Wilson, possibly the most influential missionary in Canada West, ended his association with the AMA after a stormy debate over his salary. The AMA executive committee had never considered Canada West a promising missionary field and with Wilson's resignation it was decided that there would be no further increase in the number of missionaries in Canada West, unless exceptionally qualified teachers could be found, who were willing to make the necessary sacrifices. The AMA restricted its support to Theodosia Lyon, who had assumed the management of the New Canaan school after Elias E. Kirkland's departure. But she too, became embroiled in a heated controversy in 1854 when she married John Allen, a fugitive slave who reportedly already had two wives. The AMA terminated her salary after local residents accused her of adultery and demanded that she be dismissed from the school.[72]

In 1855, the Reverend David Hotchkiss had established a mission in Windsor under the auspices of the AMA, but his condescending attitudes and frequent racist remarks alienated the Black community. After arsonists burned his home and then his church in 1857, he moved his missionary operation to the Little River, Puce and Pike's Creek settlements within the Refugee Home Society colony. When the majority of his congregation emigrated to Haiti in 1862, he resigned from the AMA.[73]

Lewis Champion Chambers, a Black minister, was the last missionary in Canada West sponsored by the AMA. Chambers, a native of Cecil County, Maryland, had purchased his freedom for $1,250 in 1844. By the early 1850s, Chambers had become a minister in the AME church and served congregations within the Philadelphia Conference. In 1855, on the recommendation of Bishop Willis Nazrey, he transferred to the Canadian Conference, where he served the Dresden congregation. Three years later, Chambers became a salaried missionary with the AMA while maintaining his position as a minister. In 1864, after aiding missionaries and teachers in Canada West for sixteen years at a cost of approximately $9,000, the AMA suspended all aid. Instead the executives of the AMA decided to redirect their resources to assisting newly emancipated slaves freed by the Emancipation Proclamation. Many other benevolent groups that supported work among the fugitive slaves in Canada West had also curtailed their efforts by 1864.[74]

On April 8, 1865, Confederate General Robert E. Lee surrendered to Union General Ulysses S. Grant at Appomattox Court House in central Virginia. Nine months later, on December 18, Congress adopted the 13th Amendment to the Constitution, which abolished slavery in the United States. With the abolishment of slavery, there was no longer a need for a safe haven in Canada West. Many Blacks returned to the United States to be reunited with family members and friends. Others left to serve as teachers, political leaders, doctors, and clergymen in the Black communities of the South.[75]

Former Peel Township resident, James Curry, was among those who went on a desperate search for lost family members. He had left Peel Township in November 1851 and had settled briefly in St. Catharines before moving on to New York. While searching for his family in Person County, North Carolina, he met a group of white men who "demanded to know whose nigger he was." Defiant, Curry retorted, "I am no man's nigger. I am a free citizen of the United States." Accusing him of sauciness, the men attacked Curry and attempted to shoot him as he fled. Curry escaped unscathed and reported the incident to Union Army Major General A. Ames in Raleigh, who dispatched a squad of cavalrymen to arrest the men. In the meantime, civil authorities seized Curry and charged him with assault. After learning that the occupying military forces had arrested white citizens, Provisional Governor W. W. Holden intervened and demanded their immediate release. Ames refused to release his prisoners and in retaliation civil authorities began proceedings against Curry. The outcome of the power struggle between the military and civil authorities is unknown, but the situation was certainly a precarious one for Curry.[76]

As an increasing number of families returned to the United States, the communities designed specifically for Blacks began to dissolve. The British-American Institute, after struggling for years amidst poor leadership and financial problems closed in 1868. Plagued by factionalism and accusations of fraud, the Refugee Home Society had been in decline since 1854, following the death of Henry Bibb, and ceased operation in 1876. After the Civil War, many young adults from the Elgin Settlement moved to the South and the settlement slowly declined. The Elgin Association issued its last annual report in 1873.[77]

Similarly, many Black inhabitants of Peel and Wellesley townships moved to the United States. During a visit to the community in 1865, just months after the war had ended, Bishop Willis Nazrey noted that the small remnant of Black families, who had remained, could barely support the once prosperous BME church. Two years later the church became part of the London Circuit.[78]

Over time, most people forgot or chose to ignore the existence of the Black community once known as the Queen's Bush. Short references to an early fugitive slave settlement appeared occasionally in local newspapers and histories, but generally they did not acknowledge the diversity of the community and the extensive contributions it had made to the area.

KNOWN MINISTERS WHO SERVED THE PEEL TOWNSHIP
AME/BME CHURCH, 1841-1865

1841-1847	Jacob Dorcey, local preacher
1844-1851	Samuel H. Brown, itinerant minister
1845	Thomas Keith, local preacher
1846-1854	Henry Smith, local preacher
1851-1853	Henry Dawson, itinerant minister
1853-1856	Thomas Pearce, itinerant minister
1855-1863	Robert Johnson, local preacher
1856-1860	Samuel H. Brown, itinerant preacher
1857-1859	Richard R. Disney, itinerant preacher
1859-1862	George W. Clark, itinerant preacher
1862-1863	James Baker, itinerant preacher
1863-1865	Robert Johnson, itinerant preacher

Source: Daniel A. Payne, *History of the African Methodist Episcopal Church* (Nashville: Publishing House of the African Methodist Episcopal Sunday School Union, 1891); Minutes of the Annual Meetings of the AME Canadian Conferences, 1853-1855 and the Minutes of the Annual Conferences of the BME Church, 1856-1865.

What then does the history of the Queen's Bush bring to our understanding of the Black experience in Canada West before 1865? In many respects, the Queen Bush was unique because it was not an organized community like the Wilberforce Settlement, the British-American Institute, the Elgin Settlement or the Refugee Home Society. But, like these communities, its development grew out of the search for a new start in life and the desire for land. The community also provided its diverse residents with a sense of place and independence. Moving into the Queen's Bush as squatters had been a gamble, one that, in the end, most Black farmers lost. Of course, they shared this fate with many other early settlers who, all along the frontier, had cleared and cultivated land they did not own. Many of these settlers were ultimately forced off the land for the same reason they had become squatters in the first place – the lack of sufficient capital. The situation in the Queen's Bush, however, was aggravated by the fact that many Black residents, who might have had an opportunity to acquire land, were prevented from doing so by the racial prejudices and unfair tactics of Crown Land Agents and wealthier white settlers.

Regardless of its outcome, the Queen's Bush settlement should not be dismissed as a failure. Those Black families who had settled in the Queen's Bush could claim many accomplishments. Through their hard work and sacrifice they transformed the wilderness into one of the largest Black communities in Canada West. They established schools, churches, social organizations, and laid the foundation for the future settlement of Wellesley and Peel townships. From the missionary teachers, many children obtained an education, which provided them with skills to better their lives. Undoubtedly, the biggest benefit of the Queen's Bush settlement and others like it – was that it served as a refuge from the demeaning and brutal oppression of slavery. It also provided a mechanism of economic survival and provided the opportunity for many ex-slaves to become accustomed to the fundamental values of middle-class society, develop a consciousness of civic responsibility and political cohesion. The community also constituted an important anti-slavery symbol, for it discredited pro-slavery claims that slaves were content with their lives in bondage and that members of the Black race were inferior and could not exist equally with whites. As such, communities like the Queen's Bush contributed to the anti-slavery movement and the final abolition of slavery. Moreover, and perhaps most importantly, the existence of this community prompted many slaves to strike out for a freedom which otherwise they might not have sought. Despite the disappearance of the Queen's Bush settlement, its story remains a vital part of the Black History of Ontario.

EPILOGUE

THROUGHOUT THE LATE nineteenth century Wellesley and Peel townships continued to be a rural farming area. The community of Glen Allan in Peel Township, attracted a few more businesses and homes, but it remained essentially a small, orderly village. Agriculture and small-scale manufacturing were the main commercial activities in the community.

In 1864, James Hart, James Irvine, Vincent Douglass and James Douglass were the only Blacks listed in the Wellesley Township section of the *Waterloo Gazetteer and General Business Directory*. Similarly, in 1867, only twenty-two men, who can be identified as the heads of Black households were reported in the Peel Township census. The Reverend Samuel H. Brown and his second wife, Ellen, were among the small number of original Black settlers who remained in the township. Brown hosted revivals and camp meetings on his farm and continued to conduct services at the BME church, but by 1871 he considered farming his primary occupation. Brown became seriously ill in early April 1881 and his doctor diagnosed the problem as an inflammation of the bladder. After suffering for twenty-two days, the Reverend Samuel H. Brown died on April 27, at

Tombstone of Reverend Samuel H. Brown. Photograph by Linda Brown-Kublish.

age 86. He had lived in Peel Township for thirty-seven years and had served as a religious leader for over half a century. The editor of the Berlin *Berliner Journal* newspaper noted his passing with a simple obituary, which recognized Brown as one of Peel Township's earliest settlers. Ellen Brown died June 16, 1887, and was buried beside her husband in the AME/BME church cemetery.[1]

In 1907, a correspondent writing for the *Guelph Weekly Mercury & Advertiser* acknowledged Mrs. Joseph Armstrong, Mrs. George Baldwin, Albert Douglass, John Mallot, and Mary A. Lawson as the last of the original Black settlers still living in Peel Township. With

The church on the 4th Line of Peel Township, Wellington County, that
was used by the neighbouring Black residents. The church was known
locally as the "Colored" Church. Courtesy of the Wellington County
Archives PH#5786.

the outbreak of the First World War, many more rural people, both
Black and white residents, migrated to urban areas in search of jobs,
higher wages and stability. Without a congregation, the Peel
Township AME/BME church closed in about 1918.[2]

In 1920, Mrs. Joseph Mallot, Mrs.Ceceila Mallot and George
Mallot, the last Black family in Wallenstein, moved to Brantford
where they established a store.[3] Members of the Mallot family had
lived in Peel Township for seventy-nine years and their departure was
noted with great sadness in the community. To commemorate their
departure, the Mallot's friends and neighbours organized a commu-
nity-wide farewell party. During the festivities they were presented
with a purse of money and the following address was read before the
assembled guests:

The Hisson family of Glen Allan, Peel Township, Wellington County,
outside their home. Identified (from left to right): Annabelle
(b. January, 1912); Father, Edward John Hisson (1881-1949); Elsie;
Mother, Mabel M. (Lawson) Hisson (1890-1974). Standing at the back
is grandmother, Mary A. Lawson, holding baby Ada (b. 1918). The girl
beside the dog could not be identified, photo 1920. Courtesy of the
Wellington County Archives, PH#5786.

We, as friends and neighbors of this family, which is
now leaving our community, wish to present to them
a token of our appreciation and good will. Being one
of the oldest settlers and with many of us for many
years, we shall feel your absence from our midst. The
strain of the departure will no doubt rest heavy
upon you, who have spent all your lives in this district,
knowing each and every passing face, and in going
among strangers, we hope, you will find with the
efforts of your sons, new friends, who will make your
life pleasant. In concluding, we, as your friends and
neighbors, take great pleasure in presenting to you

this purse, as has been a custom of this community,
and we assure you that you have the best wishes of us
all.[4]

Over the years many former residents returned to Peel Township
to see friends and to visit their ancestral home. A few individuals,
such as Mabel M. Lawson, even returned to stay. Lawson, born in
1890 on the family farm in Peel Township, was the daughter of Mary
A. and William Lawson and the granddaughter of fugitive slave,
Dangerfield Lawson. Like so many other young adults, Mabel had left
the rural community to search for employment elsewhere. She had
moved to Guelph where she found a job as a domestic and, on April,
26 1911, she married Edward John Hisson, who worked in a local stove
factory. Shortly after their marriage, the couple decided to settle in
Peel Township and they moved to a fifteen-acre farm just west of
Glen Allen. Between 1912 and 1928 Mabel Lawson Hisson bore seven
children, but only Norman, their oldest son, remained in the area.
After the death of his father, Edward, in 1949, and his mother Mabel,
in 1974, Norman Hisson was recognized as the last surviving descendant of the early Black pioneers still living in the area. He lived in
Glen Allan until the mid-1990s, when he too finally moved away.[5]

Because the missionaries were a significant part of the history of
the Queen's Bush, at least between the years 1839 and 1853, their experiences after leaving the community are also offered. In 1841, William
Raymond and his family accompanied the thirty-nine Africans
involved in the Amistad Affair to Sierra Leone, along with James
Steele and Henry R. and Tamar Wilson. The group left New York City
on November 26 on board the *Gentleman*. The ship not only encountered several severe storms during the Atlantic crossing, but the
Africans also became suspicious of their white travelling companions
fearing that they would be returned to slavery. Trouble erupted
between the missionaries and Africans when the *Gentleman* docked
for fresh water at Santiago in the Cape Verde Islands. In Porto Prayo

In 1979, Norman Hisson visited the graves of his ancestors in the abandoned Peel Township AME/BME Church cemetery. Courtesy of the Kitchener-Waterloo Collection of Photographic Negatives, Dana Porter Library, University of Waterloo, ON, N2L 3G1.

Harbor, the Africans' leader, Cinque, traded tools and supplies intended for the new mission for fresh food. His actions angered the missionaries and the distrust between the two groups intensified. After an exhausting voyage, the *Gentleman* docked in Freetown, Sierra Leone on January 15, 1842. Henry and Tamar Wilson, uneasy about the animosity between the missionaries and the Africans, refused to remain in Freetown and travelled on to Liberia. Before a mission could be established, the Africans had abandoned Raymond and Steele. Although their future in Sierra Leone looked doubtful, the two men selected the Kaw-Mendi village on the Jong River for their missionary station. William Raymond died November 26, 1847, of yellow fever and was buried at the Kaw-Mendi Mission. At the time of Raymond's death, his wife Eliza, was in Massachusetts visiting friends and relatives. After learning of her husband's death she moved to Nova Scotia, where she later married Phineas Banks. Eliza Ruggles Raymond Banks died in 1908 in Aylesford, Nova Scotia.[6]

John S. Brooks developed a close friendship with Susan Teall during his 1852 visit to Peel Township. Following his return to Sierra Leone, the two missionaries regularly corresponded with each other and eventually Brooks proposed to Teall. They were married on March 14, 1855, in Good Hope, Sierra Leone. After the wedding the couple moved to the Tappan Mission at Boom Falls, which Brooks had established during the previous year. In September Susan Teall Brooks developed a debilitating fever and Johns S. Brooks took his desperately ill wife to Good Hope for medical treatment. She died September 30, just six months after her arrival in Sierra Leone. She is buried in the Good Hope Cemetery.[7]

On July 21, 1856, John S. Brooks married E. T. Lavers of Freetown, Sierra Leone, who died shortly thereafter. In July 1858, Brooks married an African woman, who died in May 1859 while giving birth to their daughter, Rose.[8] Despite his personal tragedies, Brooks enlarged his missionary efforts during the following years establishing yet another mission called Salem Hill. His letters to AMA officials reveal a man who was in perpetually poor health. On one occasion he confided to George Whipple, of the AMA that "my nervous system is much affected. I often fear insanity – many of these difficulties would doubtless disappear by skillful treatment in America."[9] Yet, Brooks remained in Africa teaching and ministering to the local residents. He learned the Mendi language and created a written alphabet, and even established a plantation where he grew coffee and cotton. He hoped the cultivation of these crops would become substitute economic ventures to the local slave trade. Brooks also became responsible for several young children who were the sisters and cousins of his late wife. On February 19, 1861, he married his fifth wife, a Miss Proctor, who was an African and a member of Freetown's elite Black society. She had been educated in Europe and spoke English, French, and several African languages, which proved useful to Brooks' missionary work.[10]

With a new wife and a large family to support, Brooks asked for a larger salary, but D. W. Burton, senior missionary at the Kaw-Mendi Mission, denied the request. Rejected by Burton, Brooks presented his case to AMA executives. When they failed to respond to his letters, Brooks withdrew money from the AMA's Freetown bank account. His behaviour, as well as the fact that he had married another African woman, caused friction between him and his colleagues. In anger Brooks resigned from the AMA. In his letter of resignation, he described the racist attitudes of his colleagues, complaining that his previous wife had suffered greatly from their verbal abuse and that he refused to subject his new wife to the same insults.[11]

Brooks opened a trading post on the grounds of the Kaw-Mendi Mission. Local residents demanded that he close the store, because they had donated the land for missionary use only. The missionaries also objected to the trading post and accused Brooks of selling guns and liquor to the native population. Brooks further alarmed the missionaries when he hired members of the Tucker family, who were well-known slave traders, to work in the store. John S. Brooks died in Sierra Leone sometime between 1862 and 1866.[12]

On April 27, 1853, Elias E. and Fanny Kirkland, along with their children, Fidelias, Isaac, Jennitt and Olive, left New Canaan, Canada West and moved to Seoni in Jackson County, Michigan, where they took up farming. In 1862, the Kirklands moved again to Homestead Township in Benzie County, where they founded the village of Homestead. By 1875 the Kirkland family was living near Otsego Lake in Otsego County and Elias E. Kirkland had returned to the missionary field as an agent for the Home Missionary. In August 1876, Fanny Kirkland drafted the family's last known letter to the AMA, in which she enclosed a five-dollar donation in support of the organization's missionary work.[13]

APPENDIX A: BIOGRAPHICAL SKETCHES OF THE BLACK PIONEERS IN THE QUEEN'S BUSH SETTLEMENT

This list of the Black pioneer settlers known to have lived in the Queen's Bush between 1839 and 1865 is based on a variety of sources including: wills, the census, tax, assessment, land, marriage and death records, as well as newspaper articles, cemetery transcriptions and the Queen's Bush petitions. It is unlikely that researchers will ever be able to identify, much less compile information on every individual who resided in the Queen's Bush. Nevertheless, the following biographical sketches are offered as a beginning. It is hoped that this information will assist those genealogical researchers who are descendants of the early Black inhabitants of the Queen's Bush settlement.

David Ambush appears on the 1847 Queen's Bush petition.[1]

Thomas Amoss appears on the 1847 Queen's Bush petition.[2]

Deliah Anderson (1826-?), was the Maryland-born daughter of Richard and Elizabeth Gasby Anderson. She married Mr. Harris with whom she had at least two children, Eliza, born 1848, and William, born 1851. By 1861 she was a widow and lived in Peel Township with her two children. On March 16, 1861, Deliah married Thomas Johnson, a Peel Township labourer who had been born in Maryland in 1821 to John and Prillia Smith Johnson. Thomas Johnson had also been previously married and had at least one son, Remus, from the marriage.[3]

In 1871, Remus Johnson worked as a labourer and lived with his stepmother and father, who also made a living as a labourer. Twenty-two year old, Eliza Harris and her two young children, Mary A. and Elias, also lived in the Johnson household.[4]

Esther Anderson (1779 – ?), in 1861, was an eighty-two-year-old American-born widow who resided in Peel Township.[5]

Joseph Anderson arrived in Peel Township in July 1843 and settled on lot 18, concession 3. Within two years he had cleared and cultivated six acres of land. His name appears on the 1847 Queen's Bush petition.[6]

James Armstrong arrived in Peel Township in November 1842 and settled on lot 10, concession 3.[7]

Joseph Armstrong (1830 – ?), was a Peel Township labourer. He and his wife, Susan, were natives of the United States. By 1861 the Armstrong's had three children: Francis, born 1851; Lydia, born 1855, and Stephan, born 1859. All three children had been born in Canada.[8]

Lewis Armstrong appears on the 1847 Queen's Bush petition.[9]

Robert Armstrong appears on the 1847 Queen's Bush petition.[10]

James Atkinson was one of many Black settlers who borrowed money from John S. Brooks.[11]

Hampton/Hamilton Bailey arrived in Peel Township in June 1842 and settled on the north half of lot 17 on concession 3. By 1846 he had built a house and had cleared eight acres of land. His name appears on the 1843 and 1847 Queen's Bush petitions.[12]

Daniel Banks (1796 – ?) was a native of Virginia. In 1832, he lived in the Colbornesburg Settlement, where he had claimed seventy acres, of which three were cleared and cultivated. Tax assessors valued his property at £16.8. By the following year he had moved to the Queen's Bush where in about 1837, he married his wife Francey, who had been born in 1816 in New York. In 1851, the couple lived in a log shanty in Peel Township with their eight children: Rachael, born 1838; Clarsie, born 1839; Lenia Jermiach, born 1840; Ann, born 1842; Caroty, born

1844; Maria T., born 1845; Sarah A., born 1847; and John C, born 1850.[13]

John Banks registered his land claim at the Elora land office on January 8, 1846. The land office clerk made a notation beside Banks' name indicating that he was an old man.[14]

John Benson appears on the 1847 Queen's Bush petition.[15]

Robert Bond appears on the 1847 Queen's Bush petition.[16]

Jackson G. Borin (1811-?) was a Kentucky-born Wellesley Township labourer.[17]

Mark Boston arrived in Peel Township in March 1845 and settled on the front half of lot 10 on concession 4. Like many of the community's Black residents, Boston sought financial assistance from John S. Brooks. Boston eventually left Peel Township and moved to Maryborough Township in Wellington County.[18]

George Bowie arrived in Peel Township in December 1842. He settled in the centre of lot 16, concession 3 and within four years had constructed a log house and had cultivated four acres of land. Bowie's name appears on the 1843 Queen's Bush petition.[19]

John Brown (1816 – ?) was a Wellesley Township farmer and a native of Virginia. In 1835, Brown and his wife, Lucinda Green were living in Upper Canada when their daughter, Sarah, was born. In 1836, they had a son Daniel, followed by George in 1837 and Nathan in 1841. It is unknown where the Browns lived during this time period, but in 1842 they were in St. Catharines where their daughter Dorothea Elizabeth (also appears as Elizabeth Dorothea) was born. The following year John Brown moved with his family to Wellesley Township where at least four more children, Charlotte, Hannah, Alice, and Susan, were born between 1845 and 1849.[20]

In 1851, fifteen-year old, Daniel Brown attended school, but he also worked as a servant for Michael Peter Empey, who operated a general merchandise store in Hawksville.[21]

On May 17, 1859, Elizabeth Dorothea Brown married Moses Pope, Jr., who was the son of Moses and Mary Ann (Selby) Pope, of Peel Township.[22]

Lenord Brown appears on the 1847 Queen's Bush petition.[23]

Paola Brown left the Cobornesburg Settlement sometime between 1833 and 1834. He moved to Hamilton where he became an anti-slavery lecturer and often spoke out against racial discrimination.[24] To reach a broader audience, Brown published one of his speeches entitled, *Address Intended to be Delivered in the City Hall, Hamilton, February 7, 1851, on the Subject of Slavery*, which compared the treatment of slaves in the United States to the institution of slavery practised in other countries in ancient and modern times. Throughout the well-written text, Brown demonstrated that American slavery was the most abusive and inhumane form of the institution ever practised. His fiery speech bitterly attacked southern slaveholders and he warned them: "I call God, I call Angels, I call Men, to witness, that your destruction is at hand, and will be speedily consummated, unless you repent."[25]

William Brown (1826 – ?) was a native of Maryland. In the 1851 Peel Township census, he is listed as a married man, but his wife does not appear in the household. Nor was his occupation reported in the census. Daniel Brown, a twenty-six year old labourer and a native of New York was the only other member of the household.[26]

William A. Brown arrived in Peel Township in the fall of 1843 and settled on the west half of lot 12, concession 3. In 1846, Brown registered his claim at the Elora land office, but he was unable to meet the down payment. He promised the land agent that he would pay as soon as possible.[27]

Henry Butler (1828 – ?) was a Canadian-born Woolwich Township labourer.[28]

Lewis Butler in May 1841 settled on the east half of lot 2, concession 5 in Peel Township. By March 1846, he had approximately ten acres cleared and lived in a log shanty.[29]

Robert Campbell arrived in Peel Township in August 1843 and settled next to Joseph Armstrong on the west half of lot 15 on concession 3.[30]

William Cary appears on the 1847 Queen's Bush petition.[31]

John Cavey appears on the 1847 Queen's Bush petition.[32]

Fred Clery registered his claim for land on lot 10, concession 3 on October 6, 1846. Clery had lived on the property since May 1845, but had not cleared any land.[33]

Solomon Conaway and his family were members of the Colbornesburg Settlement. In 1832, the township assessor reported that Conaway and his wife had five children, two boys and two girls under the age of sixteen, and one older daughter. The assessor noted that the family had cleared and cultivated three acres on Crook's Tract, Broken Front Concession 2 valued at £30. The following year, the Conaway family settled in the Queen's Bush as squatters. In 1842, Solomon Conaway took the oath of allegiance and, in 1843, he and his sons Joseph and William added their names to the Queen's Bush petition.[34]

John Cooper arrived in Peel Township in March 1844 and settled on the west half of lot 17, concession 6. Cooper registered his claim on June 17, 1845, but by July the property had been transferred to Duncan McArthur.[35]

Lewis Crague/Creig was a bachelor, who lived in the Colbornesburg Settlement. He later moved to the east half of lot 1, concession 5 in Wellesley Township, where he became involved in a dispute over the legality of his claim with Mr. Hale, another Black settler.[36]

William Henry Crawford, on December 2, 1845, registered his claim for a tract of land on the south half of lot 9, concession 5 in Peel Township. Crawford's name appears on the 1847 Queen's Bush petition.[37]

Joseph Cromwell and his wife, Celia, had been born sometime between 1816 and 1818 in Nova Scotia. Their three oldest children, Margaret, Joseph Jr. and George, had also been born in Nova Scotia between 1843 and 1846. On June 27, 1846, the Cromwell family arrived in Peel Township along with Jacob Peterson and his family. The two families formed a partnership and settled on the south half of lot 13, concession 4. Dennis Johnson, who had abandoned the property for unknown reasons, had previously claimed the land. The Cromwells had at least two more children while living in Peel Township, Mary Ann, born in 1850, and William, born in 1851.[38]

Ticy Cullen (1814 – ?) was an American-born resident of Peel Township and a member of the Roman Catholic church.[39]

John Davis reported to the 1861 Peel Township census enumerator that he had been born in the United States in 1801. However, in the next decennial census he gave his date of birth as 1798. His wife, Harriet did not report her age at all for the 1861 census, but in 1871 she gave her age as eighty. In 1861, twenty-four year old, Rachel and two-year old, Musella, lived with John and Harriet Davis.[40]

Lewis Davis (1838 – ?) was a native of New York. The 1851 Peel Township census taker enumerated Lewis with the Dennis and Eliza Jackson family. Ten-year-old Moses Davis lived on the next farm with the Daniel Youbanks family.[41]

Rean Davis appears on the 1847 Queen's Bush petition.[42]

Aslon Dickson appears on the 1847 Queen's Bush petion.[43]

Joseph Diges signed the 1850 Queen's Bush petition. His signature is unclear, but his first name was probably Joseph. In 1851, a Joseph Digs worked in Galt (now part of Cambridge) as a cooper.[44]

Richard Randolph Disney (June 24, 1830 – April 20, 1891) served as a minister at the Peel Township BME church from 1857 to 1859. Highly respected, Disney moved up the ranks in the church hierarchy and succeeding appointments included churches at Windsor (1861-64), St. Catharines (1864-69) and Toronto (1869-72). In 1872, Disney became the minister of the Chatham church and served as Bishop Willis Nazrey's assistant. When Nazrey died on August 22, 1875, Disney became the second Bishop of the BME church. He encouraged the reunification of the BME and AME denominations, which took place in 1884. With reunification, Disney became Bishop of Ontario, Nova Scotia, Demerara (British Guiana), the West Indies, Bermuda, and South America.[45]

Fearing a loss of their distinctive identity, a majority of the BME congregations and their ministers refused to acknowledge reunification. Subsequently, delegates held a general conference in 1886 to re-establish the BME church and elected the Reverend Walter Hawkins as their general superintendent. Despite the division,

Disney continued his ministerial duties in Canada until 1888 when church leaders transferred him to Greenville, Mississippi. Disney died in Baltimore, Maryland, on April 20, 1891 and was buried in Chatham, Ontario, near the grave of Bishop Willis Nazrey.[46]

Thomas Douglas appears on the 1847 Queen's Bush petition.[47]

Vincent Douglass had been born about 1791 or 1797. He and his wife, Martha, and their children, Charles, Maria, Vincent Jr. and Agnes, had been born into slavery in Virginia. Sometime after the birth of Agnes in 1838, the Douglass family escaped and fled to Canada. In 1843 the family lived on fifty acres on lot 21, concession 14, in Wellesley Township, where another son, Albert, was born the following year. The Douglass family later moved to a farm on lot 14, concession 2, in Peel Township.[48]

On October 26, 1877, Vincent Douglass died of unknown causes. The terms of his will stated that after all debts and funeral expenses had been paid, his beloved wife Martha was to receive $50 and the use of their home and furnishings. His son, Albert, inherited the family farm with the condition that he support his mother until her death, which occurred on April 3, 1897. Two other sons, Charles and Thomas, each received $25.[49]

Albert Douglass married Mary Ann Lee on August 11, 1870, in Peel Township. The Reverend Samuel H. Brown performed the ceremony, witnessed by Henry Frances and Mary Ann Stewart. Mary Ann Lee Douglass had been born in Brantford on June 15, 1850. Her father, William Barnard Lee, had been born in Niagara-on-the-Lake in 1812 and was the son of Peter Lee, who had served in the Corps of Colour during the War of 1812. Her mother, Eleanor Jane Smith, was from County Cork, Ireland. When Mary Ann Lee was just a young girl, her parents divorced. Her father moved to Artemesia Township in Grey County where he married Roselia Adams and they had one son, William Bernard Lee, Jr.[50]

Albert and Mary Ann Douglass had twenty-one children, but only seven survived to adulthood. The children were: George L.; Albert Harvey; Aubrey; Oscar Raymond; Olive Estella, Cora Winnie and Hector Wendall. Mary Ann Douglass died March 14, 1912, of chronic bronchitis and what her doctor described as a general breakdown in health. Her husband died May 19, 1913, of appendicitis. They are buried in the Peel Township AME/BME cemetery beside their daughter, Cora Winnie. After the death of Albert and Mary Ann Douglass, the family farm was sold with the proceeds being equally divided among their children, who by then had migrated to the United States or other areas of Canada.[51]

Charles Douglass, the oldest son of Vincent and Martha Douglass, in 1861 lived in Artemesia Township, Grey County, with his wife, Mary. However, by 1871 he was a widower and had returned to his parents' home with his two daughters, Margaret and Levina. Douglass married his second wife, Isabella Johnston, and the couple had at least one child, Albert. Just two days before Christmas in 1879, Douglass became a widower for the second time when his wife Isabella died. By 1901, Douglass had returned to Grey County where he lived near Collingwood with his daughter Effie, his son-in-law, George Cooper and their twelve-year-old son, Edward. His son, Albert, also lived in Grey County and on December 28, 1904, he married Elizabeth Morton in the Owen Sound Methodist Church. Charles Douglass died in Collingwood at age 78 on January 14, 1912. Many of his descendants still live in Grey County today.[52]

William Duncan settled on the south half of lot 17, concession 2 in Peel Township in March 1844. Within two years, Duncan had cleared nine acres of land and had built a house and barn.[53]

James Dunn had been born about 1808 or 1815 in New York. His wife, Margaret (Nancy), was also a native of New York and had been born sometime between 1807 and 1823. The Dunns lived in Upper Canada as early as 1835 when their son Mathew was born. Between 1843 and 1850 the Dunns had at least five more children: Tarina, James Jr., Dennis, David and Louisa. In March 1845, the family moved to Peel Township, where they settled on the front half of lot 18, concession 1, but they later moved further north to concession 5. In 1851, eighty-five year old Sarah Dunn, a native of New York, lived with the family.[54]

As an adult, David Dunn helped his father manage the family's eighty-six acre farm. He died on December 29, 1916, at age 68, as a result of blood poisoning caused by a sliver of wood that ran into his finger while he was chopping wood, and became infected. He is buried in the Peel Township AME/BME cemetery.[55]

Leucinda Eady (1797 – ?) had been born in Pennsylvania. In 1851, she was the head of a Peel Township household that included: Estus Thomson, age 20, Lucinda Pain, age 14, and Eliza Eady, age 9.[56]

Ben Edy (sometimes spelled Ady or Eddy) may not have known his exact place and date of birth or he purposefully provided false information to census takers. In 1851, he reported to the census taker that he and his wife, Margaret (nee Piper), had been born in Canada in 1811 and 1815 respectively. In the next decennial census, they reported that they had been born in the United States in 1823 and 1825. Between 1839 and 1860 Margaret Edy bore at least eight children, Ben Jr., Eliza/Elizabeth, Julia, Melop, Nancy, Margaret, Mary, and Burnet.[57]

On September 26, 1860, Elizabeth Edy married Jacob White, who was the son of Samuel and Hannah Gray White of Peel Township.[58]

The Ady/Edy/Eddy was a common surname among early Black settlers in Canada West. There were other families with this name in Chatham, Brantford, Owen Sound and in Oro Township in Simcoe County.[59]

John Francis (1809 – ?), and his Canadian-born wife Ann, arrived in Peel Township in September 1843 and settled on lot 10, concession 3. By 1851 the couple had three children: John T., born 1848; Lucinda, born 1841, and Robert, born in 1850.[60] Financial problems forced Francis to borrow money from John S. Brooks. When Thomas Vipond later tried to collect the debt, he thought the prospects of Francis repaying the loan were, "not very good, but may pay."[61]

Robert Freeman (1822 – ?) was a Canadian-born Peel Township farmer. In December 1850, the Baptist minister, the Reverend James Sims, married Freeman and Catherine Anderson, who had been born in 1828 in Baltimore, Maryland. One of the witnesses at the wedding was Lyvis Anderson, who may have been a relative. By the following year, the Freemans lived in a one-storey log cabin with their newborn daughter, Maryan L. Their neighbour, James Freeman, a bachelor who had been born in Canada in 1823, may have been Robert's brother.[62]

George Galaway/Gallaway arrived in Peel Township in December 1844 and settled on the north half of lot 16, concession 2. On March 13, 1846, he registered his claim, but the following October he changed his application to lot 16, concession 3.[63]

James Gelrest signed the 1850 Queen's Bush petition.[64]

Robert Gent appears on the 1847 Queen's Bush petition.[65]

Tho Gibbs (1808 – ?) was a native of Kentucky. Details of his early life are unknown, but he arrived in Canada on January 10, 1840 and, by February 1841, had settled in Peel Township on lot 22, concession 1. During the next two years, Gibbs built a one-storey log house and cleared eight acres of land. On February 20, 1843, Gibbs married Ann Candora Thompson. The Reverend Stephen Brownell performed the wedding, witnessed by Thomas Proudlove and Jacob Dorcey. The Gibbs had at least two children: Miles, born 1843, and Selicetee E., born 1848. On January 11, 1847, Gibbs took the British oath of allegiance.[66]

Priscilla Giffen (1844 – ?) was a native of the United States. In 1861 she lived in Peel Township.[67]

Thomas Gillis appears on the 1847 Queen's Bush petition.[68]

James Glast appears on the 1847 Queen's Bush petition.[69]

John Goins arrived in Peel Township in March 1844 and shortly thereafter formed a partnership with David King. The two men farmed the west half of lot 8 on concession 1. On July 10, 1845, John Goins married Matilda Williams. Baptist minister, the Reverend James Sims, performed the ceremony, witnessed by James T. Elliott and Moses Prater. John and Matilda Goins were natives of Maryland, but discrepancies in the census make it difficult to determine their exact dates of birth. John Goins was probably born sometime between 1798 and 1800, while his wife may have been born between 1817 and 1820. In 1861 the Goins had eight children: John Jr., Sam, Robert, Recinda, Charles, Francis, Jeremiah and Roxann.[70]

Matilda Goins appears to have died sometime between 1861 and 1871, as she is not listed in the 1871 Peel Township census. Instead, a woman named Ellen, who had been born in 1804, was enumerated as John Goins' wife.[71]

William Gordon (1797 – ?) was a Peel Township farmer who lived on the west half of lot 16, concession 3. Gordon and his wife, Margaret, who had been born in Ireland, left the township sometime between 1851 and 1861.[72]

Edward Grandison (1791 – ?) was a labourer who lived on lot 9, concession 5 in Peel Township. Grandison, his wife, Lucinda, and their children (Lewis, Mary, Jane, Millis and Margaret) had been born in the United States. Sometime after Margaret Grandison's birth in 1857, the family moved to Peel Township where at least one more child, Rebecca, was born in 1860. The Grandison family were members of the Baptist Church.[73]

Jeremiah Green (1811 – ?) in 1851 was a widower who lived in the Wellesley Township home of Melinda Tucker, a forty-eight-year-old widow. Nineteen-year-old Jeremiah Tucker, seventeen-year-old Hester M. Tucker and twenty-two-year-old William Green also lived in the household. By 1871 Jeremiah and William Green had moved to Peel Township.[74]

Massene Hale signed the 1850 Queen's Bush petition.[75]

David Hall arrived in Peel Township in April 1843 and settled on the front half of lot 21, concession 1. Within three years, Hall had built a house and cleared eight acres of land. His name appears on the 1847 Queen's Bush petition.[76]

John Hanes (1806 – ?) was a Peel Township farmer. He and his wife, Eliza were from Maryland, but their children (John Jr., Emily, and Quellen) had all been born in New York between 1834 and 1842. By 1851 the family had moved to Peel Township.[77]

Major Harding (1798 – ?) and his wife, Martha, and their children, (Martha, born 1833; Robert, born 1835 and Racheal, born 1844) were natives of the United States. Although, the census does not indicate an exact place of birth, other than the United States, oral family tradition states that the Hardings were from Virginia. Major Harding and his twelve-year-old son, Robert appear on the 1847 Queen's Bush

petition, suggesting that the family moved to Peel Township sometime between 1844 and 1847.[78]

On May 4, 1856, Robert Harding married Celia Zebbs of Peel
Township. The Reverend Jacob Libertus performed the wedding and
the witnesses were Mary A. Zebbs and Richard Travis. Celia
Harding's date of death is unknown but, by 1861, Robert Harding had
married Elizabeth Travis, who had been born about 1840 in the
United States. By 1867 Robert and Elizabeth Harding had moved to
the Elgin Settlement where they raised seven children.[79]

In the 1861 Peel Township census, five-year-old Sarah A. Harding
was enumerated with Major and Martha Harding. Sarah Harding's
relationship to the couple is unclear, but at age sixty, Martha Harding
may have been her grandmother.[80]

George Harper (1819 – ?) was an American-born Peel Township
labourer. His wife, Sophia had also been born in the United States in
1821. The Harper's children, Fidelia, Jonathan, David, and Mary A.,
had been born between 1841 and 1851 in Canada West.[81]

George Harris appears on the 1847 Queen's Bush petition.[82]

James Harris appears on the 1847 Queen's Bush petition. In 1871, a
James Harris, who had been born in 1820, was enumerated in Peel
Township with his wife, Ann. Ten-year-old Georgina Osborne lived
with the couple, along with twenty-one-year-old Henry Francis.
Harris and Francis made a living by farming.[83]

John H. Harris (1805 – ?) farmed in Peel Township along with his
wife, Elisa M. and son, Quill. The Harris' were originally from the
United States.[84]

Mark Harris (1823 – ?) arrived in Peel Township in March 1842, along
with London and Luke Harris. The exact relationship of these three

men is unknown, but they may have been brothers. Luke Harris settled on the north half of lot 11, concession 2, but in 1846 he moved
with Isaac Jecks to lot 14, concession 2. Mark and London Harris
claimed 100 acres on the west half of lot 15, concession 2, and within
one year they had cleared and cultivated six acres. All three men
appear on the 1843 and 1847 Queen's Bush petitions but, by 1861, only
Mark Harris remained in the township. Mark Harris eventually married and he and his wife, Mary, had at least three children: Martha,
born 1852, James, born 1857, and Sarah, born 1859.[85]

Mathew Harris appears on the 1847 Queen's Bush petition.[86]

Robert Harris married Mary Ann Burton on March 19, 1850. The
Reverend James Sims performed the wedding, witnessed by Henry
White and Thomas Elwood.[87]

Wildon Harris appears on the 1847 Queen's Bush petition.[88]

Jane Harrison (1815 – ?) was an American-born Peel Township resident. In 1861 she lived with twenty-two-year-old, Samuel Harrison,
who may have been her son.[89]

Joseph Harrison (1821 – ?) in 1861, lived in Wellesley Township with
his wife, Emma, and their children: Edward, born 1845; Harriet, born
1851; Emma, born 1851, and Mabel, born 1854.[90]

James Hart was born in Maryland sometime between 1821 and 1826.
His wife, Maryann, who had been born in 1827 was also a native of
Maryland, while their oldest daughter Eliza M. had been born in New
York in 1844. James Hart appears on the 1847 Queen's Bush petition,
suggesting that the family left the United States sometime between
1844 and 1847. Between 1848 and 1850 the Hart's had at least three
more children: Hanna A., John and William.[91]

By 1861 it appears that Maryann and William Hart were deceased and Hannah had died of dropsy at age twelve. James Hart had also moved his family, which included his new wife Emily and his children (John, Mary J., Emaline and Solomon) from Peel Township to Wellesley Township.[92]

Thomas Hart (1819 – ?), was a Maryland-born Peel Township farmer. His wife, Jane, had been born in 1815 in New York.[93]

In 1851, the Peel Township census taker enumerated four young girls (Ellen, Mary E., Sarah J. and Francis E. Hart) who ranged in age from two to eight years, as living by themselves. They were natives of New York and may have been the children of Thomas and Jane Hart.[94]

Tom Holland had been born a slave in Maryland. After his escape he settled in the Queen's Bush, where his brother William joined him in 1860. The Hollands later moved to Bronte.[95]

James Howard settled on lot 8, concession 3, in Peel Township in March 1844. His name appears on the 1847 Queen's Bush petition.[96]

Lewis Howard arrived in Upper Canada in April 1829. In 1832 he lived in the Colbornesburg Settlement, along with his wife and six children, two boys and four girls. In 1832, the Woolwich Township tax assessor surveyed Howard's one hundred acre farm. With only three acres cleared and cultivated, he assessed the farm at £22.8. In 1833, the Howard family left the Colbornesburg Settlement and moved to the Wellesley Township section of the Queen's Bush community. Howard's name appears on the 1843 Queen's Bush petition and on May 9, 1849, he took the British oath of allegiance.[97]

Griffith Hughes lived in the Colbournesburg Settlement, along with his wife and three children. The Hughes family were probably recent arrivals to the community in 1832, because the tax assessor did not report the location of their farm or assess the value of their property. The family left the Colbornesburg Settlement by the following year.[98]

Enn Hunt (1855 – ?) lived with the Daniel Youbanks family in 1861, along with sixteen-year-old, Nilo Hunt, who may have been his brother. Ten-year-old William Hunt lived with the Moses Prater family and may have been a second brother. All three children were natives of Canada.[99]

William Irvine (1813 – ?) and his wife, Martha, (1825-?) were from the United States. Their oldest daughter, Rebecca, had also been born in the United States in 1852. The couple's younger children, Catherine, born in 1855, and Murray M., born in 1860, had been born in Canada, which suggests that the family moved to Canada sometime between 1852 and 1855. Irvine worked as a labourer in Peel Township.[100]

Dennis Jackson (1795 – ?) was a Virginia-born Peel Township farmer. In October 1843, he settled on the front half of lot 11 concession 2, and within three years he had built a home and had cleared five acres of land. On March 7, 1850, he married Elizabeth Hardin, who had been born in 1817 in Tennessee. Baptist minister, the Reverend James Sims, performed the ceremony, witnessed by Robert J. Evans and Broocks Edmonds. The couple had at least four children: Susan, Thomas, Major and Rachel. The Jacksons were one of the few Black families who still lived in Peel Township in 1871.[101]

James Jackson arrived in Peel Township in December 1842 and began clearing his claim on the front half of lot 16, concession 3. By 1846 he had built a home and had cleared five acres of land. His name appears on the 1847 Queen's Bush petition.[102]

John R. Jackson (1872 – 1964) as a third-generation resident of Peel Township, had a keen interest in the community's history. In 1955, he wrote a brief article about his family and the township's early schools for the *Drayton Advocate*. According to Jackson, his grandfather John arrived in the township in March 1846 and settled on lot 10, concession 2. John R. Jackson's father, William, attended the Mount Pleasant School and later purchased a farm on the east half of lot 16, concession 2.[103]

John R. Jackson died in 1964, some time after his wife Jessie Hought Jackson who had passed away in 1941. They are buried in the Glen Allen Union Cemetery along with several of their children including John Arlington, who died April 1, 1909, at age 7.[104]

Robert Jackson (1805 – ?) along with his wife Mary, and children, William, Mary F., and Charlot J. had been born in the United States. Sometime after Charlot Jackson's birth in 1837, but before 1839 when their son Moses was born, the Jackson family moved to Upper Canada. In 1841, the Jacksons celebrated the birth of another daughter, Isabella. Two years later, the same year that son Aron was born, the family settled on lot 10, concession 3, in Peel Township. In 1846, Jackson registered his claim at the Elora land office, but he did not have the down payment and deferred payment until the next year. Due to his poor financial situation, Jackson frequently borrowed money from John S. Brooks. Thomas Vipond tried to collect the outstanding loan, but he eventually gave up, stating that Jackson was "poor, won't pay unless forced."[105]

Sometime between 1847 and March 1850, the Jackson family moved to Galt, (now part of Cambridge), where Robert Jackson established a barbershop with his thirteen-year-old son, Moses. His oldest son, William, found employment as a labourer, but by 1854 he too worked as a barber and lived on Victoria Street.[106]

James was mentioned in W.E. McKenzie's history of Peel Township, published in the *Guelph Weekly Mercury & Advertiser* in 1907. McKenzie noted that "a colored man named James was the pioneer on lot 3, concession 6. He sold [his farm] to Joseph Powley."[107]

John James appears on the 1847 Queen's Bush petition.[108]

Samuel James (1786 – ?) was a Canadian-born Peel Township farmer. His wife, Mary C. was also a native of Canada, born in 1794. Their children included: Freeman, born 1825; Coleman, born 1828; Charles, born 1832; Leaney, born 1839; and Collan, born 1841.[109]

Coleman James married Lucy Scipio, of Peel Township, on April 27, 1855. The Reverend Reid performed the ceremony, witnessed by Richard Travers and Alex Watson.[110]

Dennis Johnson appears on the 1847 Queen's Bush petition.[111]

Jeremiah Johnson arrived in Peel Township in March 1844 and settled on the south half of lot 14, concession 3. Within two years he had built a log shanty and had cleared five acres. Johnson registered his claim at the Elora land office on March 15, 1846, but he did not have the down payment and requested a two-week deferment. A Jerry Johnson appears on the 1847 Queen's Bush petition.[112]

John Johnson was among the group of American Black immigrants who drafted a petition in late 1828 asking the government's permission to purchase a block of land in the Clergy Reserves on the Grand River. After government officials denied the request, Johnson along with several other settlers, established the Colbornesburg Settlement. In 1832, Johnson opened the dedication ceremonies for the community's new church and schoolhouse. After the Colbornesburg Settlement disbanded, Johnson moved to Wellesley Township and he married Leuretta Jacobs in Elmira on May 9, 1843. The Reverend Stephen Brownell performed the wedding, witnessed by Thomas

Vipond and Lewis Howard. Johnson appears on the 1847 Queen's Bush petition and on March 12, 1849, he took the British oath of allegiance.[113]

Robert Johnson (1801 – ?), was a native of the United States, along with his wife, Harriette. Sometime after the birth of their daughter Rebecca in 1842, the Johnsons moved to Canada West. On June 23, 1845, the Johnson family settled on the rear half of lot 13, concession 4, in Peel Township. Dennis Johnson, Robert's brother, lived with the family, but later left the community. Between 1845 and 1859, Harriette Johnson bore at least six more children: Mores, Matilda, Priscilla, Jacob, Abt and Joseph. Between 1855 and 1863, Johnson served the Peel Township AME/BME church as a local preacher. In 1863 he became an itinerant minister for the congregation.[114]

Thomas Johnson appears on the 1847 Queen's Bush petition.[115]

William Johnson (1808 – ?), and his wife, Jane Elizabeth, were natives of Kentucky and lived on lot 21, concession 14 in Wellesley Township. Like so many other struggling families in the Queen's Bush, Johnson borrowed money from John S. Brooks. In 1854, tax assessors valued the Johnson's fifty-acre farm at $116.[116]

Margaret Johnston (1821 – ?), lived in Peel Township in 1861 with her children: Dennis, born 1850 and Amelia, born 1854. They were all natives of Canada.[117]

Robert Johnston appears on the 1847 Queen's Bush petition.[118]

William Johnston appears on the 1847 Queen's Bush petition.[119]

Levi Jones (1818 – ?) was a Wellesley Township labourer. The 1851 Wellesley Township census enumerator reported that Jones was white, however, his name appears on the 1850 Queen's Bush petition, which according to the document was drafted only by Black inhabitants of the community. This may suggest that Jones was indeed of African ancestry. His wife, Elizabeth, was English and they had six children: James, Almira, Eli, Mary, Henry and William.[120]

Thomas Keith in 1843, had four acres of land cleared and fenced on lot 18, concession 1, in Peel Township. It is unknown if Keith had a family, but his name appears on the 1843 and 1847 Queen's Bush petitions. At the July 31, 1846, annual meeting of the AME Canadian Conference, religious leaders admitted Keith to the church as minister on trial. His work must have met with their approval because the following year Keith was elevated to the position of minister on probation.[121]

Cecil Kenny (1856 – ?) lived in Peel Township with Solomon and Jane Tibbs in 1861.[122]

Augustus Kerr appears on the 1847 Queen's Bush petition.[123]

George Kerry moved to Peel Township in February 1844 and settled on the north half of lot 9, concession 3. He never made any improvements to the property and eventually left the township.[124]

Charles K. Knox was described by Thomas Vipond as "colored & poor. Shiftless."[125]

Elwood Knox borrowed money from John S. Brooks. After he failed to collect the over-due loan, Thomas Vipond described him as "colored & unemployed, but he may pay."[126]

Thomas E. Knox was described by Thomas Vipond as "colored & responsible."[127]

Dangerfield Lawson, according to the 1851 Peel Township census, was born in 1806 in Virginia, however family oral tradition states that he lived in Hagerstown, Maryland, when he escaped from slavery at age sixteen. His owner succeeded in capturing him and during a struggle Lawson strangled the man to death. With the help of abolitionists, Lawson escaped to Canada West and, in 1842, while living in York County, he took the British oath of allegiance. In May 1844, he moved with his family to Peel Township and they settled on the west half of lot 17, concession 7. In 1851, the Peel Township census enumerator reported that Lawson was married, but eighteen-year-old, Molly Ann Lawson, a single woman, was the only other person listed in the household. Dangerfield Lawson had probably died by 1861 as he does not appear in that decennial census. His death had certainly occurred prior to an 1867 *Elora Observer and Salem and Fergus Chronicle* newspaper article about Peel Township's early pioneers, which made a reference to him.[128]

Henry Dangerfield Lawson was the oldest son of Dangerfield Lawson. Discrepancies in the census make it difficult to determine his exact date of birth, but it must have occurred between 1838 and 1841. In 1861, Henry, along with his brother William and younger sister Elizabeth, lived with the Reverend Samuel H. Brown. Henry and William Lawson worked as farm labourers on Brown's one hundred acre farm. By 1871, Henry Lawson had married Sophia and they rented a house next door to William Lawson's farm on lot 15, concession 5. Henry Lawson worked as a labourer in the community. Henry and Sophia Lawson had a large family, which included: Ellen Jane, Sophia, Agnes, Hannah, Henry, James, Jacob, Herbert and Phillip.[129]

Ellen Jane Lawson (1868 – 1948), moved to Guelph at age twenty, where she found employment as a cook and maid. She eventually married William Arthur Jewell (c.1856 – 1929), a native of England, who worked for the Canadian Pacific Railroad. The couple had four children: William Arthur, Jr.; Ina Hanrietta, Percy Cornelius and Douglas Nelson.[130]

Henry and Herbert Lawson also moved to Guelph and another sister, Sophia, married a member of the Mallot family who also lived in the city. Phillip Lawson moved to Washington, D.C.[131]

Dangerfield Lawson's second oldest son, William (1843 – January 8, 1899), married Mary A., a Canadian who had been born in 1850. The couple owned a fifty-acre farm on lot 15, concession 5, in Peel Township, where they raised their children: Joseph, Cecilium, Elizabeth, Samuel and Mabel. William Lawson died at age fifty-six and his obituary in the *Drayton Advocate* noted that he had been a respected member of the community.[132]

John Lawson (1821 – ?), his wife Elizabeth, and their two oldest children, Ester and Samuel, had been born in the United States. Sometime after Samuel Lawson's birth in 1851, but before John Jr.'s birth in 1856, the family moved to Canada. Another son, Ephraim, was born in 1859. The Lawson family lived on a farm in Peel Township.[133]

L. Alexander Lawson (1879 – 1924) is buried in Peel Township in the AME/BME cemetery.[134]

Mary J. Lawson (1873 – December 28, 1909) was the wife of Joseph Miller and is buried in the Peel Township AME/BME cemetery.[135]

Henry Lepscombe settled on the front half of lot 11, concession 4, in Peel Township in December 1844. On July 27, 1848, Lepscombe's twelve-year-old stepdaughter, Georgina French, died after a wooden shelf fell on her head. Although he vehemently denied the charges, rumours began to circulate throughout the community that Lepscombe had murdered the young girl. Many neighbours suspected Lepscomb because his wife had recently given birth to twins and they, too, had suddenly died. It was widely believed Lepscombe had killed all three children because he was not their father. The accusations led to an inquest by local coroners, who determined the deaths were coincidental.[136]

John Lero arrived in Peel Township in December 1842 and established a farm on the rear half of lot 21, concession 1. John and Cuesley Lero appear on the 1847 Queen's Bush petition.[137]

John W. Levi lived in Flamboro West before moving, in December 1842, to lot 16, concession 2, in Peel Township. Within three years Levi had built a house, a barn and had cleared eighteen acres of land. His name appears on the 1843 Queen's Bush petition. On May 9, 1849 he took the British oath of allegiance.[138]

Henson/Anson Lewis (1801 – ?) was a fugitive slave from Maryland. On December 2, 1842, he settled on the south half of lot 12, concession 2, in Peel Township. Lewis' name appears on the 1843 Queen's Bush petition. Financial problems had forced him to borrow money from John S. Brooks and, on an 1850 list of Brooks' debtors, there is a notation indicating that Lewis "is good for property." In 1851, Lewis was unemployed and lived with fugitive slaves, Moses and Nancy Prater. His financial situation appears to have improved by 1862, because he purchased fifty acres in the northeast section of lot 12, concession 2.[139]

In 1948, Robert Armstrong published a brief memoir about growing up in Peel Township in the *Drayton Advocate*. In the article, Armstrong recalled that he had frequently visited Lewis as a child and had been enthralled by his stories about slavery and his escape from bondage.[140]

Isaac Lewis moved to Peel Township in October 1843 and settled on the east half of lot 13, concession 2. By October 1846 he had built a house and had cleared six acres of land, but when he registered his claim at the Elora land office he had to defer payment until January 1847. Lewis' name appears on the 1843 Queen's Bush petition.[141]

Thomas Lewis in May 1845, registered his claim for a section of land on lot 13, concession 2 in Peel Township.[142]

Jacob Libertus/Lybertus: (1817 – ?) had lived in Hillsborough, Vermont before moving to Canada West in September 1841, along with his white wife Hannah.[143] In 1851, Jacob and Hannah Libertus lived in a one-storey frame house in Glen Allan with their children: Phylura, (also known as Fidelia), born 1845; Philae, born 1847; Phylina, born 1850; and twins, Theodore and Theodora, born 1851. Jacob Libertus served briefly as a minister in the Wesleyan Methodist church, but then joined the Christian Church. He died sometime following the birth of his last child, Jacob T. in 1859, but before 1861 when his wife was listed as a widow in the census.[144]

William Libertus was a doctor who resided on the east half of lot 16, concession 2, in Peel Township. He later moved to Glen Allan where he continued to practise medicine for many years.[145]

Lewis Lightfoot arrived in Peel Township in October 1845, and settled on the west half of lot 11, concession 3.[146]

John Little and his wife Eliza's escape from slavery, as described in Benjamin Drew's book, *The Narratives of Fugitive Slaves in Canada*, make them among the best-known inhabitants of the Queen's Bush. Despite his success as a farmer in the community, John Little sold his Peel Township farm to John Martin in 1862 and emigrated to Haiti. The Haitian emigration movement had begun in 1858, when Fabre Geffrard assumed the presidency of the Caribbean island and promised Black immigrants free land and agricultural equipment. To oversee his immigration program, Geffrard had appointed James Redpath, a Scottish journalist living in the United States, to the position of General Agent of Emigration to Haiti. Redpath had promoted emigration through his weekly newspaper the *Pine and Palm*, which he published in Boston and in New York City. Prospective settlers could also request a free copy of the 192 page book entitled, *A Guide to Hayti*, which included a detailed map of the country and a list of essential supplies immigrants would need. In response to the interest in Haiti among Canadian Blacks, Redpath had hired several agents, who lectured across the province and organized emigration clubs in Toronto, Hamilton, Chatham and St. Catharines to assist emigrants with travel arrangements.[147]

By the early 1860s, the Haitian emigration movement had gained momentum in Canada West. Many families were lured by the promise of free land, while others were attracted to the opportunity to unite with other Blacks in the development of their own nation. Only the young and fit were advised to move to Haiti, but anyone could emigrate, as long as they could pay the fare. Numerous vessels sailed to Port-au-Prince from New York City, but the *Joseph Grice*, the *King Brothers* and the *Isabella Beauman*, were regularly commissioned to transport settlers. Depending on the weather, the voyage down the Atlantic coast could take from two to three weeks. The best time to arrive in Haiti was between September and May.[148]

At least 113 individuals emigrated from Canada West to Haiti in 1861. One major colonization group originated in Toronto and consisted of fifty-four men, women and children. Known as the Stokes Colony, in honor of their leader J.W. Stokes, the group left Toronto on September 27 and travelled by train to New York City. A week later they set sail for Port-au-Prince on board the vessel *Helen Augusta*.[149]

Nothing is known of John Little's fate in Haiti, but many settlers died of disease or suffered enormous losses because the Haitian government failed to uphold its promises. Eventually, unfavorable reports about Haiti's deplorable living conditions, unsanitary water and poor agricultural conditions began to reach North America. By the end of 1862, the Haitian emigration movement began to decline.[150]

John Little (1821 – ?) was a Maryland-born Peel Township farmer. In 1851 he reported to the census taker that he was married, but his wife was not listed in the household. Twenty-two-year-old Mathew Little, two-year-old Emmilea Little and ten-year-old Henry Lee were the only other individuals recorded in the household.[151]

John Little (1811 – ?) was an American-born Peel Township farmer. In 1861 he was enumerated with his wife, Martha, who had been born in 1831 in the United States. The couple had one daughter, Amelia, age ten. Fifteen-year-old Susan Smith lived with the family.[152]

Henry Ed Lloyd (1807 – ?) was an American-born farm labourer. In 1861 he worked for the Lloyd Wilson family in Peel Township.[153]

Lige Loban signed the 1850 Queen's Bush petition.[154]

Josephus/Joseph Mallot (1799 – ?) was born a slave in Alabama and worked as a cook on a Mississippi River steamboat. He was eventually able to purchase his freedom and had settled in Ohio, where he later joined a group of settlers who moved to Upper Canada in the late 1820s and established the Colbornesburg Settlement in Woolwich Township, Waterloo County. In 1832, Mallot, his wife Lucinda Brown, and their son Janul, lived on 150 acres in Crook's Tract, Broken Front Concession 2 in Woolwich Township. With only four acres cultivated with crops, the assessed value of the property was £33. By the following year, the family had cleared three additional acres and Lucinda Mallot had given birth to their daughter Margaret.[155]

After the Colbornesburg Settlement disbanded, the Mallots moved to Bloomingdale where their children, Catherine (also known as Caroline) and Joseph Jr., were born in 1836 and 1837, respectively. By 1840 the family had moved to Waterloo Township. The tax assessor did not report the exact location of the Mallot's home, but he assessed their property at £7.[156]

The Mallot family finally found a permanent home in March 1841 when they settled on the south half of lot 18, concession 1, in Peel Township. Between 1840 and 1845 Lucinda Mallott gave birth to at least three more children: John Michael, James Wilson and Hanna.[157]

It appears that Lucinda Mallot had died by 1850, because on April 17 of that year, Joseph Mallot married Mary Ann Lightfoot of Peel Township. The Baptist minister, the Reverend James Sims performed the ceremony, witnessed by Thomas Vipond and Preston Gallaway.[158]

Joseph Mallot, Jr. and his brothers regularly worked for John Bulmer, a native of England, whose farm was also on lot 18, concession 1. In 1862, for reasons unknown, Bulmer gave John Michael and James Wilson Mallot twenty-five acres of land.[159] As Joseph Mallot Sr. does not appear in the 1861 Peel Township census, nor is he mentioned in the deed, it is reasonable to assume that he was deceased by then.

Joseph Mallot Jr. married Fanny Carter, the eldest daughter of John Carter. The couple had at least one child, Sarah, born 1858, and they adopted three boys. Joseph Mallot Jr. died on September 8, 1910, at his home in Wallenstein after a long illness.[160] A correspondent for the *Elmira Signet*, who reported Mallot's death, stated that he "will be very much missed in the neighbourhood. He was held in the highest estimation by all who knew him, his jovial disposition made him many friends and gave him a welcome everywhere."[161]

John Michael Mallot lived in Glen Allen, where he worked as a labourer and carpenter.[162]

In 1871, James Mallot lived with his wife, Matilda P., and their two children, William James and Eliza Jane, on William Close's farm in Peel Township. Mallot worked as a labourer on the farm, but by 1910 he had moved his family to Guelph.[163]

Joseph Mallot Sr.'s daughter, Caroline, married Silas Green, Jr., of Wellesley Township on April 16, 1862. Green was the thirty-seven-year-old son of Silas and Charlotte Greene, and a native of Virginia.[164]

Annie Delia Mallot (1884-August 12, 1903), lived in Wallenstein and worked as a servant. She died at age nineteen and is buried in the Peel Township AME/BME cemetery.[165]

Louisa Mallot married Daniel Brown on January 26, 1848. Primitive Methodist minister, the Reverend Matthew Nichols performed the wedding, witnessed by the Reverend Samuel H. Brown and Barnard Smith.[166]

Silvester Matton appears on the 1847 Queen's Bush petition.[167]

James Marel signed the 1850 Queen's Bush petition.[168]

Tomes Marel signed the 1850 Queen's Bush petition.[169]

Henry Miller appears on the 1847 Queen's Bush petition.[170]

Mary Miller (1796 – ?) in 1871 was seventy-five-years-old and a resident of Peel Township.[171]

Major Mingo (1796 – ?) was American-born. His name appears on the 1843 and 1847 Queen's Bush petitions. In 1851 he lived in Waterloo Township, where he worked as a labourer.[172]

Joseph Molton (1799-?) had been a slave in Virginia before moving to Peel Township, where he farmed fifty acres before they were "swallowed up by lawyers." After losing his farm, Molton lived in Guelph before settling in Stratford, Ontario.[173]

Alfred Moodie (1828 – ?) was an American-born Peel Township labourer. His wife, Mary Ann, had been born in the United States in 1821. Mary Ann Moodie bore two children before the family moved to Canada: Hannah, born 1853 and Margaret, born 1854. In the mid-1850s, the Moodies moved to Peel Township where their children, Lorinda and Alfred Jr. were born in 1858 and 1860, respectively.[174]

James Moreton (1815 – ?) was born in the United States but eventually moved to Peel Township. The 1861 Peel Township census taker indicated that Moreton was married, but his wife was not listed in the household with him. However, four children were reported in the household: William, age 19; Catherine, age 12; John, age 6; and Solomon, age 5.[175]

Martha Munro (1835 – ?) was listed in the 1861 Peel Township census as married and the mother of Harriet, age two, but her husband does not appear with the family.[176]

Robert Norris (1801 – ?) and his wife, Mary, were from Virginia and farmed in Peel Township. In 1851 eight-year-old Mary Lee lived with the couple.[177]

Henry Osborn (sometimes spelled Ausbin or Busbin), was born in Maryland in 1801 according to the 1851 Peel Township census, although the 1861 census indicates his birth date as 1795. Information about his wife also differs between the taking of each census. In 1851, she appears as Ellen with a birth date of 1805, while her name is listed as Helen with a 1795 birth date in the 1861 census.[178]

The Osborns lived in Upper Canada as early as 1835 when their son David was born. Their second son, Moses, was born in 1837. In October 1842, the Osborn family moved to Peel Township and settled on the west half of lot 19, concession 3. Henry Osborn's name appears on the 1843 Queen's Bush petition, along with the names of his sons, although they were only eight and six years old at the time. By 1861 Osborn had given up farming full-time and found employment as a labourer.[179]

David Osborn married Sarah and the couple had three children:

Barnet, born 1857; Alomin, born 1859, and Regina, born 1860. In 1867, David Osborn worked as a labourer and lived with his family in Peel Township on lot 19, concession 2.[180]

John O'Neal arrived in Peel Township in February 1844 and settled on the south half of lot 15, concession 6. By June 1845 he had built a log shanty and had cleared eight acres of land.[181]

William Palmer Sr. was the progenitor of at least three generations of the Palmer family who lived in Peel Township. William Palmer Sr. had been born a slave in Kentucky sometime between 1819 and 1825. After his escape, he moved to Ohio where he married Martha (Matty). William Palmer's two oldest sons, William Jr. and Nellson, were born in Ohio in 1842 and 1843. In June 1844, the family moved to Peel Township, where they settled on lot 10, concession 4. Between 1845 and 1862, Martha Palmer bore at least eight more children: Mary, James, Margaret A., Henry, Samuel, Joseph, Martha and George. In 1851 when the Peel Township census taker enumerated the family, Samanthy Palmer, an Ohioan, was reported as the daughter of William and Matty Palmer. With her age being given as sixteen, she was more likely one of William's relatives and not his daughter.[182]

In 1871, William Palmer Sr. was the head of a large family that included his wife, nine children, two daughters-in-law and three grandchildren. William Palmer Sr. worked as a lime burner in Glen Allan, but he and his sons, William Jr. and James, also rented eight acres of land on lot 5, concession 3. William Jr. and James, along with their nineteen-year old brother, Henry, also worked as a labourers and their ten-year-old sister, Martha, was a domestic servant. William Palmer Sr.'s other children, Margaret A., Samuel, Joseph and George, were between the ages of nine and twenty, and also lived at home. All of the Palmer children were literate, but only seventeen-year-old Samuel regularly attended school regularly. William Palmer Jr. and his wife, Rachel, had two sons: James, born in 1867 and

William, born in 1870. James Palmer and his wife Roxana had a four-month-old son, John.[183]

Adam Pary arrived in Peel Township in September 1845 and settled on the south half of lot 10, concession 5.[184]

James Penelton arrived in Peel Township in May 1842 and settled on the west half of lot 2, concession 5. Within four years Penelton had built a house and cleared approximately six acres of land. His name appears on the 1843 Queen's Bush petition.[185]

Moses Pope Sr. and his wife, Maryann Selby, were both born in 1802 in the United States. In 1836, the couple lived in Toronto where their son, Moses Jr., was born. By 1847, the Popes had settled in Peel Township, where Maryann Pope gave birth to her children: Francis, Maryann, Henrietta, John, Sylvester and Miner.[186]

On May 17, 1859, Moses Pope Jr. married Elizabeth Dorothea Brown, the daughter of John and Lucinda Brown (nee Green) of Wellesley Township. Moses and Elizabeth Pope had at least two sons, William, born in 1859, and John, born in 1860.[187]

On November 15, 1866, the *Berliner Journal* reported the death of Moses Pope of Waterloo. The brief obituary state that "owing to a quarrel in his home [Pope] had not eaten anything for several days, devoured six cans of oysters and two pounds of tallow on Friday evening. He soon became very ill and died on Saturday night."[188]

Abner Posey (1837 – ?), as a teenager, worked as a servant and labourer for William Johnson of Wellesley Township. In 1861, Posey lived in St. Thomas, where he continued to find employment as a labourer. Posey's parents are unknown, although a Jacob Posey appears on the 1847 Queen's Bush petition.[189]

Jeremiah A. Powell was born a slave about 1798 in North Carolina.

He arrived in Upper Canada on June 3, 1838 after purchasing his freedom and, by 1841, he was living in York County. In June 1844, Powell moved to Peel Township where he established the first farm on lot 16, concession 7. On January 17, 1846, he took the British oath of allegiance.[190]

William Nell, in his history of Peel Township, published as a series of articles in the *Elora Observer and Salem and Fergus Chronicle* between 1866 and 1867. He described Powell as "a man of passionate, vindictive temper, but possessed of considerable knowledge of various subjects, and was very fond of debating. He was hard-working and honest, and in many respects superior of the generality of his race."[191]

Jeremiah Powell's wife, Mary Ann, had been born in 1818 in Delaware. The couple had at least five children: Sarah A., born 1838; Sophia, born 1844; Soloman, born 1846; David, born 1847, and Mary Ann, born 1849. Jeremiah Powell eventually sold his farm to William Rainey and moved his family to Normanby Township, where he died sometime before 1867.[192]

Benjamin Richardson arrived in Peel Township in November 1843 and settled on the west half of lot 17, concession 2. Within three years he had built a house and cleared five acres of land. His name appears on the 1847 Queen's Bush petition.[193]

Lewis Robeson appears on the 1847 Queen's Bush petition.[194]

Robert Robson appears on the 1847 Queen's Bush petition.[195]

John Rose signed the 1850 Queen's Bush petition.[196]

George Ross appears on the 1847 Queen's Bush petition.[197]

John Ross (1815 – ?) was a native of Virginia. In 1851, he lived in a log shanty in Peel Township.[198]

John Ross (1842 – ?) lived with the Solomon and Jane Tibbs family in Peel Township in 1861. Seventeen-year-old Thomas Ross also lived with the family. Both teenagers had been born in the United States.[199]

Leucinda Ross (1801 – ?) was a Viriginia-born Peel Township resident. The 1851, Peel Township census enumerator listed her as a married woman, but no other family members were reported living in the household.[200]

George Selby/Silby (1806 – ?) and his wife were natives of New York. Due to discrepancies in the census, it is unclear whether Selby's wife's name was Eliza or Louisa, although her date of birth was reported as 1825. George Selby moved to Peel Township in December 1843 and settled on lot 17, concession 4. The Selby's children included: Samuel, born 1849; Ellen, born 1855 and James, born 1858.[201]

John Sims appears on the 1847 Queen's Bush petition.[202]

Charles Smith (1806 – ?) was a Maryland-born Peel Township farmer. His wife, Elizabeth, had been born in New Jersey in 1811. Charles Smith borrowed money from John S. Brooks and when Thomas Vipond failed to collect the overdue loan, he reported to the AMA that Smith "hasn't any prospects. Poor."[203]

H. Smith appears on the 1847 Queen's Bush petition.[204]

Henry Smith (1802-c.1854) was from Kentucky and arrived in Peel Township in March 1844, where he settled on the south half of lot 19, concession 2. His wife, Margaret, had been born in Canada in 1819. The Smith's children included: Charles, born 1833; John, born 1835; Henry, Jr., born 1837; Peter, born 1840; Susan, born 1843; Arthur, born 1845, and Melinda, born 1849. In 1846, church officials admitted Henry Smith to the AME church on trial as a minister. He served the

Peel Township AME church as a local preacher until at least 1853. Smith does not appear among the list of AME ministers in the *Minutes of the Sixteenth Annual Conference of the African Methodist Episcopal Church, 1854,* so it may be possible that he had died by then. The 1861 census lists his wife, Margaret, as a widow.[205]

John Smith (1795 – ?) and his wife, Fluvella, were natives of the United States. The couple's two daughters, Amelia and Sarah, were born in Canada in 1842 and 1850, respectively.[206]

George Stewart appears on a list of individuals who owed money to John S. Brooks. A notation beside his name indicates that he was "colored & may pay."[207]

Jacob F. Stewart was born in Maryland and probably did not know his exact date of birth because various records list his birth date as 1808, 1824, 1826 or 1829. Stewart had initially settled in Peel Township on the west half of lot 10, concession 3, but later moved to lot 16, concession 2. On March 18, 1847, Steward married Mary Ann Knox, a Quaker from Philadelphia, Pennsylvania. The Baptist minister, the Reverend James Sims performed the ceremony and the witnesses were Robert Jackson and Charles B. Knox. The Stewarts had at least one child, Ann, who was born in 1853. Mary Ann Stewart died March 22, 1886, at age 70. Her husband, Jacob, died December 18, 1888. They were buried beside each other in the Peel Township AME/BME cemetery.[208]

John Stewart appears on the 1847 Queen's Bush petition.[209]

Henrietta Still (1817 – ?), by 1861, was a widow raising two children, seventeen-year-old Charles and twelve-year-old Sophia, in Peel Township. Henrietta and her children had been born in the United States.[210]

Peter Edward Susand (1803 – ?) lived in Wellesley Township as early as 1843 on a fifty acre farm on lot 1, concession 12. However, sometime between 1851 and 1853, the Susand family moved to Berlin (present-day Kitchener), where Peter E. Susand established several different businesses.[211]

Peter and his English-born wife, Elizabeth, had ten children: Nathaniel, born 1833; Lavina Daphney, born February 1836; Annetta Victoria, born 1838; Henry, born 1839; Angelina, born 1841; William Alfred, born June 15, 1843; Othello Leopold, born February 8, 1845; Theodore, born 1846; Mary Jane, born September 4, 1848 and Elizabeth Ellen, born January 4, 1850.[212]

The names of his children testify to Susand's fondness of Shakespeare and he even published a book of poetry entitled, *The Prose and Poetical Works of Peter Edward Susand*. According to a review of the book, many of the poems described the sufferings of his people; unfortunately, only two lines of his work have survived:

> "Ye ho! Here comes a schooner!
> Eh ho! I wish she'd come a little sooner.[213]

Between 1853 and 1857, Susand instituted legal proceedings against whites who had damaged his Berlin property. The first court action took place on July 25, 1853 and involved a charge of misdemeanor against Jacob Brieler, who was fined five shillings. The second round of legal proceedings was the result of acts of vandalism a group of boys had committed against his store on May 24, 1856. In June, he had placed a notice in the *Berlin Chronicle*, stating that he would apply at the next meeting of the Berlin municipal council for indemnification for damages done by the vandals. The following year on June 8, Susand won a court case against Sebastian Dexter for a charge of misdemeanor. Several weeks later, on June 30, Justices of the Peace, Henry S. Huber and William Davidson, found A.S. Thornton, James Coleman, Casper Hett, John Roat, Fred S. Chadwick and John Croft guilty on charges of misdemeanors brought against them by Susand.[214]

On January 7, 1856, at a meeting held in the Waterloo County Courthouse, Mr. Godbold and James Potter nominated Peter E. Susand to the ballot for Berlin town councilor. At the time there was little doubt that incumbent, Dr. John Scott, would be re-elected to office and, given the keen awareness Susand had of the political and social realities of his time, it is likely that he himself never doubted the outcome. Yet, in accepting his nomination, Susand gave a speech before those assembled at the meeting. An account of his speech was printed in the *Berlin News*:

> He said the present occasion gave him much pleasure and delight and in rising to address such a large body of his honorable and well-disposed fellow citizens, he did not do so with any desire to exonerate himself, but in order to express the enthusiasm he felt towards the free, uncorrupted and glorious Institutions of Great Britain – the land of the brave and the home of the free, upon whose territory the greater light in the firmament never went down, nor, in shining lit up with its effulgent radiance, the face of a solitary slave. He confessed there was one thing which worked against him in the present highly delightful contest, which scarcely required a name, as it stared them all in the face. He hoped, however, that as men living in an enlightened age, when the blessings of education and Civil and Religious Liberty were scattered broadcast over the land, as chaff is scattered by the winds of heaven, that all distinctions of country and color would be forgotten, and that the electors would rally under the banners which marshalled the forces of the good

and true temporal warriors. There was a dark night,
a black night, a tempestuous night of peril to British
supremacy in this Province, when its most sanguine
supporters trembled as they beheld the tide of war
which act as the billows of the ocean tossed to and
fro in the arms of Boreas, from the shores of that
land the stripes on whose flag was emblematical of
the cruelty of its people towards the downtrodden
humanity of the South. Where, in this peril, was the
black man! Where he was most wanted, – at his post
– offering himself up a willing sacrifice upon the
altar of freedom. Yes! he was one of the glorious
band who fought in defense of British connection
and their own firesides – who hurled back the body
and soul-murdering legion of the slaveholder, and
cut off at the elbow the arm stretched out to grasp
the heart-strings of this young land. If he then
shared the dangers of the white man, he now
claimed the privileges of the white man. Would they
deny them to him? They might scorn to give the
black man these privileges in the hour of national
prosperity, but they would ask him at less fortunate
times to take their ball. (Cheers) He offered himself
for the suffrages of the people as an honest, a patri-
otic and philanthropic man – disposed to love all
men – and particularly well-inclined towards the
town of Berlin, whose interests should ever receive
at his hands an unlimited, and untiring care. If he
got one vote he would feel satisfied, as it would show
that he was a man, and claimed a man's Privileges.
He knew he was deficient in education, literature
and the fine arts, as he only went to school one week
in his life, but he hoped he was not deficient in good

common sense, and he had written an address to the general public that left gentlemen no room to laugh, except on the wrong side of the physiognomy. He wrote the address alone, unassisted and undisturbed, when the silent watches of the night were his only companions, and many of them had run down. It had been basely insinuated that he procured the services of a colored gentleman to write that address. He could only say there was not the slightest particle of truth in the charge (Laughter). Let the human mind rise – let it be free as the breeze playing over the bosom of the ocean, and carrying on its breath the scent of violets. The mind was not intended by the Creator to sink, but to go up from glory to glory! In conclusion, he threw himself upon them, and remained their humble servant.[215]

In the ensuing election Dr. Scott was re-elected, prompting Susand to comment in a letter to the editor:

My dear friend – Niggah is niggah in de eye of de world, but hc may hab as whitc a soul as his whitc brudder. I thanks you much for de publication of Peter Edward Susand's speech. He ain't a great man for he ain't a white man like the Doctor, but he ain't perniscuously envious, and he says to hisself that a clar conscience is worth more than all the public offices in de Kintry.[216]

In 1854, the Susand's thirteen-year-old daughter, Angelina died shortly followed by the death of their youngest son, Theodore, on February 16, 1861. Almost a year later, on January 16, 1862, their oldest daughter, Lavinia Daphney, died of consumption at age twenty-five.

All of the children were buried in the Mount Hope Cemetery in Berlin. Perhaps spurred by these deaths, Elizabeth Ellen, William Alfred, Othello Leopold and Mary Jane were baptized on April 13, 1862, at St. John the Evangelist Church.[217]

In 1862, Peter E. Susand moved to Guelph, where he returned to his barbering trade, while his family remained in Berlin, where they subsequently experienced significant financial problems. The reason for Susand's move is unknown, but the desperate financial situation of his family seems to indicate that he may have abandoned them.[218]

In 1865, Elizabeth Susand finally reported herself as a "widow" on the Berlin assessment records. Whether she truly was a widow or simply found it was the easiest way for her to deal with the situation is unknown. However, no obituary or burial record has been found for Peter Edward Susand in either Waterloo or Wellington counties. By this time, Elizabeth Susand and her children lived on North Queen Street in a home owned by Louis Breithaupt. She had opened a fancy goods shop and candy store where she sold molasses candy, known as "Susand's Taffy." By 1867, her business ventures were prospering and her economic situation had improved. Two years later she was able to purchase property on the west side of Foundry Street.[219]

William Alfred and Henry Susand eventually left Berlin and, in 1870, they lived in Bay City, Michigan, where they worked as barbers. William Susand's wife, Victoria, was a native of Virginia and worked as a seamstress, while Henry's wife, Mary, hailed from Kentucky and found employment as a hairdresser.[220]

On July 13, 1863, Annetta Victoria Susand married Samuel Huff of Hespeler. Nothing more is known of the couple, but in the same year Mary E. Huff was buried in the Susand family plot at the Mount Hope Cemetery in Berlin.[221]

Elizabeth Ellen Susand died on August 31, 1880, at age thirty, and was also buried in the Mount Hope Cemetery. On January 10, 1881, at the parsonage of St. John the Evangelist Church, Mary Jane Susand married Alfred Fennemore Powell, who lived in Kingston, New York, where he worked as a waiter. The previous December, Mrs. Elizabeth Susand had made her will stipulating that Mary Jane was to be the sole beneficiary of her estate and shortly thereafter, she joined her sons in Michigan.[222]

Cornelus Tailer appears on the 1847 Queen's Bush petition.[223]

Peter Tailer appears on the 1847 Queen's Bush petition.[224]

George Tebla appears on the 1847 Queen's Bush petition.[225]

Calib Thomas had been born in the United States in 1847. In 1861 he lived with the Robert Harding family in Peel Township.[226]

James Thomas arrived in Peel Township on November 10, 1843, and homesteaded on the front half of lot 9, concession 3. Within three years he had built a house and cleared five acres of land. In October 1846, Thomas filed his claim at the Elora land office, but deferred payment until January 1847. His name appears on the 1847 Queen's Bush petition.[227]

Susan Thomas (1808 – ?), in 1861, was the head of a household that included nineteen-year-old Isabella Johnston, eighteen-year-old Charles Lawson and thirteen-year-old Joseph Jackson. The two teenage boys were employed as labourers.[228]

William Thomas (1829 – ?) was an American-born Peel Township labourer. His wife, Elizabeth, had been born in the United States in 1827. The Thomas' had at least four children: Matilda, born 1846; Elizabeth, born 1851; Charles, born 1855, and Alex, born 1868. Their two oldest daughters were natives of the United States, but their sons had been born in Canada West, suggesting that the family moved to Canada sometime between 1851 and 1855.[229]

William Thomas (1798 – ?) and his wife, Charlotte, were from the United States. In 1861, they lived in Wellesley Township with seventy-year-old Mrs. Scott and ten-year-old G. Burlington.[230]

James Thornton (1801 – ?) and his wife, Elizabeth, were natives of the United States. In April 1845, they settled on lot 17, concession 3, in Peel Township, but later moved to lot 13, concession 4. By 1861 the couple had four children: Mary, born 1849; James, born 1852; Isahah, born 1854, and Elias, born 1857. Two-year-old Joseph Curtman also lived with the family.[231]

Solomon Tibbs (1800 – ?) and his wife, Jane, had at least seven children: Mary, born 1837; Nehemiah, born 1839; Solomon, Jr., born 1843; L. Jane, born 1847; Charity, born 1850; Samuel, born 1856, and James C., born 1858. The couple's four oldest children had been born in the United States, but the youngest two had been born in Canada West, indicating that the family probably moved to Canada between 1850 and 1856. The Tibbs family lived in Peel Township.[232]

Thomas Tibbs (1814-?) and his wife, Ann, were from the United States. However, their four children, Celekto, Lettica, Isikeah and Silus, had been born in Canada between 1849 and 1859.[233]

Richard Tibbs in 1861 was a single, nineteen-year-old American-born Peel Township labourer.[234]

John Tillman arrived in Peel Township in August 1842, and settled on the southeast half of lot 14, concession 3. Within just three years he built a house and cleared twenty acres of land.[235]

Thomas Tobbert appears on the 1847 Queen's Bush petition.[236]

Richard Traverse (1819-?) his wife Polleana and their daughters

(Ropana, born 1851, and Rebecca, born 1853) were natives of the United States. In the fall of 1853, the Traverse family settled on the east half of lot 4, concession 1, in Peel Township. Between 1855 and 1860, the couple had at least four more children: Mary, John R., Lucinda and Charles.[237]

George Washington (1808 – ?) was a Peel Township farmer. He and his wife, Harriet, and their children were natives of the United States. The name of their son is identified only as H. in the 1861 census and their daughter's name is unreadable.[238]

Samuel White had been born into slavery in Maryland in 1786 or 1793. His wife, Hannah Gray, had also been born in Maryland in 1786 or 1802. Their two oldest children, Henry and Sarah, however, had been born in Virginia in 1828 and 1832, respectively. The family escaped from slavery and arrived in Canada by 1834 when their son, David, was born. In the fall of 1842, the family settled on lot 19, concession 1, in Peel Township. Samuel and Hannah White's other children included: Jacob, Elizabeth and Frederick.[239]

In 1846, Samuel White made four acres of land available to John S. Brooks for the site of the Mount Hope School. The agreement stipulated that Brooks could use the property as long as the school remained opened. Brooks obviously forgot about the agreement because after his department from Peel Township in 1849, his power of attorney placed the land on the market for sale. White had to write to Lewis Tappan, of the AMA to rectify the problem. Samuel White's name and that of his sons appear on the 1843 and 1847 Queen's Bush petitions. In 1852, White put his farm on the market for sale, but could not find a buyer or decided to remain in the community. He still lived in the township in 1861, although he eventually sold his farm to John Fenton.[240]

In 1861, Samuel White's oldest son, Henry, worked as a labourer. He and his wife, Susan, rented a house and a half-acre of land on lot 13, concession 4. The couple had four children: Simon, Alfred, Samuel and Hanna. On August 1, 1876, Susanna Ellen White, who was most likely Henry White's wife, died at age twenty-eight and was buried in the Peel Township AME/BME cemetery.[241]

Jacob White, at age twenty-three, married seventeen-year-old, Elizabeth Edy White on September 26, 1860. She was the daughter of Benjamin and Margaret (Piper) Edy of Peel Township. Like his brother, Jacob White worked as a labourer.[242]

Scott White arrived in Peel Township on June 23, 1845, and settled on the south half of lot 13, concession 5.[243]

Samuel Williams arrived in Peel Township in July 1844, and claimed fifty acres on the front half of lot 20, concession 1. His neighbour, John Little, operated a farm on the back half of the lot. By 1845, Williams had constructed a house and cleared four acres of land. His name appears on the 1847 Queen's Bush petition.[244]

William Willson appears on the 1847 Queen's Bush petition.[245]

Benjamin Wilson (1810 – ?), his wife Irene, and their son, Winfield, were natives of United States. Sometime after Winfield Wilson's birth in 1852, but before 1855, when their daughter Elizabeth was born, the Wilsons moved to Canada West. They had two more daughters, Martha and Mary.[246]

Lloyd Wilson (1809 – ?) was an American-born Peel Township farmer. His wife, Polly, had been born in 1811 in the United States. She was the mother of at least two children: Peter, born 1847, and Sophia, born 1849. Both children had been born in the United States.[247]

William Wilson in January 1846, filed a claim for his homestead on the north half of lot 12, concession 4 in Peel Township. His name appears on the 1847 Queen's Bush petition.[248]

Sarah Winn in 1871, was a widow, who lived with the Reverend Samuel H. Brown and his wife Ellen. Her sons, Rickmond, Richard and Samuel, who ranged in age from three to nineteen, also lived in the household. The previous year her children, Moses and Helen, had died of whooping cough.[249]

Daniel Youbanks had been born in Virginia in 1795 or 1797. He moved to Peel Township on March 25, 1846 with his wife Elizabeth, a native of Canada. The couple's children included: William, born 1826; Anbel, born 1830; Ellen, born 1832; Hanna, born 1839; Thomas, born 1845, and Sarah, born 1857. In April 1864, Daniel Youbanks purchased a fifty-acre farm on lot 12, concession 3, and two months later he sold four acres to Joseph Powley for one hundred dollars.[250]

George Yelley appears on the 1847 Queen's Bush petition.[251]

APPENDIX B: PETITIONS[1]

1. Petition to James Durand MP, 1842

James Durand, MP at Dundas, received the following petition in the fall of 1842. He had requested that the families in the Queen's Bush submit a list of their names, but unfortunately the list is not included with the petition.

Honorable & Respected Sir,

According to your late request, that we should furnish you with a list of the inhabitants (Families) in the "Queensbush," as (sic) also of the cleared land of the same, – we herewith transmit such list to you.

We are aware that an apology for our boldness of squatting into the Queens Bush the way we have done, should be reasonalbly looked for. We would therefore beg leave to state to you that we are most of us, Emigrants, who came to this country without the means of buying land, either cultivated or wild, – and that we had therefore no means of making a living except as Day Labourers, which is by the way no very easy way of getting a living; but to which we would have still cheerfully submitted, could we have got places to live with our families and constant employment, but we could get neither one nor the other. It is true, we owe many obligations to the older Settlers of Waterloo and Woolwich for employment and temporary places of residence; but a strong emigration, as you are no doubt well aware, cannot, for any length of time, be supported, or support itself, in this manner. Taking these things into consideration, we thought it would be best for ourselves and Families, if we would go into the woods and cultivate that soil, which we saw that was at any rate, as long as it was unsettled of no more use than being a rendezvous of the wolf and the Bear, – comtemplating at the same time, once to buy the land we have taken in possession, should it be sold upon such conditions that we could buy it and we are sincerely glad that there is a prospect of its being surveyed out. At the same time we would beg to state that a report is abroad that the late Lord Sydenham should have recommended that no wild land should be sold any more except for <u>Cash</u>. We will by no means question the propriety of this plan in a general point of view; but in our case it would be hard indeed, as it would be impossible for most, if not all of us, to buy our land in this way; whereas as we would have a prospect of buying it, were it to be sold upon installments. We would therefore beg that you would use your influence that it may be sold upon as favorable conditions as possible, as also that the lots will not be made so large. We think that 200 hundred acres would be a good size for a lot. In the whole we hope, and have full confidence, that you will do the best for us you can; and we are withall truly thankful that you have taken up our cause and have done what you have done already.

To James Durand, Esqr. MP

Dundas

The Settlers of the Queens Bush

P.S. We would prefer, by far, having the lots surveyed out from <u>North</u> to <u>South</u> – from <u>North</u> to <u>South</u> length ways.

2. Petition to Charles Metcalfe, Governor General, 1843

On April 24, 1843, Charles Metcalfe, the Governor General, received a petition from the inhabitants of the Queen's Bush, which included a list of names. The letter B follows the names of those individuals who have been identified as being of African descent by the author.

To His Excellency The Right Honorable Sir Charles Theopilus Metcalfe, Knight Grand Cross of the Most Honorable Military Order of the Bath, one of Her Majesty's Most Honorable Privy Council, Governor General of British North America; and Captain General, and Governor-in-Chief; in and over the Province of Canada, Nova Scotia, New Brunswick, and the Island of Prince Edward, and Vice-Admiral of the same, etc. etc. etc.

The Humble Petition

Showeth, that your petitioners the Inhabitants of the Queens Bush now labouring under many disadvantages on account of the state of the Lands on which we have settled not being surveyed consequently, we have no regular Roads and being a distance of fifteen miles to the nearest mill, and your Petitioners being extremely poor having lately emigrated from England and from the Southern states where we have suffered all the horrors of Slavery and having no means of purchasing land, your Petitioners humbly pray that your Lordship will take our case into consideration and if agreeable to your Lordship's humanity to make us a grant of Land it will be most thankfully received by Lordship's dutiful and Loyal Petitioners and your Petitioners as is duty bound will ever pray

Thomas Vipond

Isaac H. Vipond

James Sims

Thomas Keith (B)

Daniel Charles

James Thomas (B)

Samuel White (B)

George Harrison

Henry Murphy

Jeremiah Belding

? Dickson

Henry White (B)

Cuilen Vincent

John Brown (B)

Daniel Brown (B)

George Brown (B)

Nathan Brown (B)

Josephus Malott Sr. (B)

Sytruober (?) Malott (B)

James Carey

George W. Thomas

Samuel Thomas

Matthew Giffen

Jacob Dorcey (B)

Peter Dorsey (B)

John Malott (B)

Josephus Malott Jr. (B)

Levy Johnson

Thomas Gibbs (B)

Robert Clarkes

Vincent Douglass, Sen. (B)

Vincent Douglass Jr. (B)

Jophnenos Belding

Thomas H. Douglass

Hezkiah Belding

Jeremiah Belding

George Belding

Isaac Johnston

Philomet Workman

Hamton Bailey (B)

John W. Levy (B)

John Ness

John Brooks (B)

Charles W. Douglass

Isaac Franklin

Henry Osborn (B)

Robert Jackson (B)

Anotin Dickson

Edward Blackwall

Samuel Brown (B)

John Howard

Frederic Albert

Alfred Munro

Samuel Simons

Phineinus Hale

Lewis Bulter (B)

Wesley Lero (B)

John Lero (B)

James Penelton (B)

Daniel Aghurt

John Jackson (B)

Jacob Defink, Sen

Johannes Defink

Jacob Defink

David Lewis

George Duncan

Charles Duncan

Joseph Armstrong (B)

David White (B)

Samson White (B)

Josiah Brown

George Harris

Lewis Lightfoot (B)

P.E. Susand (B)

Andrew Johnston

Joseph Harris

Joseph Harris

Robert Carey

Major Mingo (B)

London Harris (B)

Luke Harris (B)

Mark Harris (B)

George Bovie (B)

Matthew Harris (B)

Robert Robinson

Cornelius Robinson

Lewis Howard (B)

Isaac Lewis (B)

John Lewis

Jeremiah Thomas

William Workman

Edward Johnston

Henry Brewer

John Johnston

Wesley Johnston

Barnet Howard

Barnet Smith

Daniel Banks (B)

John Banks (B)

Henson Lewis (B)

Peyton Harris

John Robinson

Thomas Proudham

John Proudham

John Little (B)

Peter Sims

James M. Mallot (B)

Owans Ott

Solomon Conaway (B)

Josephes Armstrong (B)

William Conaway (B)

Hillig Ott

Adam Ott

Jacob Aepite

Richard James

Scott James

David Osborne (B)

Moses Osborne (B)

John Tillman

William Vipond

Gilbert O. Field

James Sim

Henry Blackwell

James Blackwell

3. Petition to the Governor General, 1847

In June 1847, Henry Miller delivered another petition on behalf of the Black inhabitants of the Queen's Bush to the Governor-General of Canada, which stated:

To His Excellency the right Honourable the Elgin and Kincardine, Captain general and govenor-in-Chief of Her majesty's provinces of Canada New Brunswick Nova Scotia and of the Island of Prince Edward and govenor general of all Her Majestys provinces on the Continent of North America and High Admiral of the same

The Humble petition of the Undersigned Coloured Inhabitants of the Queensbush in the townships of Wellesley and Peele most Humbly Therwith

That your pettrs has settled on these lands for many years and under Every difficulty has mad Improvements on the lots of land that your pettrs hav taken up by making roads fencing and Cultivating these land Your pettrs Having no Capital to Comence with makes your pettrs not able to purchase these lands Except that Your pettrs is granted time to pay it by instalments which Your pettrs will do if allowed to pay the same and we earnestly intreat your Excellency favour to grant your pettrs this their Humble request for if your pettrs is driven from our little Homes our distress will be great not knowing what to do. Many of your pettrs hav large families to suport and no means of suporting them if your pettrs Hs to leave these lands that your pettrs Has settled upon now we are loyal subjects to our sovering Queen Victoria every man and when the outbreak of '37 took place we turned out to a man in defence of the Country and done our duty as soldiers and is ready and willing at any time to the same. We therfore leave our Case before Your Excellency in hopes that Your Excellency will give it a favourable consideration and as in Duty bound Will Ever pray.

Pettrs on the within mentioned lands:

Henry Osburn

William Gordon

Henry Miller

Dangfeld Lawson

Jeremiah Powel

James Dunn

George Tebla

Moses Pope

Johnson Johnson

Denis Johnson

Thomas Amess

William Craford

William Burton

John Smith

Hamilton Bailey

Benjeman Richardson

Joseph Mallot

Silvester Matton

Jacob White

Major Harder

John Palmer

Thomas Gilis

London Harris

Wildon Harris

Mark Harris

Mathew Harris

James Thomas

Luke Harris

Denis Jackson

James Howard

John James

John Francis

Major Mingo

Josep Anderson

James Thornton

Benjeman Willson

George Ross

Cornelos Tailer

Petter Tailer

Saml Brown

H. B Lepscomb

James Glast

Robert Jackson

John Brown

William Johnston

Ben Eddy

Robert Robson

Charles Smith

Moses Prater

James Jackson

William Burton

Lewis Robeson

George Yelley

H. Smith

John Benson

William Thomas

Thomas Johnson

Jerry Johnson

Thomas Knox

John Stewart

Robert Freeman

James Harris

Jacob Dorsey

David Ambush

Thomas Keeth

Rean Davis

James Douglas

Vinnis Douglas

Augusta Kerr

Robert Bond

Robert Johnston

Lewis Armstrong

Joseph Armstrong

Robert Armstrong

Thomas Tobbert

Ashlon Dickson

John Carey

William Willson

John Davis

John Sims

Samuel White

Samuel Williams

Lenord Brown

Robert Gent

David Hall

George Harris

Robert Harden

James Hart

Thomas Douglas

William Cary

John Little

If your Excellancy will please give the bearer of the Petition Henry Miller as he would the Same.

Henry Miller (His mark)

4. Petition to Lord Elgin – 850

In 1850, ten black residents of the Queen's Bush sent another petition:

His Excellency the Right Honorable James, Earl of Elgin and Kincardine, Baron Elgin K.J. Governor General of British north America and Captain General and Governor in chief in and over the Provinces of Canada, Nova Scotia, New Brunswick and the Island of Prince Edward and Vice Admiral of the same etc. etc.

May it please your Excellency
The petition of the Undersigned Men of Colour
Humblely showeth

That there was a proclamation issued in the year 1840 to the effect that every man of colour assisting in putting down the Rebellion of the year 1837 & 1838 by going to the Queens Bush was to get a deed of 50 acres of land with the privilege of purchasing 50 acres more of the Lot if able to do so.

That your petitioners in consequence removed with their families to the aforesaid Queen's Bush and Located in it.

That after nine years privations & hard labour your petitioners succeeded in clearing on an average 20 acres of Land with corresponding improvements.

That your petitioners are now informed by Mr. Gayters, Crown Land Agent in Elora that their farms and improvements are in the Market.

Your petitioners therefore humbly entreat you will take their Case into your humane consideration and petitioners will as is duty bound ever pray

Massene Hale	Tomes Marel
Lige Loban	Joep Diges
Thomas Jones	John Rose
Samel	John Marel
Levie Jones	James Gelares

NOTES

Prologue: An Overview of the Black Experience in Canada West

1.   Excerpt from the song, "The Free Slave," written by American abolitionist, George W. Clark, from the *Provincial Freeman*, Mar. 25, 1852.

2.   Jason H. Silverman, *Unwelcome Guests: Canada West's Response to American Fugitive Slaves, 1800-1865* (New York: Associated Faculty Press, 1985) 1; Robin W. Winks, *The Blacks in Canada: A History* (New Haven: Yale University Press, 1971) 1-2.

3.   William Renwick Riddell, "The Slave in Canada," *Journal of Negro History* vol. 5 (New York: Association for the Study of Negro Life and History, July 1920) 264; Winks, *Blacks in Canada*, 3.

4.   Winks, *Blacks in Canada*, 12; Silverman, *Unwelcome Guests*, 2.

5.   Winks, *Blacks in Canada*, 4-5, 9.

6.   Riddell, "The Slave in Canada," 273, 305.

7.   Winks, *Blacks in Canada*, 29-30; Silverman, *Unwelcome Guests*, 3.

8.   Winks, *Blacks in Canada*, 30; Silverman, *Unwelcome Guests*, 3-4.

9.   Winks, *Blacks in Canada*, 46-47; Silverman, *Unwelcome Guests*, 55.

10.   Riddell, "The Slave in Canada," 317-320; Daniel G. Hill, *The Freedom Seekers: Blacks in Early Canada* (Agincourt, ON: Society of Canada Ltd., 1981) 15-17; Winks, *Blacks in Canada*, 96-99.

11.   Silverman, *Unwelcome Guests*, 14.

12.   Wilbur H. Seibert, *The Underground Railroad From Slavery To Freedom* (New York: Russell & Russell, 1898) 5; John Hope Franklin and Loren Schweninger, *Runaway Slaves: Rebels on the Plantation* (Oxford: Oxford University Press, 1999) 210-212; Adrienne Shadd, Afua Cooper & Karolyn Smartz Frost, *The Underground Railroad: Next Stop, Toronto!* (Toronto: Natural Heritage, 2002) 74, 75.

13.   Silverman, *Unwelcome Guests*, 23.

14.   Jermain Wesley Loguen (1813–1872), was born Jarm Logue in Davidson County, Tennessee. His mother was a slave and his father, David Logue, was a white

plantation owner. Around 1835 Logue escaped from bondage and settled in
Hamilton, Upper Canada, where he acquired an education. He later moved to
Syracuse, New York, where he established a school and assumed the name Jermain
Wesley Loguen. He also operated an Underground Railroad station. According to
Loguen, he assisted approximately 1,500 fugitive slaves in their escape to freedom.
In 1842, Loguen became an ordained African Methodist Episcopal Zion (AMEZ)
minister. In the 1850s, with the support of the American Missionary Association,
Loguen served as an itinerant minister throughout western New York and helped
to organize numerous AMEZ churches. After the passage of the Fugitive Slave Law
in 1850, Loguen endorsed violent means to end slavery and encouraged abolitionists
to ignore the law. On October 1, 1851, Loguen assisted the Syracuse Vigilance
Committee in their rescue of William "Jerry" McHenry, a fugitive slave imprisoned
in the Syracuse jail. Fearing imprisonment for his participation in the rescue,
Loguen fled to St. Catharines, Canada West, where he worked briefly as a missionary
with Hiram Wilson. He also became an anti-slavery lecturer for the Anti-slavery
Society of Canada. In 1852, Loguen returned to Syracuse and resumed his anti-slavery
activities. In 1859, he published his autobiography *The Rev. J.W. Loguen, as a Slave
and as a Freeman*. After the Civil War, Loguen continued his missionary work
among the freedmen and, in 1868, he became a bishop in the AMEZ church. He died
in Saratoga Springs, New York, in 1872. C. Peter Ripley, *The Black Abolitionist
Papers, Volume 11, Canada, 1830-1865* (Chapel Hill: University of North Carolina
Press, 1986) 198-199; Jermain Loguen, *The Rev. J.W. Loguen, as a Slave and as a
Freeman*. Syracuse: J.G.K. Truair & Co., 1859.

15. Frederick Douglass (February 1817–February 20, 1895), was born Frederick
Augustus Washington Bailey in Talbot County, Maryland. In 1838, after escaping
from bondage, he adopted the name Frederick Douglass. Along with his family,
he settled in New Bedford, Massachusetts, and, in 1841, became a lecturer for the
Massachusetts Anti-slavery Society. A gifted orator, Douglass quickly became
recognized as America's leading Black abolitionist. Because of his eloquence as a
speaker, many people doubted Douglass' slave heritage, so in 1845 he published his
autobiography entitled *The Narrative of the Life of Frederick Douglass*. Between 1845
and 1847, Douglass successfully toured Great Britain as an anti-slavery lecturer and
raised money to purchase his freedom. In 1848 after returning to the United States,
Douglass founded the *North Star*, a weekly reform newspaper. The paper was later
replaced with the *Frederick Douglass Paper* (1851-1859) and *Douglass's Monthly*
(1859-1863). Douglass criticized Black colonization and emigration schemes,
believing that free Blacks should not abandon their homeland or those still held in
bondage. Like his friend Jermain W. Loguen, Douglass encouraged anti-slavery
supporters to reject the Fugitive Slave Law of 1850 and aided John Brown's October 16,
1859, attack on Harper's Ferry, Virginia. During the Civil War, Douglass persuaded
President Abraham Lincoln to use Blacks as soldiers and he became a recruiting
agent for the 54th and 55th Massachusetts regiments. After the war, Douglass
received several government appointments while continuing his fight against racial
injustice. He died February 20, 1895, in Washington, D. C. Ripley, *Black Abolitionist*

Papers, 312-313; Frederick Douglass, *My Bondage and My Freedom*, New York: Miller, Orton & Mulligan, 1855.

16.   Loguen, *The Reverend J.W. Loguen*, 339.

17.   For more information on Black culture in early Toronto, see Shadd *et al*, *The Underground Railroad: Next Stop Toronto!* and Catherine Slaney, *Family Secrets*, Toronto: Natural Heritage, 2003.

18.   Winks, *Blacks in Canada*, 144-146.

19.   Silverman, *Unwelcome Guests*, 53. For further information on the subject see Leon F. Litwack, *North Of Slavery: The Negro In The Free States, 1790-1860*. Chicago: University of Chicago Press, 1961.

20.   Samuel Ringgold Ward (October 17, 1817–c.1866), was born the son of slave parents in Maryland. In 1820, the Ward family escaped from slavery and settled in New Jersey. Always fearful of being captured by slave catchers, the family moved to New York City in 1826, where Ward received his education in the classics and theology. Ward worked as a teacher in New Jersey and New York until 1839 when he became an ordained minister in the Congregational Church. During the same year he accepted an appointment as a lecturer for the American Anti-slavery Society. In 1840, he became associated with the American & Foreign Anti-slavery Society. Throughout the 1840s Ward worked as a minister and as an advocate for Black freedom and political rights. He also helped to establish several newspapers including the *True American* and the *Impartial Citizen*. On October 1, 1851, Ward assisted his friend Jermaine Loguen and the Syracuse Vigilance Committee to rescue fugitive slave, William "Jerry" McHenry, from jail. After the rescue attempt Ward feared imprisonment and fled to Montreal, then to Toronto, where he worked for the Anti-slavery Society of Canada (ASC) as a touring lecturer. In Windsor, in March 1853, he, along with Mary Ann Shadd, founded the *Provincial Freeman* newspaper. However, the following month, the ASC sent him to Great Britain to solicit funds for fugitive slaves living in Canada. He successfully toured Great Britain for two and a half years and, in 1855, he published *Autobiography of a Fugitive Negro: His Anti-slavery Labours in the United States, Canada and England*. In 1855, Ward left England and settled in Kingston, Jamaica, where it is believed he died in 1866. Ripley, *Black Abolitionist Papers*, 293; Samuel Ringgold Ward, *Autobiography of a Fugitive Negro: His Anti-slavery Labours in the United States, Canada and England*, New York: Arno Press, 1968 reprint edition; Dumas, Malone, ed., *Dictionary of American Biography, Volume 14* (New York: Charles Scribner's Sons, 1936) 440.

21.   Ward, *Autobiography of a Fugitive Negro*, 29.

22.   Stanley Campbell, *The Slave Catchers: Enforcement of the Fugitive Slave Law, 1850-1860* (Chapel Hill: University of North Carolina Press, 1970) 25, 51.

23.   *Voice of the Fugitive*, Oct. 22, 1851.

24.   Harriet Tubman (c.1820–1913), was born on a plantation near Bucktown in Dorchester County, Maryland. Around 1844 she married John Tubman, a free Black man. When her master died in 1849, Tubman, fearing that she would be sold, ran away. She settled in Philadelphia, Pennsylvania, but moved to St. Catharines, Canada West, after the enactment of the Fugitive Slave Law in 1850. She returned to Maryland and Virginia at least nineteen times to lead approximately three hundred slaves to freedom. She rescued several family members along with relatives of fugitive slaves already living in Canada West. Known as the "Moses of her People," Tubman gained a reputation as one of the most daring and successful conductors on the Underground Railroad. During the Civil War, she served the Union army as a spy and nurse. Tubman died in 1913 in Auburn, New York. Sarah H. Bradford, *Harriet: The Moses of Her People* (Gloucester: Peter Smith, reprint edition 1981); Adrienne Shadd, "The Lord Seemed to Say Go: Women and the Underground Railroad Movement," in Bristow, Peggy, coordinator, *'We're Rooted Here and They Cant't Pull Us Up': Essays in African Canadian Women's History* (Toronto: University of Toronto Press, 1994) 41-68.

25.   Daniel G. Hill, "Negroes In Toronto, 1793-1865," *Ontario History*, vol. 55 (Toronto: Ontario Historical Society, June 1963) 77-85; *Pine and Palm*, Sept. 7, 1861, Sept. 28, 1861, Nov. 30, 1861; Ripley, *Black Abolitionist Papers*, 25-26.

26.   Jason H. Silverman, "The American Fugitive Slave in Canada: Myths and Realities," *Southern Studies*, vol. 19 (Natchitoches, LA: Southern Studies Institute, Fall 1980) 217-218.

27.   Winks, *Blacks in Canada*, 142-144.

28.   For the most comprehensive literature on all three communities see: William Pease and Jane Pease, *Black Utopia: Negro Communal Experiments in America*. Madison: State Historical Society of Wisconsin, 1963.

29.   Ronald G. Walters, *Antislavery Appeal: American Abolitionism After 1830* (Baltimore: Johns Hopkins University Press, 1976) 60.

30.   Michael F. Hembree, "The Question of 'Begging': Fugitive Slave Relief in Canada, 1830-1865," *Civil War History*, vol. 37 (Kent, OH: Kent State University Press, December 1991) 314-315; *Friend of Man*, Mar. 14, 1838, July 24, 1839; Letter from Fidelia Coburn Brooks to Lewis Tappan, November 16, 1847, American Missionary Association Archives, Amistad Research Center, Tulane University, New Orleans, hereafter cited as AMAA; *American Missionary*, vol. 2 (New York: American Missionary Association, November 1848) 5.

31. Donald Simpson, "Negroes in Ontario From Early Times to 1870," Ph.D. dissertation, University of Western Ontario, 1971, 349.

32. Mary Ann Shadd (October 9, 1823–June 1893), was born in Wilmington, Delaware, to Abraham D. and Harriet Shadd, both free Blacks. A shoemaker by profession, Abraham Shadd became a prominent leader in the Black community. He served as a delegate at the annual meetings of the American Anti-slavery Society and at the conventions for the Free People of Color. Influenced by her father, Mary Ann Shadd dedicated herself to the cause of improving the conditions of her race. After completing her education in 1839, she taught in schools in Delaware, New York and Pennsylvania. In 1849, she published *Hints for the Colored People of the North*, which dealt with the themes of Black independence and self-respect. In 1851, as a result of the Fugitive Slave Law of 1850, Shadd moved to Windsor, Canada West, where she assumed her most influential role as a spokesperson and leader in the Black community. In 1852, she published *A Plea for Emigration, Or Notes on Canada West, in its Moral, Social, and Political Aspect: With Suggestions Respecting Mexico, West Indies and Vancouver's Island for the Information of Colored Emigrants*, in which she concluded that Canada West was the most favourable destination for Black emigrants. More importantly, she provided detailed information about Canada West, including the climate, land prices, agricultural production, employment opportunities, racial equality, education and politics. In March 1853, she began publishing the *Provincial Freeman* in Windsor with Samuel Ringgold Ward. In 1854, Shadd moved the newspaper to Toronto and the following year to Chatham. Despite these moves and numerous staff changes, Shadd was the newspaper's most prominent editor until its demise in 1859. In January 1856, Shadd married Toronto barber, Thomas J. Cary, who died four years later. Following his death, Mary Ann Shadd Cary managed a school in Chatham between 1860 and 1863, but continued to be an energetic anti-slavery spokesperson. During the Civil War she worked as a recruiting agent for the United States Army. After the war, Cary taught briefly in Detroit, Michigan, but eventually moved to Washington, D.C., where she found employment as the principal of a Black elementary school from 1872 until 1884. In 1883, at age 60, she graduated from Howard University with a degree in law. Until her death in 1893, Shadd advocated equal rights for women and Blacks. Harold Hancock, "Mary Ann Shadd: Negro Editor, Educator and Lawyer," *Delaware History*, vol. 15 (Wilmington: Historical Society of Delaware, April 1973) 187-194; Jason H. Silverman, "Mary Ann Shadd and the Search for Equality," *Black Women in United States History, Volume 4* (Brooklyn, NY: Carlson Publishing Inc., 1990) 86-100; Jane Rhodes, *Mary Ann Shadd Cary: The Black Press and Protest in the Nineteenth Century*. Bloomington: Indiana University Press, 1998.

33. *Provincial Freeman*, June 24, 1854.

34. Winks, *Blacks in Canada*, 339-342; Letter from Fidelia Coburn Brooks to George Whipple, July 4, 1849, AMAA; Letter from Isaac Rice to William Harned, September 8, 1847, AMAA.

35. *American Missionary*, vol.1 (New York: American Missionary Association, December 1846) 10.

36. *Colored American*, February 20, 1841.

37. Silverman, *Unwelcome Guests*, 81-82,87; Winks, *Blacks in Canada*, 219.

38. Silverman, *Unwelcome Guests*, 83-87.

39. Silverman, *Unwelcome Guests*, 88-89; Winks, *Blacks in Canada*, 339.

40. *True Wesleyan*, Dec. 5, 1846, Jan. 1, 1848; Letter from Elias E. Kirkland to George Whipple, October 18, 1851, AMAA; *American Missionary*, vol. 2 (New York: American Missionary Association, February 1848) 31; Daniel A. Payne, *History of the African Methodist Episcopal Church* (New York: Johnson Reprint Corporation, 1968 reprint edition) 119, 124; Richard Wright, ed., *Encyclopaedia of the African Methodist Episcopal Church* (Philadelphia: Book Concern of the AME Church, 1947) 345; Winks, *Blacks in Canada*, 355-356.

41. Janet Duitsman Cornelius, *Slave Missions and the Black Church in the Antebellum South* (Columbia: University of South Carolina Press) 25; Silverman, *Unwelcome Guests*, 91-93; Hill, *Freedom Seekers*, 138-139; James Lewis, "Religious Nature of the Early Negro Migration to Canada and the Amherstburg Baptist Association," *Ontario History*, vol. 58 (Toronto: Ontario Historical Society, 1966) 121, 125, 130; Winks, *Blacks in Canada*, 340-343.

42. Chris Padgett, "Hearing the Antislavery Rank-and-File: The Wesleyan Methodist Schism of 1843," *Journal of the Early Republic*, vol. 12 (West Lafayette, IN: Society for Historians of the Early Republic, Spring 1992) 64; *True Wesleyan*, Jan. 17, 1846.

43. Silverman, *Unwelcome Guests*, 105-108; Silverman, "The American Fugitive Slaves in Canada," 220-221.

44. Winks, *Blacks in Canada*, 394.

45. Henry Walton Bibb (1815–August 1, 1854), was born in Shelby County, Kentucky, the son of Mildred Jackson, a slave. His father was James Bibb, a slave-holder. Bibb had numerous brutal masters, and finally escaped from bondage in 1837. He settled initially in Ohio, but in 1838 returned to Kentucky to rescue his family from slavery. During the rescue attempt Bibb was captured, but managed to escape. He tried unsuccessfully two more times to free his family. During his third rescue attempt he was re-enslaved and transported to New Orleans with his family. Undaunted, Bibb escaped again only to be captured once more and sold to a Native American in the Indian Territory. In 1841, Bibb made his fifth and final successful escape. He settled in Detroit, Michigan, where he acquired an education and became an active anti-slavery spokesman. An articulate speaker, Bibb gave anti-

slavery lectures in New York, Ohio and Michigan. In 1845, Bibb tried once more to rescue his family, but gave up when he learned that his wife had become the mistress of her master. In 1848, Bibb married Mary Miles, a free Black abolitionist of Boston. The following year he published his autobiography entitled *Narrative of the Life and Adventures of Henry Bibb, An American Slave.* After the enactment of the Fugitive Slave Law in 1850, the Bibbs fled across the border to Sandwich, Canada West. Mary Bibb briefly managed a fugitive slave school, but in January 1851 the couple began publishing the *Voice of the Fugitive,* a weekly reform and anti-slavery newspaper. In 1853, as result of several factors, including a rivalry with Mary Ann Shadd, editor of the *Provincial Freeman,* and competition from American newspapers, Bibb ceased publication of his newspaper. Henry Bibb died on August 1, 1854, at age 39. Ripley, *Black Abolitionist Papers,* 109-110; Winks, *Blacks in Canada,* 396-397; Fred Landon, "Henry Bibb, A Colonizer," *Journal of Negro History,* vol. 5 (New York: Association for the Study of Negro Life and History, October 1920) 437-447; Henry Bibb, *Narrative of the Life and Adventures of Henry Bibb, An American Slave* (New York: The author, 1849); Afua Cooper, " 'Doing Battle in Freedom's Cause': Henry Bibb Abolitionism, Race Uplift, and Black Manhood 1842-1854," Ph.D. dissertation, University of Toronto, 2000.

46.   *Voice of the Fugitive,* January 1, 1851.

47.   *Ibid,* December 3, 1851.

48.   *Ibid,* February 12, 1851.

49.   *Provincial Freeman,* April 4, 1857.

50.   *Provincial Freeman,* March 25, 1854. For further discussion about Shadd and the *Provincial Freeman* see Rhodes, *Mary Ann Shadd Cary,* 70-134, and Alexander Murray. "The Provincial Freeman: A New Sources for the History of the Negro in Canada and the United States," *Journal of Negro History* vol.2 (New York: Association for the Study of Negro Life and History, April 1959) 123-135.

51.   Hill, *Freedom Seekers,* 75; Silverman, *Unwelcome Guests,* 114-119.

52.   Augustus R. Green (?–1878), was born in Virginia to free Black parents. The family eventually moved to Pennsylvania where Green acquired an education and developed an interest in the ministry. In 1841, he joined the AME Ohio Conference and tried unsuccessfully to establish a manual labour school for Blacks near Columbus, Ohio. In 1848, he returned to Pittsburgh, Pennsylvania, where he became superintendent of the AME Book Concern and editor of the church's publication, *The Christian Herald.* During the 1850s he supported Black emigration to Canada West, but he opposed the formation of the BME church. Despite his opposition to the schism, he moved to Windsor, Canada West, in 1860 and joined the BME church. In 1862, he was expelled from the church and became the bishop of the newly

formed Independent Methodist Episcopal Church. After the Civil War, Green moved to Washington, D.C. After rejoining the AME church, he received a ministerial appointment in Vicksburg, Mississippi, in 1876. He died two years later while tending the sick during a yellow fever epidemic. Ripley, *Black Abolitionist Papers*, 495-496; Floyd J. Miller, *The Search for a Black Nationality: Black Emigration and Colonization, 1787-1863* (Chicago: University of Illinois Press, 1975) 146, 156, 158, 161.

53.   Winks, *Blacks in Canada*, 221-223, 261, 396; Ripley, *Black Abolitionist Papers*, 365, 112; Silverman, *Unwelcome Guests*, 119.

54.   John James Edmonstoune Linton (1804–1869) emigrated to Upper Canada from Perthshire, Scotland, in 1833. Linton settled in Stratford where he worked as a teacher, notary public and clerk. An outspoken critic of slavery, he condemned all fellowship with pro-slavery churches. Ripley, *Black Abolitionist Papers*, 365; Winks, *Blacks in Canada*, 221-223.

55.   Ripley, *Black Abolitionist Papers*, 365; Winks, *Blacks in Canada*, 221-223, 261, 397.

56.   Jason H. Silverman and Donna J. Gillie, " 'The Pursuit of Knowledge Under Difficulties': Education And The Fugitive Slave In Canada," *Ontario History*, vol. 74 (Toronto: Ontario Historical Society, June 1982) 95-112; Hill, *Freedom Seekers*, 148-151; Robin Winks, "Negro School Segregation in Ontario and Nova Scotia," *Canadian Historical Review*, vol. 50 (Toronto: Canadian Historical Society, June 1969) 171-173; *True Wesleyan*, Dec. 5, 1846, Jan. 1, 1848; *Colored American*, Mar. 13, 1841.

57.   Hill, *Freedom Seekers*, 149; Winks, *Blacks in Canada*, 365-366; Winks, "Negro School Segregation," 171-173.

58.   In 1840, the Act of Union joined Upper Canada and Lower Canada into one colonial entity, the Province of Canada, thus creating Canada West (now Ontario) and Canada East (now Quebec).

59.   Winks, "Negro School Segregation," 174, 176; Silverman, "The American Fugitive Slave," 224-226; Silverman, *Unwelcome Guests*, 129-130, 134.

60.   Benjamin Drew, *The Refugee: Or The Narratives of Fugitive Slaves In Canada* (Toronto: Coles Publishing Co., 1981 reprint ed.) 348.

61.   Winks, *Blacks in Canada*, 373; Winks, "Negro School Segregation," 175-176, 179: Silverman, *Unwelcome Guests*, 135-136.

62.   Shadd, *A Plea For Emigration*, 33.

63.   Drew, *Narratives of Fugitive Slaves*, 341. For more information about education see Hildreth Houston Spencer, "To Nestle in the Mane of the British Lion: A

History of Canadian Black Education, 1820-1870," Ph.D. dissertation, Northwestern University, 1970.

Chapter 1: "We Marched Right Into the Wilderness"

1.   The chapter title is adapted from a sentence in John Little's narrative in Drew, *Narratives of Fugitive Slaves in Canada,* 216.

2.   *Colonial Advocate,* Oct. 4, 1832; Richard C. Wade, "The Negro in Cincinnati, 1800-1830," *Journal of Negro History,* vol. 39 (New York: Association for the Study of Negro Life and History, January 1954) 43-57; Marily Baily, "From Cincinnati, Ohio to Wilberforce, Canada: A Note on Antebellum Colonization," *Journal of Negro History,* vol. 53 (New York: Association for the Study of Negro Life and History, October 1973) 427-429.

3.   On April 26, 1819, in order to ensure continued work on the remote Penetanguishene Road, the Executive Council of Upper Canada decreed that tracts of land in Oro Township be given to settlers who were willing to perform settle-ment duty. Very few whites responded to the offer, but four Blacks did request land grants. By 1827 the settlement had nearly failed, but in that year Peter Robinson, newly appointed as commissioner of Crown Lands, concentrated his efforts on encouraging settlement in the township. Instead of paying the usual four shillings per acre, he permitted Blacks to pay only one. The discount attracted many Blacks and it was the only Black settlement to receive government sponsorship. Gary E. French, *Men of Colour: An Historical Account of the Black Settlement on Wilberforce Street and in Oro Township, Simcoe County, Ontario, 1819-1949* (Stroud, ON: Kaste Books, 1978) 10-18; Silverman, *Unwelcome Guests,* 24-25.

4.   French, *Men of Colour,* 23-27.

5.   Pease and Pease, *Black Utopia,* 46-62; Fred Landon, "Agriculture Among Negro Refugees in Upper Canada," *Journal of Negro History,* vol. 21 (New York: Association for the Study of Negro Life and History, July 1936), 304-312; "Documents: Banishment of the People of Colour from Cincinnati," *Journal of Negro History,* vol. 8 (New York: Association for the Study of Negro Life and History, July 1923), 331-332; Baily, "From Cincinnati, Ohio to Wilberforce, Canada," 428-430. For further discussion about the Wilberforce Settlement see Austin Steward, *Twenty-two Years a Slave, and Forty Years a Freeman; Embracing a Correspondence of Several Years While President of Wilberforce Colony, London, Canada West.* New York: Negro Universities Press, reprint edition, 1968.

6.   Waterloo, Wellington and Grey counties were not established from the District of Wellington until 1854. However, for the sake of clarity the terms Waterloo County and Wellington County have been used throughout the text.

7.   *Illustrated Atlas of Wellington County, Ontario,* (Toronto: Walker & Miles, 1877) 9, 110; W.V. Uttley, "Woolwich Township - Its Early Settlement," *Waterloo Historical Society Annual Volume,* vol. 21 (Kitchener: Waterloo Historical Society, 1933) 10-11; Winterbourne Women's Institute Tweedsmuir History Collection, Kitchener Public Library, Kitchener, Ontario, hereafter referred to as KPL.

8.   Bishop Brown may have been Morris Brown, a free Black who had been born on January 8, 1770, in Charleston, South Carolina. He had served as assistant minister at the Bethel African Methodist Episcopal church in Philadelphia, Pennsylvania, before he became bishop of the AME church on May 25, 1828. Clarence Walker, *A Rock in a Weary Land: The African Methodist Episcopal Church During the Civil War and Reconstruction* (Baton Rouge: Louisiana State University Press, 1982) 20-21.

9.   *Colonial Advocate,* Aug. 2, 1832; Oct. 4, 1832.

10. 1834 Gore District Census and Assessment, Woolwich Township.

11. Fred Landon, ed., "The Diary of Benjamin Lundy Written During His Journey Through Upper Canada January, 1832," *Ontario Historical Society Papers and Records,* vol. 19 (Toronto: Ontario Historical Society, 1922) 116, 122.

12. "1833 Gore District Census and Assessment," Woolwich Township; "1834 Gore District Census and Assessment," Woolwich Township.

13, This map was adapted from the one in Daniel Hill's, *The Freedom-Seekers: Blacks in Early Canada,* 65.

14. *Elmira Signet,* Sept. 29, 1910; Hill, *Freedom Seekers,* 52, 95, 150, 154; *Guelph Herald,* Nov. 2, 1847; Archives of Ontario, R.G. 1, C1-1, Volume 42, Petitions 1827-1856 (Queen's Bush).

15. Jean Hutchinson, *History of Wellington County* (Grand Valley: Landsborough Printing Ltd., 1997) 7; *True Wesleyan,* Dec. 5, 1846.

16. *True Wesleyan,* Aug. 28, 1847.

17. Edwin C. Guillet, *The Pioneer Farmer and Backwoodsman, Volume 1* (Toronto: Ontario Publishing Co. Ltd., 1963) 311-312; Cecil J. Houston and William J. Smyth, *Irish Emigration And Canadian Settlement* (Toronto: University of Toronto Press, 1990) 132-134; *Elora Observer and Salem and Fergus Chronicle,* June 7, 1867.

18. *True Wesleyan,* Aug. 28, 1847; Guillet, *Pioneer Farmer and Backwoodsman,* 48-56.

19. Drew, *Narratives of Fugitive Slaves in Canada,* 219.

20. *Ibid*, 198.

21. *Ibid*, 198.

22. *Ibid*, 200-201.

23. *Ibid*, 200.

24. *Ibid*, 202.

25. *Ibid*, 204.

26. *Ibid*, 204.

27. *Ibid*, 205-206.

28. *Ibid*, 224; Emma Williams, *Historic Madison* (Jackson, TN: McCowat & Mercer Press, 1972) 121, 198.

29. Drew, *Narratives of Fugitive Slaves in Canada*, 225.

30. *Ibid*, 225.

31. *Ibid*, 225.

32. *Ibid*, 207.

33. *Ibid*, 208-212, 221, 226.

34. Stuart Sprague, ed., *His Promised Land: The Autobiography of John P. Parker, Former Slave and Conductor on the Underground Railroad* (New York: W.W. Norton & Company, 1996) 138.

35. Drew, *Narratives of Fugitive Slaves in Canada*, 216.

36. *Ibid*, 216.

37. *Ibid*, 217-218.

38. *Ibid*, 217.

39. Henry Stauffer Huber (June 18, 1819–September 3, 1872) was born in Lancaster County, Pennsylvania, the son of Peter and Veronica Souder Huber. The Huber family moved to Upper Canada in 1822. When Henry was still a young man, he went into the mercantile business with Jacob S. Shoemaker, the founder of

Bridgeport. In 1851, Huber formed a partnership with Charles Henry Ahrens and together they operated a general store and foundry in Berlin. A community leader, Huber was a Crown Land Agent, a Justice of the Peace, a founder of Berlin's grammar school and served as a school trustee for twenty-five years. He also served as a Reeve of Berlin in 1857 and from 1859 to 1864. Helen Warner, "The Mennonite Heritage of the Huber Family: Oxford and Waterloo Counties, Ontario". Student essay, August 1990; *Berliner Journal*, Sept. 5, 1872; Undated newspaper article in the Henry S. Huber File, KPL; W.V. Uttley, *A History of Kitchener, Ontario* (Waterloo: Chronicle Press, 1937) 86.

40. *True Wesleyan*, Aug. 28, 1847; Drew, *Fugitive Slaves in Canada, 218*; Elora Agency Applications, Applicants for Land, Peel Township, entry dated Oct. 6, 1846, Wellington County Museum and Archives, Fergus; hereafter cited as WCMA; Robert W. Kerr, P.L. S. "Memorandum of the Clerances (sic) of the Settlers," Held with Surveyors Letters, Township of Peel, Archives of Ontario.

41. *Elora Observer and Salem and Fergus Chronicle*, May 10,1867; *Guelph Weekly Mercury and Advertiser*, Oct. 24, 1907.

42. Drew, *Narratives of Fugitive Slaves in Canada*, 218.

43. *Ibid*, 218.

44. *Ibid*, 218, 233.

45. *Elora Observer and Salem and Fergus Chronicle*, May 10, 1867.

46. *True Wesleyan*, Aug. 28, 1847; George Klinck, "The Early Days of Elmira," *Waterloo Historical Annual Volume*, vol.15 (Kitchener: Waterloo Historical Society, 1927) 289; Drew, *Narratives of Fugitive Slaves in Canada, 219*.

47. Letter from James Curry to Lewis Tappan, April 30, 1851, AMAA; *True Wesleyan*, Aug. 28, 1847; Edwin C. Guillet, *The Pioneer Farmer and Backwoodsman, Volume 2* (Toronto: Ontario Publishing Co., Ltd., 1963) 214.

48. *Elora Observer and Salem and Fergus Chronicle*, June 7, 1867; Hutchinson, *History of Wellington County*, 14.

49. Moses Chambers (March 23, 1788–April 20, 1858), was a farmer and merchant. In 1835, he represented Person County at the North Carolina Constitutional Convention and from 1836 to 1840 he served as a representative to the North Carolina General Assembly. Moses married his wife, Lucy, in about 1810 and they had eight children, four sons and four daughters. In 1820, Chambers owned eighteen slaves; nine males and nine females, ranging in age from under ten to forty years old. Madeline Eaker, ed., *The Heritage of Person County, 1981* (Roxboro, N.C.:

Person County Historical Society, 1981) 195-196; "1820 United States Census," North Carolina, Person County.

50. *Liberator*, Jan. 10, 1840. I discovered James Curry's biography in John Blassingame, *Slave Testimony: Two Centuries of Letters, Speeches, Interviews and Autobiographies* (Baton Rouge: Louisiana State University Press, 1977) 128-144.

51. *Liberator*, Jan. 10, 1840.

52. *Ibid.*

53. *Ibid.*

54. *Ibid.*

55. Elizabeth Cook Stevens, "From Generation to Generation: The Mother and Daughter Activism of Elizabeth Buffurn Chace and Lillie Chace Wyman," Ph.D. dissertation, Brown University, 1993, 47; *Liberator*, Jan. 10, 1840.

56. Letter from Hiram Wilson to Lewis Tappan, June 9, 1851, AMAA; Letter from James Curry to Lewis Tappan, April 30, 1851, AMAA; Archives of Ontario, R.G. 1, C1-1, Volume 42, Petitions 1827-1856 (Queen's Bush).

57. Charles T. Torrey (November 21, 1813–May 9, 1846), was born in Scituatee, Massachusetts, and graduated from Yale in 1833. He became an ordained minister in the Congregational Church in 1836, but soon realized that he was not suited for the demands of pastoral life. As a student he had become interested in the anti-slavery movement and, in the fall of 1838, became the editor of the *Massachusetts Abolitionist*. He eventually resigned his position to become a freelance reporter. In 1842, while reporting on the Convention of Slaveholders in Annapolis, Maryland, delegates discovered that he was an abolitionist and had him arrested. The ensuing court case attracted national attention. After his acquittal, Torrey worked unsuccessfully as the editor of the *Tocsin of Liberty* and later the *Albany Patriot*. At the end of the year he moved to Baltimore, Maryland, where he began assisting runaway slaves. He aided approximately four hundred fugitive slaves from Virginia and Maryland, many of whom, like the Praters, eventually settled in the Queen's Bush. In 1844, he was arrested and imprisoned in the Baltimore Penitentiary where he died on May 9, 1846. Dumas Malone, ed., *Dictionary of American Biography, Volume 18* (New York: Charles Scribner's Sons, 1936) 595; Wilbur H. Seibert, *The Underground Railroad from Slavery to Freedom* (New York: Russell & Russell, 1898) 168-169.

58. *True Wesleyan*, Oct. 17, 1846; Joseph C. Lovejoy, *Memoir of Rev. Charles T. Torrey, Who Died in the Penitentiary of Maryland, Where he was Confined for Showing Mercy to the Poor* (New York: Negro Universities Press, 1969, reprint edition) 186.

59. According to Sophia Burthen Pooley, Brant also owned Simon Ganseville and a Mr. Patten, who may have been Prince Van Patten. Drew, *Narratives of Fugitive Slaves in Canada*, 194. For additional information see: *Brantford Weekly Expositor*, Aug. 23, 1900; Brantford Historical Society Publication Committee, "Prince Van Patten: A Loyal Servant of Joseph Brant," *Brantford Historical Society Quarterly*, vol. 2 (Brantford: Brantford Historical Society, Winter 1995) 2.

60. Drew, *Narratives of Fugitive Slaves in Canada*, 192-193.

61. Robert Pooley/Poolly lived in Waterloo Township at least during the years 1825 to 1828. In the 1825 Waterloo Township census he is listed as the head of the household. Three men over age sixteen and one female under age sixteen also lived in the household. Pooley/Poolly operated a twenty-five acre farm on lot 5, west end of Broken Front Concession. "1825 Canadian Census," Gore District, Waterloo Township; "1826 Canadian Census," Gore District, Waterloo Township; "1827 Canadian Census," Gore District, Waterloo Township; "1828 Canadian Census," Gore District, Waterloo Township.

62. Drew, *Narratives of Fugitive Slaves in Canada*, 192-195.

63. *London Free Press*, Jan. 18, 1969; Elora Agency Applications, Applicants for Land, Peel Township, entry dated October 22, 1846, WCMA.

64. Drew, *Narratives of Fugitive Slaves in Canada*, 195-197.

65. *Elmira Signet*, Sept. 23, 1910; "1834 Gore District Census and Assessment," Woolwich Township; "1840 Gore District Census," Waterloo Township; Archives of Ontario, R.G. 1, C1-1, Volume 42, Petitions 1827-1856 (Queen's Bush).

66. Drew, *Narratives of Fugitive Slaves in Canada*, 191.

67. *Elmira Signet*, Aug. 1, 1935.

68. Drew, *Narratives of Fugitive Slaves in Canada*, 216-217.

Chapter 2: "Many Are the Trials We Have to Encounter"

1. The chapter title is from a sentence in a letter written by Fidelia Coburn to Lewis Tappan, March 18, 1847, AMAA.

2. *Oberlin Evangelist*, Jan. 1, 1845.

3. Letter written by William Raymond to Sarah Kinson, July 23, 1846, printed in the *Oberlin Evangelist*, Feb. 3, 1847.

4.   Letter written by William Raymond to George Thompson, n.d., printed in the *Oberlin Evangelist*, Feb. 2, 1848; *Hartford Daily Courant*, Dec. 21, 1841; *American Missionary*, vol. 2 (New York: American Missionary Association, April 1848) 45.

5.   Letter from William Raymond to W. Garrison, November 13, 1836, AMAA; *American Missionary*, vol. 2 (New York: American Missionary Association, April 1848) 45; Letter from Stedman W. Hanks to Lewis Tappan, November 12, 1841, AMAA; Letter from Stedman W. Hanks to William Raymond, November 9, 1841, AMAA.

6.   John Myers, "American Antislavery Society Agents and the Free Negro, 1833-1838," *Journal of Negro History*, vol. 52 (New York: Association for the Study of Negro Life and History, July 1967) 215, 218; *American Anti-slavery Society, Fourth Annual Report* (New York: American Anti-slavery Society, 1837) 19; Ripley, *Black Abolitionist Papers*, 159-160; *True Wesleyan*, Oct. 31, 1846; Harriet Martineau, *Martyr Age of the United States of American with an Appeal on Behalf of the Oberlin Institute in Aid of the Abolition of Slavery* (Newcastle Upon Tyne, England: Newcastle Upon Tyne Emancipation and Aborigines Protection Society, 1840) xv; Samuel Fletcher, *A History of Oberlin College From Its Foundation Through the Civil War* (Oberlin, OH: Oberlin College, 1943) 246; James Fairchild, *Oberlin: The Colony and the College, 1833-1883* (Oberlin, OH: E. J. Goodrich, 1883) 135; *Colored American*, Feb. 6, 1841; Lawrence T. Lesick, *The Lane Rebels: Evangelicalism and Antislavery in Antebellum America* (Metuchen, NJ: Scarecrow Press, 1980) 6, 181, 183.

7.   *Oberlin Evangelist*, Feb. 3, 1847; *American Missionary*, vol. 2 (New York: American Missionary Association, April 1848) 45; Leone Banks Cousins, "Woman of the Year-1842: The Early Life of Eliza Ruggles," *Nova Scotia Historical Quarterly*, vol. 6 (Halifax, N.S.: Petheric Press, December 1976) 352; F. Douglas Reville, *History of the County of Brant* (Brantford, ON: Hurley Printing Co., Ltd., 1920) 97; Landon, *Diary of Benjamin Lundy*, 120-121; Hill, *Freedom Seekers*, 13, 51.

8.   Landon, *Diary of Benjamin Lundy*, 121.

9.   *Colored American*, Mar. 13, 1841; Robin Winks, "Negro School Segregation in Ontario and Nova Scotia," *Canadian Historical Review*, vol. 50 (Toronto: Canadian Historical Society, June 1969) 171-173.

10.   Winks, *Blacks in Canada*, 367; William Raymond Collection, AMAA; Cousins, "Woman of the Year-1842: The Early Life of Eliza Ruggles," 351-352.

11.   Letter from Hiram Wilson to George Whipple, May 1, 1848, AMAA.

12.   Cousins, "Woman of the Year-1842: The Early Life of Eliza Ruggles," 352-353.

13.   French, *Men of Colour*, 47; Letter from William Clarke to George Whipple, July 6, 1849, AMAA; Letter from John Roaf to Joshua Leavitt, October 14, 1841, AMAA;

Letter from A.F. Williams to Lewis Tappan, October 2, 1841; Bethesda Congregation Church Minutes, 1859-1865, Simcoe County Archives, Minesing, ON; Oro Historical Committee, *A History of Oro Schools, 1836 to 1966* (Oro, ON: Oro Township School Board, 1967) 28; "1861 Canadian Census," Simcoe County, Innisfil Township.

14. The Amistad Affair involved Mendians from Sierra Leone who had been captured in the spring of 1839 by slave hunters. Despite a Spanish law which prohibited the importation of slaves from Africa into Spain's dominions, the Mendians had been transported to Cuba. In Havana two planters had bought fifty-three of the Mendians, falsely declaring that they were domestic slaves, and had shipped them on the schooner *L'Amistad* to Puerto Principe. While en route, the Mendians had rebelled, killing the captain and one crew member. The Mendians had then ordered the remaining crew members to return to Africa. For two months the crew, fearful for their lives, had sailed east during the day and then zigzagged to the north at night. Sighting the schooner off the coast of Long Island, New York, Lieutenant Gedney of the United State Coast Survey had become suspicious and seized the ship. He took the ship to the nearest port, New London, Connecticut, where the Mendians had been charged with piracy and murder.

Lewis Tappan and a group of abolitionists organized a defense committee that eventually took the case to the Supreme Court. Ultimately, the Mendians were judged to be free men with the inherent right to self-defense. After the final ruling, the abolitionists had settled the Mendians in Farmington, Connecticut, while further funds were to be raised to repatriate them to Africa. Keenly interested in the Mendians' plight, William Raymond responded to Tappan's requests for teachers. In November 1841, Raymond and three other missionaries accompanied the Mendians back to Sierra Leone. For further information about the Amistad Affair see Christopher Martin, *The Amistad Affair* (New York: Abelard-Schuman, 1970); *Hartford Daily Courant*, Oct. 21, 1841, Nov. 1, 1841, Dec. 21, 1841; *True Wesleyan*, Mar. 18, 1848; *American Missionary*, vol. 2 (New York: American Missionary Association, April 1848) 45.

15. Letter from Thomas Vipond to Lewis Tappan, January 29, 1850, AMAA; Letter from H.A. Lizer to Lewis Tappan, October 22, 1849, AMAA; 1851 Canadian Census, Canada West, Waterloo County, Wellesley Township.

16. Letter from Thomas Vipond to Lewis Tappan, January 29, 1850, AMAA; *Liberty Standard*, Feb. 15, 1843; Archives of Ontario, R.G. 1, C1-1, Volume 42, Petitions 1827-1856 (Queen's Bush).

17. Morris Brown (January 8, 1770–May 9, 1849), was born free in Charleston, South Carolina. He was a shoemaker by trade but, in 1817, he became the minister of the city's AME church. In 1822, he was suspected of participating in the Denmark Vesey plot that was to lead to a slave uprising, and he left South Carolina. Brown moved to Philadelphia, Pennsylvania, where he served as assistant minister at the Bethel AME church. On May 25, 1828, church officials consecrated him as a bishop.

In 1844, while attending the annual AME Upper Canadian Conference, Brown suffered a massive stroke and never recovered. He died in Philadelphia on May 9, 1849, at age 79. Wright, *Encyclopaedia of the African Methodist Episcopal Church*, 566-567; David Robertson, *Denmark Vesey* (New York: Alfred A. Knopf, 1999) 49; Clarence Walker, *A Rock in a Weary Land: The African Methodist Episcopal Church During the Civil War and Reconstruction* (Baton Rouge: Louisiana State University Press, 1982) 20-21; Payne, *History of the African Methodist Episcopal Church*, 261-262.

18.   In 1838, Edmund Crosby became a missionary for the AME church. He was assigned to the western states and Upper Canada. Payne, *History of the African Methodist Episcopal Church*, 120, 129.

19.   George Weir became an ordained deacon in the AME church in 1838, and served the Buffalo, New York, congregation. Along with Edmund Crosby, Weir supported the organization of an Upper Canadian Conference because of the rapid growth and prosperity of the Canadian congregations. Payne, *History of the African Methodist Episcopal Church*, 120, 135-136.

20.   In 1840, William H. Edwards became an ordained deacon in the AME church and received an appointment to the Toronto Circuit. In 1842, he became the itinerant minister for the St. Catharines Circuit. Church officials ordained Edwards as an elder in 1844 and he returned to Toronto, where he became a prominent leader in the city's Black community. During the same year he travelled to England to solicit funds to build a church for his congregation. Payne, *History of the African Methodist Episcopal Church*, 129, 145, 178; Ripley, *Black Abolitionist Papers*, 80.

21.   James Harper, an ordained AME deacon, received an appointment to the London Circuit in 1840. In 1842, he became an ordained elder and reassigned to the Brantford Circuit. In April 1863, Harper was a member of the Toronto committee that drafted an address to Canadian Blacks entitled "Address to the Colored Citizens of Canada." The address acknowledged the Civil War raging in the United States and President Abraham Lincoln's efforts to emancipate slaves. Payne, *History of the African Methodist Episcopal Church*, 129, 145; Ripley, *Black Abolitionist Papers*, 513.

22.   Alexander Helmsley (1790–1855), was born a slave in Queen Anne's County, Maryland. At age 23 he escaped and fled to New Jersey. Arrested in 1836 as a fugitive slave, he faced re-enslavement. David Paul Brown, a lawyer took Helmsley's case before the New Jersey Supreme Court, which ruled in his favour. Realizing that his freedom remained precarious, Helmsley moved with his family to St. Catharines, Upper Canada, in 1837. In 1840, he became an ordained deacon in the AME church and received an appointment to the St. Catharines Circuit. During the same year he took the oath of allegiance to become a British citizen. In 1842 he became an elder in the AME church. Hemsley ministered to congregations throughout the province until he died of dropsey on November 15, 1855. Payne, *History of the African Methodist Episcopal Church*, 129, 145, 360; Ripley, *Black Abolitionist Papers*, 260;

Drew, *Narratives of Fugitive Slaves*, 32-40; Donald A. McKenzie, *Upper Canada Naturalization Records, 1828-1850* (Toronto: Ontario Genealogical Society, 1991) 79.

23.   Jeremiah Taylor (?–1856), in 1840, became the itinerant minister for the Brantford Circuit. In 1842 he was reassigned to the London Circuit, but eventually became minister of the Sayer Street BME Church in Toronto. As a result of his influence and leadership, the church became the third largest BME congregation in Canada West. In the early 1850s, Samuel Ringgold Ward criticized Taylor's style of preaching because of his use of theatrical gestures and indecent language. Ward argued that such emotional sermons only contributed to white prejudice against Blacks. Taylor died in 1856. Payne, *History of the African Methodist Episcopal Church*, 129, 144, 145, 391; Ripley, *Black Abolitionist Papers*, 235-236, 483; Daniel Hill, "Negroes of Toronto, 1793-1865," *Ontario History*, vol. 55 (Toronto: Ontario Historical Society, June 1963) 79; *Minutes of the Eighteenth Annual Conference of the AME Church and the Doings of the First Annual Assembly of the British Methodist Episcopal Church, 1856* (Chatham, CW: The church, 1856) 23.

24.   In 1840, Daniel D. Thompson received permission from AME church officials to preach on a trial basis. He received full membership into the church in 1846. Payne, *History of the African Methodist Episcopal Church*, 129, 203.

25.   Peter O'Banyan (1796–?), was a mulatto who had been born in Kentucky. In 1840, he received permission to preach in AME churches on a trial basis and eventually received an appointment to the Brantford AME church. In 1841, he took the British oath of allegiance. Although highly respected by his parishioners, church authorities often accused him of lacking interest in his duties. He officially withdrew from the church in 1857. Payne, *History of the African Methodist Episcopal Church*, 129; Ripley, *Black Abolitionist Papers*, 231-232; McKenzie, *Upper Canada Naturalization Records*, 44; *Minutes and Proceedings of the Second Annual Conference of the British Methodist Episcopal Church, 1857* (St. Catharines, CW: The church, 1857) 2.

26.   Henry Bullard attended the organizational meeting of the AME Upper Canadian Conference. Payne, *History of the African Methodist Episcopal Church*, 129.

27.   *Ibid*, 128-129.

28.   *Ibid.*

29.   Elora Agency Applications, Applicants for Land, Peel Township, entry dated Oct. 14, 1845, WCMA; Payne, *History of the African Methodist Episcopal Church*, 138, 128-129, 144-145, 178; *Der Morgenstein*, May 20, 1841.

30.   The Sims family settled near Hawksville on lot 2, concession 13, in the Township of Wellesley. Waterloo Historical Society Publication Committee,

"Biography: Reverend James Sims," *Waterloo Historical Society Annual Volume*, 29 (March 1942) 193-195; *Canadian Baptist Magazine*, (December 1841) 138; Rosemary Ambrose, *Waterloo County Churches: A Research Guide to Churches Established Before 1900*. (Kitchener, ON: Waterloo-Wellington Branch, Ontario Genealogical Society, 1993) 34; American Baptist Home Mission Society, *Baptist Home Missions in North America*, (New York: The author, 1883) 560.

31.   Archives of Ontario, R.G. 1, C1-1, Volume 42, Petitions 1827-1856 (Queen's Bush).

32.   Barbara Stewart, Phyllis Kitchen and Debbie Dietrich, ed., *The Maple Leaf Journal: A Settlement History of Wellesley Township* (Waterloo: Corporation of the Township of Wellesley, 1983) 24; "Plan of the Township of Wellesley, Surveyed by William Walker, Deputy Surveyor, Brantford, Sept. 5, 1843," KPL.

33.   Ross Cumming, ed., *Historical Atlas of Wellington County, Ontario, 1906* (Guelph, ON: Corporation of the County of Wellington, reprint edition 1972) 6; Robert W. Kerr, "Diary of the Time Occupied in Surveying the Township of Peel, 1843," WCMA.

34.   Archives of Ontario, R.G. 1, C1-1, Volume 42, Petitions 1827-1856 (Queen's Bush).

35.   Stewart, Kitchen and Dietrich, *Maple Leaf Journal*, 25.

36.   Edwin C. Guillet, *The Pioneer Farmer and Backwoodsman, Volume 2* (Toronto: Ontario Publishing Co., Ltd., 1963) 117.

37.   Louise Helen Coburn, *Skowhegan on the Kennebec* (Skowhegan, ME: self-published, 1941) 210; *Liberty Standard*, Feb. 9, 1842, Mar. 9, 1842.

38.   The photograph of Fidelia Coburn was made for the author from the book *Skowhegan on the Kennebec* (Louise Coburn), by the Maine Historical Society, with the understanding that the author would accept responsibility for the copyright, as the historical society did not own the image. Linda Brown-Kubish made repeated efforts to locate Louise Coburn, including an internet search, but to no avail. It is believed that this photograph may have been taken around 1849, and it is believed to be in the public domain.

39.   Barbara Welter, "The Cult of True Womanhood, 1820-1860," *American Quarterly*, vol. 18 (Baltimore, MD: John Hopkins University Press, Summer 1966) 151-174; Lawrence J. Friedman, *Gregarious Saints: Self and Community In American Abolitionism, 1830-1870* (New York: Cambridge University Press, 1982) 131-132. For additional information about women and the anti-slavery movement see Julie Roy Jeffrey, *The Great Silent Army of Abolitionism: Ordinary Women in the Antislavery Movement*. Chapel Hill: University of North Carolina Press, 1998.

40. Josiah Henson (June 15, 1789–1883) was born a slave near Port Tobacco in Charles County, Maryland. In the fall of 1830, Henson along with his wife and their four children escaped from bondage. The family arrived in Upper Canada on October 28, 1830, where Henson became an influential minister and prominent leader of the British-American Institute. He also gained notoriety because of his identification with the character "Uncle Tom" in Harriet Beecher Stowe's novel, *Uncle Tom's Cabin*. For more information on Josiah Henson, see *An Autobiography of the Reverend Josiah Henson*. Reading: Addison-Wesley Publishing Company, 1969, reprint edition.

41. Hannah Maria Hubbard Wilson (?–1847), during the 1830s, taught a school for Black children in the basement of the Presbyterian Church in East Troy, New York. The Reverend Daniel A. Payne, who later become Bishop of the AME Church, was the pastor of the church at the time and described Hubbard "as a woman of uncommon faith and powerful in prayer, well suited to be the wife of a missionary." Hubbard married Hiram Wilson in 1837 and taught classes at the British-American Institute in Dawn, Upper Canada. She died in Dawn at the home of Josiah Henson. Payne, *History of the African Methodist Episcopal Church*, 118; Daniel Payne, *Recollections of Seventy Years* (New York: Arno Press and New York Times, reprint edition 1968) 65-66; *True Wesleyan*, Oct. 31, 1846; Ripley, *Black Abolitionist Papers*, 320.

42. *Friend of Man*, Jan. 11, 1842; *Liberty Standard*, July 13, 1842, Feb. 15, 1843, June 14, 1843; Pease and Pease, *Black Utopia*, 64; Letter from Fidelia Coburn Brooks to George Whipple, July 4, 1849, AMAA. D. Thurston, in the June 14, 1843, *Liberty Standard*, stated that Fidelia Coburn and Elizabeth Kirkland were sisters, but no other document has been found to support this statement.

43. Sixth Annual Report of the Canada Mission, 1842 as reported in *The African*, Aug. 5, 1843.

44. *Liberty Standard*, July 13, 1842.

45. *Ibid.*

46. *Ibid.*

47. *Liberty Standard*, May 17, 1843.

48. *Ibid.*

49. *Liberty Standard*, May 17, 1843; Nov. 23, 1843; Feb. 15, 1844.

50. *Liberty Standard*, Feb. 15, 1844.

51. Silverman, *Unwelcome Guests*, 55.

52. *Liberty Standard*, May 23, 1844; Elora Agency Applications, Applicants for Land, Peel Township, entry dated Oct. 6, 1846, WCMA; Letter from Fidelia Coburn Brooks to Lewis Tappan, January 29, 1849, AMAA. John R. Jackson in his 1955 history of Peel Township schools stated that Mount Pleasant was on the southwest half of lot 13 and that its foundation was still visible. *Drayton Advocate*, Oct. 20, 1955.

53. *Liberty Standard*, May 23, 1844; *True Wesleyan*, May 2, 1846.

54. *Liberty Standard*, May 23, 1844; *True Wesleyan*, May 2, 1846; *American Missionary*, 1 (February 1847) 30.

55. *Minutes of the 7th Session of the Annual Conference of the British Methodist Church, June 1863* (Chatham, C.W.: The church, 1863) 11; Ontario Death Records, entry #019894-81, Archives of Ontario; James Mohr, ed., *The Cormany Diaries: A Northern Family in the Civil War* (Pittsburgh, PA: University of Pittsburgh Press, 1982) 131; Payne, *History of the African Methodist Episcopal Church*, 129, 138, 144; McKenzie, *Upper Canada Naturalization Records, 57.*

56. Elora Agency Applications, Applicants for Land, Peel Township, entry dated June 13, 1845, WCMA.

57. *True Wesleyan*, July 4, 1846, Aug. 8, 1846, Oct. 31, 1846, Dec. 5, 1846; *Annual Report of the American and Foreign Anti-slavery Society, 1850* (New York: American and Foreign Anti-slavery Society, 1850) 65.

58. *True Wesleyan*, Jan. 17, 1846; Aug. 8, 1846; Oct. 17, 1846.

59. *True Wesleyan*, May 30, 1846; *Liberty Standard*, Apr. 16, 1846.

60. Drew, *Narratives of Fugitive Slaves in Canada,* 196; Elora Agency Applications, Applicants for Land, Peel Township, WCMA.

61. Elora Agency Application, Applicants for Land, Peel Township, entry dated October 6, 1846; Letter from Mary W. Brooks to William Hearned, May 20, 1850, AMAA; *True Wesleyan*, May 30, 1846.

62. *True Wesleyan* May 30, 1846.

63. *Ibid.*

64. In 1907, W.F. MacKenzie described the site of the school as near the Wallenstein Canadian Pacific railway station. In 1955, John R. Jackson reported that the former schoolhouse had stood across from the station. *Guelph Weekly Mercury & Advertiser*, Oct. 24, 1907; *Drayton Advocate*, Oct. 20, 1955.

65. *True Wesleyan*, Aug. 28, 1847.

66. *True Wesleyan*, May 30, 1846, Dec. 5, 1846; Letter from Samuel White to Lewis Tappan, March 17, 1854, AMAA.

67. Letter from Fidelia Coburn Brooks to George Whipple, October 18, 1848, AMAA.

68. *True Wesleyan*, Oct. 17, 1846.

69. *True Wesleyan*, June 27, 1846, July 4, 1846, Aug. 22, 1846, Oct. 17, 1846.

70. *American Missionary*, vol. 1 (New York: American Missionary Association, December 1846) 10-11; *True Wesleyan*, Aug. 15, 1846, Feb. 6, 1847; Mohr, *Cormany Diaries*, 174; Letter from Fidelia Coburn Brooks to William Harned, June 1, 1848, AMAA.

71. *American Missionary*, vol. 1(New York: American Missionary Association, February 1847) 30-31.

72. Letter from John Brooks to Lewis Tappan, July 30, 1848, AMAA.

73. *Liberty Standard*, May 23, 1844; *True Wesleyan*, May 30, 1846; Letter from Fidelia Coburn to AMA, November 16, 1847, AMAA; *American Missionary*, vol. 1 (New York: American Missionary Association, February 1847) 30.

74. Records of the Dover Ladies Anti-slavery Society Sewing Circle, Sept. 30, 1846, June 2, 1847, Nov. 14, 1848, New Hampshire Historical Society, Concord, New Hampshire; Letter from S.C. Paine to George Whipple, October 14, 1847, AMAA; *Liberty Standard*, Feb. 15, 1844, Apr. 16,1846; *True Wesleyan*, May 2, 1846.

75. *True Wesleyan*, Jan. 17, 1846, Oct. 31, 1846, Jan, 23, 1847.

76. John Roaf (1801–1862) was born in Margate, Kent, England. In 1837, he moved to Upper Canada as a missionary with the Colonial Missionary Society and founded the Zion Congregational Church in Toronto. Roaf became active in several different reform movements. He also advocated the establishment of non-denominational public schools. Financial problems led to his dismissal in 1856. Ripley, *Black Abolitionist Papers*, 318.

77. Allen P. Stouffer, *The Light of Nature and the Law of God: Antislavery in Ontario 1833-1877* (Baton Rouge: Louisiana State University Press, 1992) 57; Letter from John Brooks to Lewis Tappan, July 11, 1848, July 30, 1848, AMAA; Letter from John Roaf to Lewis Tappan, October 14, 1841, AMAA.

78. Will of Eleazer Coburn, probated February 11, 1845, Archives of Maine, Portland, Maine; *American Missionary*, vol. 1 (New York: American Missionary Association, February 1847) 30.

79. William P. Newman (1815–1866), was born a slave in Richmond, Virginia, but escaped in the 1830s. He settled in Ohio and attended Oberlin College where he became active in the anti-slavery movement. In 1839, he joined twenty-eight other Oberlin students who refused to celebrate the 4th of July as long as slaves remained in bondage. In 1843, he left Oberlin to help establish the British-American Institute at Dawn, Canada West. During the next few years he travelled between Canada and Ohio promoting racial equality. As an agent for the Ladies Education Society of Ohio, Newman visited numerous Black communities reporting on their condition and arranging the appointment of teachers to their schools. After his ordination, Newman became pastor of the Union Baptist Church in Cincinnati, one of the oldest Black Baptist Churches in the western United States. In 1845, he resigned the position to become the Secretary of the British-American Institute's Executive Committee. After investigating the Institute's records, Newman charged Hiram Wilson and Josiah Henson with mismanagement of funds. Although, the Executive Committee agreed with Newman it refused to act on the matter and, in 1846, he resigned from the Institute.

Newman returned to the Union Baptist Church and became an agent for the Colored Orphan Asylum. After the enactment of the Fugitive Slave Law in 1850, Newman returned to Canada West and again helped to manage the British-American Institute. He resigned two years later when the British abolitionist, John Scoble, assumed control of the organization. During the next seven years Newman lived in Toronto where he remained an active social reformer. Notably, he became secretary of the Canadian Anti-slavery Baptist Association and the Provincial Union Association. In 1855, he became the editor of Mary Ann Shadd's *Provincial Freeman*, a position he held for one year. By the late 1850s, Newman was disillusioned with the idea of Canada as a homeland for Blacks and turned his attention to Black colonization in Haiti and Jamaica. Ultimately he decided that both countries were unsuitable destinations. In 1863, Newman and his family returned to Cincinnati where he resumed his ministerial duties at the Union Baptist Church. He died of cholera in Cincinnati on August 31, 1866. Ripley, *Black Abolitionist Papers*, 302-303; Pease and Pease, *Black Utopia*, 71-72; William Cheek and Aimee Cheek, *John Mercer Langston and the Fight for Black Freedom, 1829-1865* (Urbana: University of Illinois Press, 1989) 55, 119-120.

80. *North Star*, Dec. 22, 1848.

81. Dwight L. Dumond, ed., *Letters of James Gillespie Birney 1831-1857, Volume 2* (New York: D. Appleton-Century Company, Inc., 1938) 1044.

82. Simpson, "Negroes in Ontario From Early Times to 1870," 387.

83. Letter from Fidelia Coburn Brooks to George Whipple, November 23, 1847, AMAA.

84. Letter from Fidelia Coburn Brooks to George Whipple, November 23, 1847, AMAA; *American Missionary*, vol. 1 (New York: American Missionary Association,

December 1846) 10. For further discussion about clothing worn by slave children see: Wilma King, *Stolen Childhood: Slave Youth in Nineteenth Century America* (Indianapolis: Indiana University Press, 1995) 15-16.

85.   Letter from Fidelia Coburn to Lewis Tappan, March 18, 1847, AMAA.

86.   Letter from Fidelia Coburn Brooks to George Whipple, November 23, 1847, AMAA.

Chapter 3: "It is Times Here Now That Tries Men's Souls"

1.   The chapter title is adapted from a letter written by Fidelia Coburn Brooks to Lewis Tappan, Feb. 20, 1849, AMAA.

2.   *American Missionary*, vol. 1 (New York: American Missionary Association, December 1846) 11.

3.   *True Wesleyan*, Oct. 17, 1846.

4.   Letter from John S. Brooks to Lewis Tappan, December 17, 1848, AMAA.

5.   Letter from Fidelia Coburn Brooks to George Whipple, July 4, 1849, AMAA.

6.   William Paul Quinn (1788–February 3, 1873) was born in India where his father was a mahogany merchant in Calcutta. As a young man he became interested in Christianity, perhaps as a result of his contact with English Quaker merchants or sailors. Disowned by his Hindu relatives, he moved to England in the early 1800s and then to Bucks County, Pennsylvania. Soon after his arrival in the United States, Quinn joined the AME church and, in 1812, he received his license to preach. He became a successful evangelist and established numerous churches in Pennsylvania, Ohio, Indiana and Illinois. His success as an evangelist gained him the title, "Missionary of the West." On May 19, 1844 he became the fourth bishop of the AME church. He died February 3, 1873 in Richmond, Indiana. Campbell, *Songs of Zion*, 33; Wright, *Encyclopaedia of the African Methodist Episcopal Church*, 596.

7.   *True Wesleyan*, Sept. 11, 1847; Payne, *History of the African Methodist Episcopal Church*, 203.

8.   Letter from Fidelia Coburn Brooks to Lewis Tappan, November 16, 1847, January 1, 1848, January 29, 1849, AMAA; *True Wesleyan*, Aug. 28, 1847; *Oberlin Evangelist*, Oct. 13, 1847; Letter from Isaac Rice to Mrs. Selden Huntington, October 6, 1847, AMAA. For more information about the begging system in Canada West see: Michael F. Hembree, "The Question of 'Begging': Fugitive Slave Relief in Canada, 1830-1865," *Civil War History*, vol. 37 (Kent, OH: Kent State University Press, December 1991).

9.   Letter from Fidelia Coburn Brooks to Lewis Tappan, November 16, 1847, AMAA.

10.   Letter from Fidelia Coburn to Lewis Tappan, March 19, 1847, AMAA.

11.   Waterloo Historical Society Publication Committee, "Wellesley Township and its Early Settlement," *Waterloo Historical Society Annual Volume*, vol. 30 (Kitchener, ON: Waterloo Historical Society, 1943) 227; Orpheus Schantz, "Hawkesville, A Pioneer Village of Waterloo County," *Waterloo Historical Society Annual Volume*, vol. 22 (Kitchener, ON: Waterloo Historical Society, 1934) 142.

12.   Reville, *History of the County of Brant*, 97-98; Winks, *Blacks in Canada*, 146.

13.   *True Wesleyan*, Oct. 17, 1846.

14.   Letter from Fidelia Coburn to Lewis Tappan, November 16, 1847, AMAA; *Oberlin Evangelist*, Aug. 30, 1848.

15.   Letter from Fidelia Coburn to Lewis Tappan, March 18, 1847, AMAA.

16.   *True Wesleyan*, Apr. 17, 1847; Letter from Hiram Wilson to George Whipple, June 21, 1851, AMAA.

17.   "List of Missionaries Working in Canada West," compiled by Fidelia Coburn Brooks, October 28, 1849, AMAA. The fact that Ambush was "a sort of physician for a living" is intriguing and seems to imply that he did not have formal medical training. Although patent medicines were available, Ambush's knowledge of medicine may have been mostly based on the use of herbs, plants and roots. Often denied treatment by professionally trained physicians, many slaves utilized folk cures and natural medicines that had been handed down from generation to generation to cure a wide variety of illnesses. For further information about the medicinal knowledge of slaves see: Todd L. Savitt, *Medicine and Slavery: The Diseases and Health Care of Blacks in Antebellum Virginia*. Urbana: University of Illinois Press, 1978.

18.   *True Wesleyan*, Apr. 17, 1847; Elizabeth Hancocks, *County Marriage Registers of Ontario, Canada, 1858-1869, Volume 32, Waterloo County* (Agincourt, ON: Generation Press, 1996) 64; 1851 Canadian Census, Canada West, Waterloo County, Wellesley Township 85; Canadian Census, Canada West, Wellington County, Peel Township; Elora Agency Applications, Applicants for Land, Peel Township, entry dated October 6, 1846.

19.   *True Wesleyan*, Apr. 17, 1847.

20.   *Ibid.*

21.   *Ibid.*

22. *True Wesleyan*, Apr. 17, 1847; *American Missionary*, vol. 1 (New York: American Missionary Association, July 1847) 72.

23. *True Wesleyan*, Sept. 6, 1846; Letter from Fidelia Coburn Brooks to William Hearned, July 3, 1848, AMAA.

24. Letter from Fidelia Coburn to Lewis Tappan, June 19, 1847, September 10, 1847, October 14, 1847, AMAA.

25. *Elora Observer and Salem and Fergus Chronicle*, June 7, 1867; Drew, *Narratives of Fugitive Slaves*, 196-197; *True Wesleyan*, Aug. 28, 1847; *American Missionary*, vol. 1 (New York: American Missionary Association, July 1847) 72.

26. Drew, *Narratives of Fugitive Slaves*, 196.

27. *American Missionary*, vol. 1 (New York: American Missionary Association, July 1847) 72.

28. *True Wesleyan*, Oct. 17, 1846.

29. Archives of Ontario, R.G. 1, C1-1, Volume 42, Petitions 1827-1856 (Queen's Bush). For more information about the role of Blacks in the Patriots War, also known as the Rebellion of 1837-1838 see: Ged Martin, "British Officials and Their Attitudes to the Negro Community, 1833-1861," *Ontario History*, vol. 66 (Toronto: Ontario Historical Society, June 1974) 78-88; Ernest Green, "Upper Canada's Black Defenders," *Ontario Historical Society Papers and Records*, vol. 27 (Toronto: Ontario Historical Society, 1931) 365-391. See also Peter Meyler and David Meyler, *A Stolen Life: Searching for Richard Pierpoint*. Toronto: Natural Heritage, 1999.

30. *Guelph Herald*, Nov. 2, 1847.

31. Letter from Andrew Geddes to Commissioner of Crown Lands, October 14, 1847, Archives of Ontario.

32. Payne, *History of the African Methodist Episcopal Church*, 178, 213; *True Wesleyan*, Oct. 30, 1847, Jan. 1, 1848.

33. *True Wesleyan*, Oct. 30, 1847.

34. *Oberlin Evangelist*, July 21, 1847.

35. *Oberlin Evangelist*, July 21, 1847; *True Wesleyan*, Dec. 23, 1848; Silverman, *Unwelcome Guests*, 56.

36. Arthur Tappan (May 22, 1786–July 23, 1865) was a successful businessman,

philanthropist and abolitionist. He supported numerous humanitarian and reform causes, especially those that related to the anti-slavery movement. In 1840, Tappan withdrew from the American Anti-slavery Society to form the American and Foreign Anti-slavery Society, acting as its first president. Dumas Malone, ed., *Dictionary of American Biography, Volume 18* (New York: Charles Scribner's Sons, 1936) 298-300.

37.   Lewis Tappan (May 23, 1788–June 21, 1873) like his brother, Arthur, was a prominent New York City businessman and philanthropist. He also participated in numerous religious and social reform movements throughout his life. Malone, *Dictionary of American Biography, Volume 18*, 303-304. For more information see Bertram Wyatt-Brown, *Lewis Tappan and the Evangelical War Against Slavery.* Cleveland, OH: Press of Case Western Reserve University, 1969.

38.   Joshua Leavitt (September 8, 1794–January 16, 1873) was a Congregational minister, journalist and religious activist. Dumas Malone, ed., *Dictionary of American Biography, Volume 15* (New York: Charles Scribner's Sons, 1936) 84-85. For more information see Hugh Davis, *Joshua Leavitt: Evangelical Abolitionist.* Baton Rouge: Louisiana State University Press, 1990.

39.   Gerrit Smith (March 6, 1797–December 28, 1874) was a New York abolitionist and social reformer, who supported causes such as temperance, anti-slavery and women's suffrage. He encouraged John Brown's raid on Harpers Ferry, Virginia, but believed in political action as a means to end slavery. He was among the leaders who formed the Liberty Party and from 1853 to 1854 he served as a U.S. Congressman. Dumas Malone, ed., *Dictionary of American Biography, Volume 15* (New York: Charles Scribner's Sons, 1936) 270-271.

40.   George Whipple (1805–1876) attended Lane Seminary in Ohio, but transferred to Oberlin College as a Lane Rebel along with Hiram Wilson. After graduation he became principal of the school's Preparatory Department and professor of Mathematics. He was a founder of the Western Evangelical Missionary Society and became the corresponding secretary for the AMA soon after it organized. He worked for the AMA until his death in 1876. Lesick, *Lane Rebels,* 191; Ripley, *Black Abolitionist Papers,* 185; Oberlin College, *Oberlin College Alumni Directory, 1960* (Oberlin, OH: The author, 1960) section 3, part B.

41.   Augustus F. Beard, *A Crusade of Brotherhood: A History of the American Missionary Association* (New York: Kraus Reprint Company, 1970 reprint ed.) v-vii; Lesick, *Lane Rebels,* 191.

42.   *Oberlin Evangelist,* May 27, 1847; Winks, *Blacks in Canada,* 197; Fred Landon, "Amherstburg Terminus of the Underground Railroad," *Journal of Negro History,* vol. 10 (New York: Association for the Study of Negro Life and History, January 1925) 1-9.

43. Letter from Fidelia Coburn to Lewis Tappan, June 19, 1847, AMAA.

44. Letter from Fidelia Coburn to AMA, November 16, 1847, AMAA; Elizabeth Bloomfield, *Waterloo Township Through Two Centuries* (St. Jacobs, ON: St. Jacobs Printery, 1995) 403.

45. Letter from Fidelia Coburn Brooks to Lewis Tappan, November 16, 1847, AMAA.

46. Dan Walker and Fawne Stratford-Deval, *The Marriage Registers of Upper Canada/Canada West, Volume 9: Part 1, Wellington District, 1840-1852* (Delhi, ON: NorSim Research and Publishing, 1997) 63.

47. The Reverend Samuel Young was an abolitionist from New York. He had helped a runaway slave from Maryland to reach Canada West safely. However, slave catchers had pursued the runaway across the border and accused him of committing a capital crime in the United States. Upon learning of the accusations, Young had travelled to Montreal to personally testify on the fugitive's behalf. Young's testimony prevented the slave's recapture, but the man moved to the Queen's Bush in hopes of finding a safe refuge. Before returning to New York, Young decided to go to the Queen's Bush along with Hiram Wilson. During his visit, Young succumbed to a debilitating illness and died on September 11, 1847. He was buried in Wellesley Township. *Toronto Mirror*, Oct. 15, 1847.

48. Letter from Fidelia Coburn Brooks to Lewis Tappan, October 14, 1847, AMAA.

49. Letter from Hiram Wilson to George Whipple, June 21, 1851, AMAA.

50. Letter from Fidelia Coburn Brooks to George Whipple, July 4, 1849, AMAA.

51. Letter from Fidelia Coburn Brooks to Lewis Tappan, November 16, 1847, AMAA.

52. *Ibid.*

53. *True Wesleyan*, May 30, 1846, Jan. 1, 1848; 1851 Canadian Census, Canada West, Wellington County, Peel Township; Letter from Fidelia Coburn Brooks to William Harned, July 3, 1848, AMAA; Frances Hoffman, *Upper Canada Naturalization Records, Wellington District, 1842-1849* (Kitchener, ON: Waterloo-Wellington Branch, Ontario Genealogical Society, 1998) 12.

54. Letter from Fidelia Coburn Brooks to William Harned, July 3, 1848, AMAA; Letter from Fidelia Coburn Brooks to Lewis Tappan, November 16, 1847, AMAA.

55. *True Wesleyan*, May 30, 1846; Letter from Isaac Rice to Lewis Tappan, March 30, 1848, AMAA.

56. Letter from Fidelia Coburn Brooks to Lewis Tappan, November 16, 1847, AMAA.

57. Letter from Fidelia Coburn Brooks to Lewis Tappan, November 16, 1847, AMAA; Letter from Fidelia Coburn Brooks to George Whipple, November 23, 1847, AMAA; Letter from Fidelia Coburn Brooks to AMA, January 1, 1848, AMAA.

58. Letter from Fidelia Coburn Brooks to Lewis Tappan, January 1, 1848, AMAA; *American Missionary*, vol. 2 (New York: American Missionary Association, February 1848) 29.

59. *American Missionary*, vol. 3 (New York: American Missionary Association, December 1848) 10-11; Fidelia Coburn Brooks to William Harned, July 3, 1848, AMAA.

60. *True Wesleyan*, Dec. 23, 1847; Letter from Fidelia Coburn Brooks to Lewis Tappan, October 14, 1847, AMAA; Itemized list of school supplies received by John and Fidelia Brooks, April 25, 1848, AMAA; *American Missionary*, vol. 2 (New York: American Missionary Association, May 1848) 53.

61. Letter from Fidelia Coburn Brooks to William Harned, June 1, 1848, AMAA.

62. *Ibid. American Missionary* 2 (New York: American Missionary Association, August 1848) 77.

63. Letter from Fidelia Coburn Brooks to Lewis Tappan, February 20, 1849, AMAA.

64. Letter from Fidelia Coburn Brooks to William Harned, June 1, 1847, AMAA. W.F. MacKenzie in his history of Wellington County reported that fugitive slave John Little owned the first reaper in Peel Township. *Guelph Mercury and Advertiser*, Oct. 24, 1907.

65. Letter from Mary Jones to Thomas Jones, October 21, 1848, WCMA.

66. Ross Cumming, ed., *Historical Atlas of Wellington County, Ontario, 1906* (Guelph, ON: Corporation of the County of Wellington, reprint edition, 1972) 7; *Guelph Weekly Mercury & Advertiser*, Oct. 31, 1907.

67. Letter from Fidelia Coburn Brooks to William Harned, July 3, 1848, AMAA.

68. *American Missionary* 2 (New York: American Missionary Association, August 1848) 77.

69. *Ibid.*

70. Letter from Fidelia Coburn Brooks to William Harned, July 3, 1848, AMAA.

71.   Letter from Fidelia Coburn Brooks to William Harned, June 1, 1848, AMAA.

72.   Lorana Parker was a teacher at the British-American Institute at Dawn, Canada West. *True Wesleyan*, Dec. 5, 1846.

73.   William King (1812–January 5, 1895) had been born in Ireland and educated at Glasgow University. In 1833, he immigrated to the United States where he secured a teaching position in Louisiana. On January 10, 1841 he married Mary Mourning Phares, the daughter of a plantation owner. Her dowry included several slaves and despite his hatred of slavery, King became a slaveholder. By 1846 he had become a minister in the Presbyterian Church and had suffered the loss of his wife and two children. During the same year he accepted an appointment to become a missionary in Canada West for the Colonial Committee of the Free Church of Scotland. In 1849, he manumitted his Louisiana slaves and escorted them to the province, where they became the nucleus of the Elgin Settlement, named for Lord Elgin, the Governor General of the Canadas. Edwin Larwill, a local racist politician led a campaign against the Black community, but King and his supporters were able to overcome the opposition. After the American Civil War, the Elgin Settlement began to decline when many of its inhabitants returned to the United States. In 1873, the Elgin Association issued its last annual report and, in 1880, King retired from missionary life and moved to Chatham. Victor Ullman, *Look to the North Star: A Life of William King*, Toronto, ON: Umbrella Press, 1969; Ripley, *Black Abolitionist Papers*, 254-255; Winks, *Blacks in Canada*, 208-218; William Pease and Jane Pease, "Opposition to the Founding of the Elgin Settlement," *Canadian Historical Review*, vol. 38 (Canadian Historical Society, September 1957) 202-218. See also Catherine Slaney, "The Elgin Settlement" in *Family Secrets: Crossing the Colour Line* (Natural Heritage, 2003) 31-43.

74.   Letter from John S. Brooks to Lewis Tappan, July 11, 1848, AMAA; *True Wesleyan*, Sept. 16, 1848; *Oberlin Evangelist*, Aug. 30, 1848.

75.   In June 1849, the Elgin Association was incorporated, but William King did not purchase any land until October. Winks, *Blacks in Canada*, 208-218; Pease and Pease, *Black Utopia*, 84-90; *Ecclesiastical and Missionary Record*, vol. 5 (Toronto: Presbyterian Church of Canada, December 1848) 27.

76.   *Ecclesiastical and Missionary Record*, 27; Drew, *The Narratives of Fugitive Slaves in Canada*, 190; Conversation with Elise Harding-Davis, September 1993.

77.   *Ecclesiastical and Missionary Record*, 27.

78.   *Ibid.*

79.   *Ibid.*

80. *Ibid.*

81. Letter from John S. Brooks to Lewis Tappan, July 11, 1848, AMAA.

82. Letter from Fidelia Coburn Brooks to William Harned, July 3, 1848; Letter from John S. Brooks to Lewis Tappan, July 11, 1848; Letter from John S. Brooks to Lewis Tappan, July 30, 1848, AMAA.

83. Letter from Fidelia Brooks to George Whipple, October 8, 1848, AMAA.

84. *North Star*, Dec. 22, 1848; Letter from John S. and Fidelia Coburn Brooks to Lewis Tappan, April 2, 1849, AMAA.

85. *American Missionary*, 3 (New York: American Missionary Association, November 1848) 6.

86. *Oberlin Evangelist*, Oct. 10, 1849, Clara Merritt DeBoer, "Role of Afro-Americans in the Origin and Work of the American Missionary Association, 1839 - 1877," Ph.D. dissertation, Rutgers University, 1973, 141.

87. Letter from John S. Brooks to Lewis Tappan, December 17, 1848, AMAA; *American Missionary Third Annual Report* (New York: American Missionary Association, 1849) 22; *American Missionary*, vol. 4 (New York: American Missionary Association, February 1850) 38; Letter from Mary Teall to AMA, January 13, 1850, AMAA.

88. Letter from Hiram Wilson to George Whipple, July 21, 1851, AMAA; *True Wesleyan*, May 5, 1849; *Voice of the Fugitive*, Feb. 12, 1851; *American Missionary Seventh Annual Report* (New York: American Missionary Association, 1853) 49; Letter from Mary Teall to George Whipple, no date, but early 1852, AMAA.

89. Letter from Fidelia Coburn Brooks to Lewis Tappan, January 29, 1849, AMAA.

90. Letter from Fidelia Coburn Brooks to Lewis Tappan, February 20, 1849, AMAA.

91. Ibid.

92. Ibid, April 2, 1849, AMAA.

93. Ibid.

94. Letter from Fidelia Coburn Brooks to George Whipple, June 12, 1849, AMAA.

95. John English and Kenneth McLaughlin, *Kitchener: An Illustrated History* (Waterloo, ON: Wilfrid Laurier University Press, 1983) 21-22.

96. Miriam H. Snyder, *Hannes Schneider and his Wife Catharine Haus Schneider Their Descendants 1534-1939* (Kitchener, ON: Miriam Helen Snyder, 1945) 234.

97. *Berlin Chronicle,* May 27, 1857.

98. Archives of Ontario, R.G. 1, C1-1, Volume 42, Petitions 1827-1856 (Queen's Bush); Elora Agency Applications, Applicants for Land, Peel Township, entry dated January 5, 1846, WCMA; 1851 Canadian Census, Canada West, Waterloo County, Galt. The 1851 census enumerator for Galt listed Francis Burten, a fourteen-year-old boy with Lewis and Maryann Brown. He may have been the oldest son of William and Julia Ann Burten.

99. *Kitchener-Waterloo Record,* July 2, 1927; Snyder, *Hannes Schneidner,* 256, 303; *Berlin Chronicle,* May 27, 1857, Feb. 22, 1859; 1851 Canadian Census, Canada West, Waterloo County, Galt; Linda Brown-Kubisch, "In Search of Freedom: Early Blacks in Waterloo County," *Waterloo Historical Society Annual Volume,* vol. 80 (Kitchener: Waterloo Historical Society, 1993) 54; *True Wesleyan,* Jan. 29, 1848.

100. Letter from Fidelia Coburn Brooks to George Whipple, June 12, 1849, AMAA.

101. Ibid, July 4, 1849, AMAA.

102. Ibid.

103. *American Missionary Third Annual Report, 1849,* 22-23.

104. *American Missionary,* vol. 4 (New York: American Missionary Association, November 1849) 11; *American Missionary,* vol. 4 (New York: American Missionary Association, June 1950) 68.

Chapter 4: "Our Work Here is Almost Done"

1. Chapter title is adapted from a letter written by Mary Teall to George Whipple, 23 September 1851, AMAA.

2. Letter from Mary Teall to William Harned, January 13, 1850, AMAA; *American Missionary Association Fourth Annual Report* (New York: American Missionary Association, 1850) 27-28; *American Missionary Association Fifth Annual Report* (New York: American Missionary Association, 1851) 33; letter from Mary Teall to AMA, September 24, 1851, AMAA.

3. Letter from Mary Teall to AMA, January 3, 1850, AMAA; *American Missionary,* vol. 4 (New York: American Missionary Association, May 1850) 62.

4. *Voice of the Fugitive,* Mar. 12,1851.

5.   Letter from Mary Teall to William Harned, January 13, 1850, AMAA; *American Missionary*, vol. 4 (New York: American Missionary Association, February 1850) 38; Letter from James Curry to Lewis Tappan, August 12, 1851, AMAA. In his *Voice of the Fugitive*, Mar. 12, 1851 article, Henry Bibb mistakenly called Queen's Bush the Greensbush.

6.   Letter from H. A. Linzer to Lewis Tappan, October 22, 1849. AMAA.

7.   Ontario Land Records Index, entry dated September 12, 1849, Archives of Ontario; *American Missionary Association Fifth Annual Report*, 34; letter from Mary Teall to William Harned, January 13, 1850, AMAA; letter from Mary Teall to Mr. Miner, November 24, 1851, AMAA.

8.   Letter from Mary Teall to William Harned, January 13, 1850, AMAA.

9.   Letter from Mary Teall to Lewis Tappan, January 29, 1850, AMAA.

10.   Josiah B. Jackson (1810 –May 26, 1880), and his wife, Sarah Philips, lived in Peel Township with their children, Hanna P., Mary T., Edith, and Joseph W. The 1851 Peel Township census enumerator listed Thomas Johnston, a Black infant, as a member of the Jackson household. In 1849, H. A. Lizer, agent of the American Baptist Free Mission Society, who visited Peel Township on behalf of the AMA executive committee, mistakenly identified Jackson as Black. However, Thomas Vipond and Mary Teall in their correspondence to the AMA identified Jackson as white. The 1851 Peel Township census enumerator also reported Jackson as white. Jackson died May 26, 1880, at age 72 and his wife, Sarah, died on 28 September 1894, at age 77. They are buried in the Glen Allan Union Cemetery in Peel Township. 1851 Canadian Census, Canada West, Wellington County, Peel Township; letter from H. A. Lizer to Lewis Tappan, October 22, 1849, AMAA; "Copy of Thos. Vipond's Receipts," March 6, 1850, AMAA; Waterloo-Wellington Branch, Ontario Genealogical Society, *Glen Allan Union Cemetery* (Kitchener, ON: The author, 1996) 23.

11.   Ontario Land Records Index, entries dated February 9, 1847, May 5, 1847, April 9, 1848, Archives of Ontario.

12.   British courts had declared that American settlers were not legal citizens but aliens. Unless they became naturalized, Americans were unable to legally own property or enjoy political rights. David Mills, *The Idea of Loyalty in Upper Canada, 1784-1850* (Kingston, ON: McGill-Queen's University Press, 1988) 34.

13.   Letter from J. P. Bardwell to Lewis Tappan, March 27, 1850, AMAA; letter from Thomas Vipond to Lewis Tappan, January 29, 1850, AMAA; letter from Josiah B. Jackson to Lewis Tappan, February 4, 1850, AMAA.

14.   Archives of Ontario, R.G. 1, C1-1, Volume 42, Petitions and Applications 1827-1856 (Queen's Bush).

15. Letter from Mary Teall to George Whipple, September 18, 1850, AMAA.

16. Ibid.

17. Winks, *Blacks in Canada*, 195-198; Pease and Pease, *Black Utopia*, 67-71, 81, 106; Ripley, *Black Abolitionist Papers*, 159-160; Silverman, "American Fugitive Slave in Canada," 221-223; *American Missionary Association Fourth Annual Report*, 28; Ullman, *Look to the North Star*, 85-99, 126, 208.

18. Campbell, Stanley, *The Slave Catchers: Enforcement of the Fugitive Slave Law, 1850-1860* (Chapel Hill: University of North Carolina Press, 1970) 24.

19. *Annual Report of the American and Foreign Anti-slavery Society, 1851* (New York: American and Foreign Anti-slavery Society, 1851) 30-31; Fred Landon, "The Negro Migration To Canada After The Passing Of The Fugitive Slave Act," *Journal of Negro History*, vol.5 (New York: Association for the Study of Negro Life and History, January 1920) 22-36; *Voice of the Fugitive*, Nov. 4,1852; *American Missionary Association Fifth Annual Report*, 32; Winks, *Blacks in Canada*, 142-209; *Provincial Freeman*, July 29, 1854.

20. Stouffer, *The Light of Nature and the Law of God: Antislavery in Ontario 1833-1877*, 110-111, 119; Ripley, *Black Abolitionist Papers*, 18-19, 223; Fred Landon, "The Anti-slavery Society of Canada," *Journal of Negro History*, vol. 4 (New York: Association for the Study of Negro Life and History, January 1919) 33-36. See also Adrienne Shad *et al*, *The Underground Railroad: Next Stop, Toronto!*, (Toronto: Natural Heritage, 2002) 24.

21. David Hotchkiss was a Wesleyan Methodist minister from Pennsylvania. Between 1835 and 1839 he worked as a missionary in the western United States among the Choctaws and French. He arrived in Amherstburg in November 1850. Ripley, *Black Abolitionist Papers*, 117; letter from David Hotchkiss to Lewis Tappan, 20 November 1850, AMAA.

22. *American Missionary Association Fifth Annual Report*, 32-33.

23. Letter from Mary Teall to William Harned, November 18, 1850, AMAA.

24. Ibid.

25. Letter from Thomas Vipond to Lewis Tappan, January 9, 1851, AMAA; letter from Susan Teall to Lewis Tappan, January 10, 1851, AMAA.

26. Letter from Mary Teall to Brother Miner, November 24, 1851, AMAA.

27. 1851 Canadian Census, Wellington County, Peel Township; letter from Mary Teall to William Harned, February 28, 1851, AMAA; letter from Mary Teall to AMA,

March 3, 1851, March 28, 1851, 16 August 1851, September 23, 1851, AMAA; letter from the Reverend Matthew Swan to AMA, March 17, 1851, AMAA; *American Missionary Association Fifth Annual Report*, 33.

28.   Letter from James Curry to Lewis Tappan, April 30, 1851, August 12, 1851, AMAA.

29.   Ibid.

30.   Letter from Hiram Wilson to AMA, June 21, 1851, AMAA.

31.   Letter from James Curry to George Whipple, August 12, 1851, AMAA; letter Mary Teall to George Whipple, December 17, 1851, January 10, 1852, AMAA.

32.   Daniel Alexander Payne (24 February 1811–29 November 1893) was born to free mulatto parents in Charleston, South Carolina. Payne's father had been born free in Virginia, but as a child had been kidnapped and sold into slavery. He remained a slave until he reached adulthood and purchased his freedom for one thousand dollars. Payne's mother was a descendant of the Catawba Indian tribe of the Carolinas. In 1829, Payne opened a school in Charleston, which he managed until 1835 when the South Carolina state legislature enacted a law forbidding the education of Blacks. Forced to abandon his career as a teacher, Payne enrolled in the Lutheran Theological Seminary in Gettysburg, Pennsylvania, and received his license to preach in the Lutheran church in 1837. The loss of his voice in 1839 forced Payne to resign his pastorate in East Troy, New York, and for the next five years he taught in a school in Philadelphia. While in Philadelphia, Payne joined the AME church and quickly became an influential minister within the church hierarchy. He fought for an educated clergy and opposed the use of traditional African practices, such as ring shouts, in religious services. In 1848, Payne became the official historian for the denomination and, on May 7, 1852, he was elected bishop of the AME church. Between 1863 and 1876 he served as president of Wilberforce University, the first AME-owned college. Daniel A. Payne, *Recollections of Seventy Years*. Nashville, TN: Publishing House of the A. M. E. Sunday School Union, 1888.

33.   Payne, *History of the African Methodist Episcopal Church*, 257-258.

34.   *Ibid.*

35.   Ripley, *Black Abolitionist Papers*, 263; Payne, *History of the African Methodist Episcopal Church*, 258.

36.   Payne, *History of the African Methodist Episcopal Church*, 258-259. The other delegates were J.P. Campbell, G.W. Johnson, H.E. Stephens and L. Anderson.

37.   1851 Canadian Census, Canada West, Wellington County, Peel Township; 1851 Canadian Census, Canada West, Waterloo County, Wellesley Township.

38. Ibid.

39. Ibid.

40. 1851 Canadian Census, Canada West, Waterloo County, Wellesley Township.

41. Letter from Mary Teall to George Whipple, September 23, 1851, AMAA.

42. Letter from Mary Teall to William Harned, September 24, 1851, AMAA.

43. Ibid, September 23, 1851, AMAA.

44. Ibid, February 3, 1852, AMAA.

45. Letter from Thomas Vipond to Lewis Tappan, February 28, 1851, AMAA.

46. Letter from Mary Teall to Brother Miner, November 24, 1851, AMAA.

47. Ibid.

48. Letter from Mary Teall to AMA, December 17, 1851, AMAA.

49. Letter from Mary Teall to George Whipple, January 10, 1852, AMAA.

50. Ibid.

51. Letter from Mary Teal to George Whipple, dated 1852, AMAA.

52. Ibid

53. Letter from Mary Teall to William Harned, February 3, 1852, AMAA.

54. Ibid.

55. Ibid.

56. Letter from Samuel T. Teall to AMA, April 22, 1852, AMAA; letter from Mary Teall to George Whipple, May 12, 1852, July 19, 1852, AMAA; letter from Susan Teall to George Whipple, February 3, 1853, AMAA. Robin Winks in *Blacks in Canada* states that Mary Teall returned briefly to the Queen's Bush in 1859. This author did not find any evidence of Teall's visit in the correspondence of the AMA.

57. *Elora Backwoodsman*, July 1, 1852; Ward, *Autobiography of a Fugitive Negro*, 136-137, 143-149, 193, 218; Ripley, *The Black Abolitionist Papers*, 165; Ronald K. Burke, *Samuel Ringgold Ward: Christian Abolitionist* (New York: Garland Publishing, Inc., 1995) 43-52.

58. Winks, *Blacks in Canada*, 271; Ripley, *The Black Abolitionist Papers*, 20.

59. Letter from John S. Brooks to George Whipple, July 23, 1852, AMAA.

60. Robert W. S. Mackay, *The Canadian Directory* (Montreal: John Lovell, 1851). No numbers, but page 1 of the Addenda; Cumming, *Historical Atlas of Wellington County, Ontario, 1906*, 7; "Village's History Recalled Old Directory Yields Info," Jan. 4, 1971, unidentified newspaper article in the Peel Township Vertical File at WCMA; Hutchinson, *History of Wellington County*, 12, 306.

61. There were several families in Peel Township with the Knox surname, so it is unknown if this Mr. Knox was white or Black.

62. Letter from John S. Brooks to George Whipple, July 22, 1852, July 23, 1852, July 30, 1852, August 2, 1852, August 12, 1852, AMAA; Deed of Sale, August 12, 1852, AMAA. On November 30, 1857, the Reverend Henry Reid received a title to lot 3, concession 3, Ontario Land Records Index, entry dated November 30, 1857, Archives of Ontario.

63. Letter from Susan Teall to William Harned, November 8, 1852, AMAA; letter from Susan Teall to George Whipple, February 28, 1853, AMAA.

64. *Minutes of the Fifteenth Annual Conference of the African Methodist E. Church for the Canada District, 1853* (Toronto: Henry Stephens, 1853) 5, 9.

65. Letter from Mary Teall to George Whipple, March 1, 1853, AMAA.

66. Letter from Elias Kirkland to George Whipple, March 14, 1853, AMAA.

67. Letter from Susan Teall to George Whipple, February 3, 1853, AMAA.

68. Letter from Thomas Vipond to George Whipple, February 25, 1853, AMAA.

69. Letter from Susan Teall to George Whipple, April 18, 1853, AMAA.

70. Ibid, October 16, 1853, AMAA.

Chapter 5: "Most of the Colored People Living Here are Doing as Well, if Not Better, Than Once Could Reasonably Expect"

1. Quote is adapted from Thomas Elwood Knox's interview with Benjamin Drew in 1855. Drew, *Narratives of Fugitive Slaves in Canada*, 191.

2. Drew, *Narratives of Fugitive Slaves in Canada*, 197.

3. Willis Nazrey (March 5, 1808–August 22, 1875), was a native of Isle of Wight

County, Virginia. In June 1840 at the AME New York Conference, Bishop Morris Brown admitted Nazrey to the church on probation as an itinerant minister. The following year he became a deacon and in 1843 was ordained as an elder. On May 13, 1852, at the AME General Conference held in New York, Nazrey became the sixth bishop of the AME church. In 1856, he became the first bishop of the newly organized British Methodist Episcopal Church in Canada West. He died in Chatham, Ontario, and over two hundred people attended his funeral on September 2, 1875. Payne, *History of the African Methodist Episcopal Church*, 127, 134, 158, 382; Payne, *Recollections of Seventy Years*, 110; Wright, *Encyclopaedia of the African Methodist Episcopal Church*, 593; Charles Smith, *A History of the African Methodist Episcopal Church* (New York: Johnson Reprint Corporation, 1968) 111.

4.   *Minutes of the Fifteenth Annual Conference of the African Methodist E. Church for the Canada District*, 4, 5, 9-11; Payne, *History of the African Methodist Episcopal Church*, 111, 295; McKenzie, *Upper Canada Naturalization Records, 1828-1850*, 44, 57, 59, 79.

5.   *Minutes of the Fifteenth Annual Conference of the African Methodist E. Church for the Canada District*, 5, 9.

6.   Richard Warren (December 1, 1812–?), was born a slave in Gates County, North Carolina, and reared in Rutherford County, Tennessee. Despite a lack of formal training, Warren conducted worship services for slaves in his community, sometimes walking ten to twenty miles to hold the secret meetings. In 1845, Warren escaped from slavery and settled in Detroit, Michigan, where he received a license to preach in the Methodist church. For the next several years he travelled throughout Canada West and New York. In 1847, he became an ordained deacon in the AME church and received an appointment to the London Circuit. He later served AME congregations in Hamilton, Chatham and Dawn. In 1855, he published his autobiography, *Narrative of the Life and Sufferings of Rev. Richard Warren, (A Fugitive Slave)*. Richard Warren, *Narrative of the Life and Sufferings of Rev. Richard Warren, (A Fugitive Slave)*, Hamilton, C.W.: Christian Advocate Book & Job Office, 1856.

7.   *Minutes of the Fifteenth Annual Conference of the African Methodist E. Church for the Canada District*, 11.

8.   Winks, *Blacks in Canada*, 144.

9.   "Impressions of Canada West in the 1850s," *Western Ontario Historical Notes*, vol. 17 (London, ON: University of Western Ontario Library, 1961) 8.

10.   Drew, *Narratives of Fugitive Slaves in Canada*, i-ii.

11.   *Ibid*, 191.

12. *Ibid.*

13. *Ibid*, 233.

14. *Ibid*, 190.

15. *Ibid*, 190.

16. *Ibid*, 198, 219.

17. *Ibid*, 219-220.

18. *Ibid*, 197.

19. *British Constitution and Fergus Freeholder*, Jan. 4, 1858.

20. Drew, *Narratives of Fugitive Slaves in Canada*, 218.

21. *Ibid*, 218-219.

22. *Ibid*, 219.

23. *Minutes of the Sixteenth Annual Conference of the A.M.E Church in the Province of Canada Begun at Chatham, British North America, 1855* (Chatham, C.W.: Freeman Office, 1855) 8-10, 12, 16; *Minutes of the First General Conference of the British M.E. Church, 1860* (Chatham, C.W.: William Thompson & Company, 1861) 4.

24. Payne, *History of the African Methodist Episcopal Church*, 322.

25. William H. Jones (?–1915), was reared in Baltimore, Maryland. In 1852, he became the travelling agent for the AME Book Concern and published new editions of Black-authored works, including *The Life of Richard Allen* and *Colored Patriots of the Revolution*. Jones regularly visited Canada West and participated in the annual meetings of the Canadian Conference. Between 1855 and 1863 Jones served as minister of the Chatham church. A dynamic minister, Jones and his preaching attracted new parishioners and the congregation grew to over 300 members. During the early 1860s, Jones authored an eight-page booklet about the history of the BME church. In 1863 and 1864, as the Civil War raged in the United States, Jones toured the northern states with a panorama of slave and battle scenes to raise money for American sanitary aid associations. Between 1865 and 1868, he conducted a lecture tour in Great Britain to raise money for the newly freed slaves in the southern states. He eventually settled in Tennessee where he served as a minister in Black communities. Black abolitionist William Wells Brown described Jones as of a man of medium height and pure African descent. Jones died in Arkansas in 1915. Ripley, *Black Abolitionist Papers*, 487-489; *Minutes of the Eighteenth Annual Conference of the AME Church and the*

Doings of the First Annual Assembly of the British Methodist Episcopal Church, 1856 (Chatham, C.W.: The church, 1856) 5; *Pine and Palm,* Sept. 28, 1861.

26. *Minutes of the Eighteenth Annual Conference of the* A.M.E. *Church and the Doings of the First Annual Assembly of the British Methodist Episcopal Church,* 1, 7-8; Payne, *History of the African Methodist Episcopal Church,* 322, 361-362, 367, 375; Wright, *Encyclopaedia of the African Methodist Episcopal Church,* 345; Payne, *Recollections of Seventy Years,* 135.

27. *Minutes of the Eighteenth Annual Conference of the* A.M.E. *Church and the Doings of the First Annual Assembly of the British Methodist Episcopal Church,* 7-26.

28. The author made repeated attempts to locate an AME Church archives to obtain permission to use the photographs of Nazrey and Disney. Although one of the largest AME Church collections is at Wilberforce University, Jacqueline Brown, the archivist of the University, was not aware of any official church archives. She suggested that the author contact Dr. Dennis Dickerson, Historiographer of the A.M.E. Review. There was no response to her letter of September 30, 2002. As these photographs were taken in the late 1800s, it is believed that they are in the public domain.

29. *Minutes of the Eighteenth Annual Conference of the* A.M.E. *Church and the Doings of the First Annual Assembly of the British Methodist Episcopal Church,* 29-30.

30. *Minutes and Proceedings of the Second Annual Conference of the* B.M.E. *Church, 1857* (Chatham, C.W.: W.H. Thompson, 1857) 3, 4; Ripley, *Black Abolitionist Papers,* 496; Leroy Graham, *Baltimore: The Nineteenth Century Black Capital* (New York: University Press of America, 1982) 153; Wright, *Encyclopaedia of the African Methodist Episcopal Church,* 576.

31. *Minutes and Proceedings of the Second Annual Conference of the* B.M.E. *Church, 2, 3, 4; Minutes and Proceedings of the Third Annual Conference of the British* M.E. *Church in Canada, 1858,* (Chatham, C.W.: W.H. Thompson, 1858) 4, 6,7, 9.

32. *Minutes of the Fourth Session of the Annual Conference of the British* M.E. *Church in Canada, 1859* (Chatham: B.M.E. Church Conference, 1859) 17.

33. *Minutes of the Fourth Session of the Annual Conference of the* B.M.E. *Church,* 17.

34. *Ibid,* 18.

35. *Ibid, 15-16.*

36. Ripley, *Black Abolitionist Papers,* 496; *Minutes of the Fourth Session of the Annual Conference of the* B.M.E. *Church,* 10, 13, 14.

37. 1861 Canadian Census, Canada West, Wellington County, Peel Township; *Minutes of the Eighteenth Annual Conference of the A.M.E. Church*, 5; *Minutes of the Fourth Session of the Annual Conference of the B.M.E. Church*, 3, 5, 8-10; *Minutes of the First General Conference of the British M.E. Church*, 5, 6,11; *Minutes of the Fifth Session of the Annual Conference of the British Methodist Episcopal Church, 1861* (Chatham, C.W.: R. Stephenson, 1861) 4.

38. *Minutes of the First General Conference of the British M.E. Church*, 1,16.

39. *Ibid*, 10-11.

40. "Statistics from the *Canadian Baptist Register, 1857-1876* and the *Baptist Year Book for Ontario and Quebec, 1877-1878*," compiled by Judith Colwell, McMaster Divinity College, Hamilton, Ontario; Baptist Missionary Convention, *Canadian Baptist Register, 1860* (Toronto, C.W.: Globe Book & Job Office, 1859) 14.

41. Baptist Missionary Convention, *Canadian Baptist Register*, 1861 (Brantford, C.W.: Expositor Books & Job Office, 1860) 16.

42. "Statistics from the *Canadian Baptist Register, 1857-1876* and the *Baptist Year Book for Ontario and Quebec, 1877-1878*," compiled by Judith Colwell, McMaster Divinity College, Hamilton, Ontario.

43. Arthur M. Schlesinger, Jr., ed., *The Almanac of American History* (New York: Barnes and Noble, Inc., 1993) 277-278; Robin W. Winks, *Canada and the United States: The Civil War Years* (Baltimore: John Hopkins Press, 1960) 45, 184-185. The southern states that had seceded by March 4, 1861 were: South Carolina on December 20, 1860; Mississippi on January 9, 1861; Florida on January 10, 1861; Alabama on January 11, 1861; Georgia on January 19, 1861; Louisiana on January 26, 1861; and Texas on February 23, 1861.

44. 1861 Canadian Census, Canada West, Wellington County, Peel Township; 1861 Canadian Census, Canada West, Waterloo County, Wellesley Township.

45. Ibid.

46. 1861 Canadian Census, Canada West, Wellington County, Peel Township; 1861 Canadian Census, Canada West, Waterloo County, Wellesley Township.

47. *Third Annual Conference of the B.M.E. Church*, 13; Ripley, *Black Abolitionist Papers*, 487; *Minutes of the Fifth Session of the Annual Conference of the B.M.E. Church*, 10; *Pine and Palm*, Sept. 28, 1861.

48. *Minutes of the Fifth Session of the Annual Conference of the B.M.E. Church*, 10; *Minutes of the Sixth Session of the Annual Conference of the British M.E. Church in Canada, 1862* (Chatham, C.W.: I.B. Richardson, 1862) 11.

49. Charles H. Pearce (1817–1887), was born a slave in Queen Anne's County, Maryland. After purchasing his freedom he moved to New Haven, Connecticut. In 1852, he became a minister with the AME New England Conference, but later resigned and moved to Canada West where he served the Toronto AME church as an itinerate elder. In 1861, at the time of his expulsion from the BME church, Pearce was assigned to the Chatham church. After the Civil War, Pearce returned to the United States, where he was appointed superintendent of the AME church in Florida and Alabama. From 1868 to 1872, he served in the Florida senate. *Minutes of the Sixteen Annual Conference of the AME Church*, 1, 7; Ripley, *Black Abolitionist Papers*, 488-489; Clarence Walker, *A Rock in a Weary Land: The African Methodist Episcopal Church During the Civil War and Reconstruction* (Baton Rouge: Louisiana State University Press, 1982) 120-121.

50. George W. Broadie was born in Kentucky but, by the early 1850s, he had settled in Chatham, Canada West. He established a grocery store with William Sterritt and also operated a real estate business. In the mid-1850s, he became a minister in the AME church and served as secretary at the founding meeting of the BME Church in 1856. After the Civil War, Broadie returned to the United States and rejoined the AME church. He served as the AME superintendent for North Carolina and became an influential leader in Raleigh's Black community. Ripley, *Black Abolitionist Papers*, 333-334; *Minutes of the Eighteenth Annual Conference of the A.M.E. Church and the Doings of the First Annual Assembly of the British Methodist Episcopal Church*, 5, 8; *Minutes of the Fourth Session of the Annual Conference of the B.M.E. Church*, 7; Walker, *A Rock in a Weary Land*, 74.

51. Henry J. Young (1819–1874), was born in Delaware to free Black parents. In the 1830s, he received a license to preach in the Methodist Episcopal Church (South), but joined the AME church in 1840. He became an ordained minister in 1848. In 1853 he immigrated to Canada West and received an appointment to the Sayer Street AME church in Toronto. Two years later he received an appointment to the Chatham AME church and eventually became a leading member of the town's Black community. *Minutes of the Fifteenth Annual Conference of the A.M.E. Church*, 5, 6; *Minutes of the Sixteenth Annual Conference of the A.M.E. Church*, 7; Ripley, *Black Abolitionist Papers*, 332.

52. William Douglass was the presiding elder of the St. Catharines BME church in 1859. In 1860 church officials reassigned him to Toronto, but he later abandoned the position. *Minutes of the Fourth Session of the Annual Conference of the B.M.E. Church*, 3, 10; *Minutes of the First General Conference of the B.M.E. Church*, 7; *Minutes of the Fifth Session of the Annual Conference of the B.M.E. Church*, 6.

53. Edward Brook was a local preacher from Amherstburg, Canada West. *Minutes and Proceedings of the Third Annual Conference of the B.M.E. Church*, 6.

54. *Minutes of the Fifth Session of the Annual Conference of the British Methodist Episcopal Church*, 5; *Minutes of the Sixth Session of the Annual Conference of the B.M.E. Church*, 1, 4; Ripley, *Black Abolitionist Papers*, 333, 489, 496.

55. *Minutes of the Sixth Session of the Annual Conference of the* B.M.E. *Church,* 4-5; *Minutes of the Seventh Session of the Annual Conference of the British Methodist Episcopal Church, 1863* (Chatham, C.W.: British Methodist Episcopal Church, 1863) 4, 7. James Baker died sometime between June 1862 and June 1863. After his death, BME church officials assigned the Reverends Edward Gant and Samuel H. Brown to look after his children. *Minutes of the Seventh Session of the Annual Conference of the British Methodist Episcopal Church, 1863*, 4-5.

56. Alton Hornsby, Jr., *Chronology of African American History From 1492 to the Present* (Toronto: Gale Research, 1997) 69.

57. Winks, *Blacks in Canada,* 215; Winks, *Canada and the United States,* 199; Ullman, *Look to the North Star,* 212; Silverman, *Mary Ann Shadd and the Search for Equality,* 97. A. Shadd et al, *The Underground Railroad: Next Stop Toronto!* Toronto, Natural Heritage Books, 2002.

58. *Minutes of the Seventh Session of the Annual Conference of the British Methodist Episcopal Church,* 6.

59. *Ibid,* 7.

60. Hornsby, *Chronology of African American History From 1492 to the Present,* 72. For more information about Black soldiers who served in the Civil War see: Dudley T. Cornish, *The Sable Arm: Black Troops in the Union Army, 1861-1865* (Lawrence: University of Kansas Press, 1990). For more information from a Canadian perspective, see Catherine Slaney, "Off to War," "Dr. Abbott and the Civil War" and "The Grand Army of the Republic" in *Family Secrets: Crossing the Colour Line* (Toronto: Natural Heritage, 2003) 51-74.

61. *Dumfries Reformer and Weekly Advertiser,* Aug. 5, 1863.

62. Samuel G. Howe, *The Refugees from Slavery in Canada West* (Boston: Wright & Potter, 1864) 101.

63. *Ibid,* 101-104.

64. *Ibid,* 102.

65. *Ibid,* 104.

66. *American Missionary Association Sixth Annual Report, 1852* (New York: American Missionary Association, 1852) 31; Winks, *Blacks in Canada,* 224-225; Simpson, "Negroes in Ontario," 65-66.

67. Letter from the Reverend Elias E. Kirkland to George Whipple, December 27, 1850, AMAA.

68. Letter from the Reverend Elias E. Kirkland to George Whipple, December 27, 1850, AMAA.

69. Letter from the Reverend Elias E. Kirkland to William Harned, January 1, 1853, AMAA.

70. *American Missionary Association Seventh Annual Report, 1853* (New York: American Missionary Association, 1853) 49.

71. *American Missionary Association Seventh Annual Report,* 50; Letter from Mary Ann Shadd to George Whipple, April 2, 1853, AMAA; Clara Merritt DeBoer, *Be Jubilant My Feet: African American Abolitionists in the American Missionary Association, 1839-1861* (New York: Garland Publishing, Inc., 1994) 172.

72. *American Missionary Association Eighth Annual Report, 1854* (New York: American Missionary Association, 1854) 48; Letter from Theodosia Lyon to George Whipple, May 11, 1853, AMAA; letter from William C. Talbert to George Whipple, July 3, 1854, AMAA; letter from Abigail B. Martin to George Whipple, September 1, 1854, AMAA; letter from Isaac Fairfax and Don Quicksott to George Whipple, December 22, 1854, AMAA.

73. Letter from David Hotchkiss to George Whipple, May 6, 1861, May 26, 1861, AMAA; *Voice of the Fugitive,* Jan. 29, 1852; Winks, *Blacks in Canada,* 225; Ripley, *Black Abolitionist Papers,* 486; Fred Landon, "The Work of the American Missionary Association Among the Negro Refugees in Canada West, 1848-1864," *Ontario Historical Society Papers and Records,* vol. 21 (Toronto: Ontario Historical Society, 1924) 204-205.

74. *Minutes of the Sixteenth Annual Conference of the African Methodist Episcopal Church,* 4; letter from I.C. Chambers to George Whipple, August 2, 1859, AMAA; *Minutes of the First General Conference of the British Methodist Episcopal Church and the Proceedings of the Fourth Session of the Annual Conference, 1860,* 7; Ripley, *Black Abolitionist Papers,* 486.

75. Winks, *Blacks in Canada,* 215-217; Hill, *Freedom Seekers,* 86; Ullman, *Look to the North Star,* 224. For an assessment of the Black migration to the United States after the Civil War based on the census see: Michael Wayne, "The Myth of the Fugitive Slave: The Black Population of Canada West on the Eve of the American Civil War: A Reassessment Based on the Manuscript Census of 1861," *Historie Sociale/Social History,* vol. 56 (Ottawa: Les Publications Historie Sociale – Social History, Inc., November 1995) 465-485.

76. *National Anti-slavery Standard,* Aug. 19, 1865.

77. Winks, *Blacks in Canada,* 195-197, 216; Pease and Pease, *Black Utopia,* 67-71; Hill, *Freedom Seekers,* 74-76; Ullman, *Look to the North Star,* 222, 234.

78. *Minutes of the Ninth Annual Conference of the British Methodist Episcopal Church*, 33; Simpson, "Negroes in Ontario," 815; Hill, *Freedom Seekers*, 58.

Epilogue

1.   James Sutherland, *County of Waterloo Gazetteer and General Business Directory for 1864* (Toronto, C.W.: Mitchell & Company, 1864) 43-44; Henry Roswell, *Gazetteer and Directory of the County of Wellington, 1867* (Toronto, ON: The author, 1867) 63-70: *Drayton Advocate*, Oct. 20, 1955; 1871 Canadian Census, Ontario, Wellington County, Peel Township; Register of Ontario Deaths, entry 019894-81, Archives of Ontario; Waterloo-Wellington Branch, Ontario Genealogical Society, *Ten Cemeteries, Peel Township, Wellington County, Ontario* (Kitchener: Ontario Genealogical Society, 1984) 11.

2.   No official date could be located for the church closing, but Israel Martin, of Wallenstein, believed the last services were held in about 1918. *Kitchener-Waterloo Record*, July 20, 1979.

3.   Letter from Helen Hulse to Linda Brown-Kubisch, December 21, 1994.

4.   *Elmira Signet*, Mar. 4, 1920.

5.   Conversation with Marilyn E. Hisson, August 23, 1993; *Kitcherner-Waterloo Record*, July 20, 1979; Waterloo-Wellington Branch, Ontario Genealogical Society. *Glen Allan Union Cemetery* (Kitchener: Ontario Genealogical Society, 1996) 32.

6.   William A. Owens, *Black Mutiny: The Revolt on the Schooner Amistad* (Philadelphia: Pilgrim Press, 1968) 294-306; *Hartford Daily Courant*, Dec. 21, 1841; Cousins, "Woman of the Year–1842: The Early Life of Eliza Ruggles," 370-372: William Raymond Collection, AMAA; *Friend of Man*, Nov. 9, 1841: letter from Eliza Raymond to Lewis Tappan, July 29, 1850, AMAA.

7.   George Thompson, *The Palm Land; West Africa Illustrated* (Cincinnati: Moore, Wilstach, Keys & Company Printers, 1859) 298-300; 363-364; *American Missionary Association Eighth Annual Report, 1854*, 24.

8.   Clara Merritt DeBoer, "Role of Afro-Americans in the Origin and Work of the American Missionary Association, 1839-1877." Ph.D. dissertation, Rutgers University, 1973, 107-108.

9.   Letter from John S. Brooks to George Whipple, July 9, 1859, May 24, 1860, AMAA.

10.   Letter from John S. Brooks to George Whipple, November 12, 1859; August 30, 1860; February 18, 1861, AMAA. For a detailed outline of the plan to establish a

cotton plantation in Sierra Leone see: *Pine and Palm*, May 18, 1861 and DeBoer, "Role of Afro-Americans in the Origin and Work of the American Missionary Association, 1839-1877," 111-112.

11.   Letter from John S. Brooks to George Whipple, November 16, 1860, November 19, 1860, February 21, 1861, AMAA.

12.   Letter from John S. Brooks to George Whipple, August 1861, AMAA; letter from G.P. Claflin to George Whipple, March 17, 1862, June 16, 1862, AMAA; DeBoer, "Role of Afro-Americans in the Origin and Work of the American Missionary Association, 1839-1877," 113.

13.   Letter from Theodosia Lyon to George Whipple, May 11, 1853, AMAA; 1860 United States Federal Population Census, Michigan, Jackson County; Walter Romig, *Michigan Place Names* (Detroit: Wayne State University Press, 1986) 271; 1870 United States Federal Population Census, Michigan, Benzie County; letter from Elias E. Kirkland to William E. Whiting, February 1, 1875, AMAA; letter from Fanny Kirkland to W.E. Whiting, August 1876, AMAA.

Appendix A: Biographical Sketches of the Black Pioneers in the Queen's Bush Settlement

1.   Archives of Ontario, R.G. 1, C1-1, Volume 42, Petitions 1827-1856 (Queen's Bush).

2.   *Ibid.*

3.   1851 Canadian Census, Canada West, Wellington County, Peel Township; 1861 Canadian Census, Canada West, Wellington County, Peel Township; 1871 Canadian Census, Ontario, Wellington County, Peel Township; Hancocks, *County Marriage Registers of Ontario, Canada, 1858-1869, Volume 32, Waterloo County*, 67.

4.   1871 Canadian Census, Ontario, Wellington County, Peel Township.

5.   1861 Canadian Census, Canada West, Wellington County, Peel Township.

6.   Elora Agency Applications, Applicants for Land, Peel Township, entry date June 13, 1845, WCMA; Robert W. Kerr, P.L.S. "Memorandum of the Clerances [sic] of the Settlers." Held with Surveyors Letters, Township of Peel, Ontario Archives; Archives of Ontario, R.G. 1, C1-1, Volume 42, Petitions 1827-1856 (Queen's Bush).

7.   Elora Agency Applications, Applicants for Land, Peel Township, entry dated October 6, 1845, WCMA.

8.   1861 Canadian Census, Canada West, Wellington County, Peel Township.

9.   Archives of Ontario, R.G. 1, C1-1, Volume 42, Petitions 1827-1856 (Queen's Bush).

10.   *Ibid.*

11.   "List of Thos. Vipond's Receipt," March 6, 1850, AMAA.

12.   Elora Agency Applications, Applicants for Land, Peel Township, entry dated March 15, 1846, WCMA; Archives of Ontario, R.G. 1, C1-1, Volume 42, Petitions 1827-1856 (Queen's Bush).

13.   1832 Gore District Census and Assessment, Woolwich Township; 1851 Canadian Census, Canada West, Wellington County, Peel Township.

14.   Elora Agency Applications, Applicants for Land, Peel Township, entry dated January 8, 1846, WCMA.

15.   Archives of Ontario, R.G. 1, C1-1, Volume 42, Petitions 1827-1856 (Queen's Bush).

16.   *Ibid.*

17.   1851 Canadian Census, Canada West, Waterloo County, Wellesley Township.

18.   Elora Agency Applications, Applicants for Land, Peel Township, entry dated October 27, 1846, WCMA; "List of Thos. Vipond's Receipt," March 6, 1850, AMAA; letter from Josiah B. Jackson to Lewis Tappan, February 4, 1850, AMAA.

19.   Elora Agency Application, Applicants for Land, Peel Township, entry dated October 27, 1846; Robert W. Kerr, P.L.S. "Memorandum of the Clerances (sic) of the Settlers," Held with Surveyors Letters, Township of Peel, Archives of Ontario; Archives of Ontario, R.G. 1, C1-1, Volume 42, Petitions 1827-1856 (Queen's Bush).

20.   1851 Canadian Census, Canada West, Waterloo County, Wellesley Township; Hancocks, *County Marriage Registers of Ontario, Canada, 1858-1869, Volume 32, Waterloo County,* 105; Archives of Ontario, R.G. 1, C1-1, Volume 42, Petitions 1827-1856 (Queen's Bush).

21.   1851 Canadian Census, Canada West, Waterloo County, Wellesley Township.

22.   Hancocks, *County Marriage Registers of Ontario, Canada, 1858-1869, Volume 32, Waterloo County,* 105.

23.   Archives of Ontario, R.G. 1, C1-1, Volume 42, Petitions 1827-1856 (Queen's Bush).

24.   Hill, *Freedom Seekers,* 95, 150, 154.

25.   Paola Brown, *Address Intended to be Delivered in the City Hall, Hamilton, February 7, 1851 on the Subject of Slavery* (Hamilton: The author, 1851) 49. A review of Brown's publication appears in the Toronto *Globe*, June 21, 1851.

26.   1851 Canadian Census, Canada West, Wellington County, Peel Township.

27.   Elora Agency Applications, entry dated October 6, 1846, WCMA.

28.   1851 Canadian Census, Canada West, Wellington County, Woolwich Township.

29.   Elora Agency Applications, entry dated March 12, 1846, WCMA.

30.   Elora Agency Applications, entry dated October 22, 1846.

31.   Archives of Ontario, R.G. 1, C1-1, Volume 42, Petitions 1827-1856 (Queen's Bush).

32.   Ibid.

33.   Elora Agency Applications, entry dated October 6, 1846.

34.   1832 Gore District Census and Assessment, Woolwich Township; Archives of Ontario, R.G. 1, C1-1, Volume 42, Petitions 1827-1856 (Queen's Bush); McKenzie, *Upper Canada Naturalization Records*, 58.

35.   Elora Agency Applications, entry dated June 17, 1845.

36.   1833 Gore District Census and Assessment, Woolwich Township; Stewart, Kitchen and Dietrich, *Maple Leaf Journal*, 25.

37.   Elora Agency Applications, entry dated December 2, 1845; Archives of Ontario, R.G. 1, C1-1, Volume 42, Petitions 1827-1856 (Queen's Bush).

38.   1851 Canadian Census, Canada West, Wellington County, Peel Township; 1861 Canadian Census, Canada West, Wellington County, Peel Township; Elora Agency Applications, entry dated January 9, 1846.

39.   1861 Canadian Census, Canada West, Wellington County, Peel Township.

40.   *Ibid.*

41.   *Ibid.*

42.   Archives of Ontario, R.G. 1, C1-1, Volume 42, Petitions 1827-1856 (Queen's Bush).

43.   *Ibid.*

44.   Archives of Ontario, R.G. 1, C1-1, Volume 42, Petitions 1827-1856 (Queen's Bush), 1851 Canadian Census, Canada West, Waterloo County, Galt.

45.   Winks, *Blacks in Canada*, 357; Smith, *History of the African Methodist Episcopal Church*, 172; Wright, *History of the African Methodist Episcopal Church*, 576; *Proceedings of the Seventh Session General Conference of the British Methodist Episcopal Church, 1884* (Chatham, ON: The Church, 1884) 51, 54.

46.   J. William Lamb. "Disney, Richard Randolph," *Dictionary of Canadian Biography* on CD disc, Toronto: University of Toronto, 2000.

47.   Archives of Ontario, R.G. 1, C1-1, Volume 42, Petitions 1827-1856 (Queen's Bush).

48.   1851 Canadian Census, Canada West, Waterloo County, Wellesley Township; 1854 Wellesley Township Assessment Records.

49.   Waterloo-Wellington Branch, Ontario Genealogical Society, *Ten Cemeteries,* 12; Will of Vincent Douglass, dated January 19, 1878, Wellington County Courthouse; *Berliner Journal*, Apr. 15, 1897; Apr. 22, 1897.

50.   Ontario Marriage Records, 315, Archives of Ontario; Ontario Death Records, entry 033382, Archives of Ontario; letter from Lisa B. Lee to the author, July 26, 2002; email from Lisa B. Lee to the author, July 1, 2002.

51.   Email from Lisa B. Lee to the author, July 1, 2002; Ontario Death Records entry 033382, Archives of Ontario; Ontario Death Records entry 035305, Archives of Ontario; Waterloo-Wellington Branch, Ontario Genealogical Society, *Ten Cemeteries,* 12; Letters of Administration for the estate of Cora W. Douglass, April 13, 1914, Wellington County Courthouse.

52.   Email from Lisa B. Lee to the author, November 5, 2002; 1871 Canadian Census, Ontario, Waterloo County, Wellesley Township; Ontario Death Records, entry 028627, Archives of Ontario.

53.   Elora Agency Applications, Applicants for Land, Peel Township, entry dated October 6, 1846, WCMA.

54.   1851 Canadian Census, Canada West, Wellington County, Peel Township; 1861 Canadian Census, Canada West, Wellington County, Peel Township; Elora Agency Applications, Applicants for Land, Peel Township, entry dated October 6, 1846, WCMA.

55.   1871 Canadian Census, Ontario, Wellington County, Peel Township; *Drayton Advocate*, Jan. 4, 1917; Waterloo-Wellington Branch, Ontario Genealogical Society, *Ten Cemeteries*, 11.

56. 1851 Canadian Census, Canada West, Wellington County, Peel Township.

57. Ibid;

58. Hancock, *County Marriage Registers of Ontario, Canada, 1858-1869, Vol.32, Waterloo County*, 148.

59. French, *Men of Colour*, 88; 1871 Canadian Census, Ontario, Grey County, Owen Sound.

60. Elora Agency Applications, Applicants for Land, Peel Township, entry dated October 6, 1846, WCMA; Robert W. Kerr, P.L.S. "Memorandum of the Clerances (sic) of the Settlers," Held with Surveyors Letters, Township of Peel, Archives of Ontario; Archives of Ontario, R.G. 1, C1-1, Volume 42, Petitions 1827-1856 (Queen's Bush); 1851 Canadian Census, Canada West, Wellington County, Peel Township.

61. Letter from J. Bardwell to AMA, March 6, 1850, AMAA.

62. 1851 Canadian Census, Canada West, Wellington County, Peel Township; Walker and Stratford-Deval, *Marriage Registers of Upper Canada/Canada West, Volume 9: Part 1, Wellington District, 1840-1852*, 107.

63. Elora Agency Applications, Applicants for Land, Peel Township, entry dated March 13, 1846, October 27, 1846, WCMA.

64. Archives of Ontario, R.G. 1, C1-1, Volume 42, Petitions 1827-1856 (Queen's Bush).

65. Ibid.

66. Walker and Stratford-Deval, *Marriage Registers of Upper Canada/Canada West, Volume 9: Part 1, Wellington District, 1840-1852*, 15; Robert W. Kerr, P.L.S. "Memorandum of the Clerances (sic) of the Settlers," Held with Surveyors Letters, Township of Peel, Archives of Ontario; 1851 Canadian Census, Canada West, Wellington County, Peel Township; Hofffman, *Upper Canada Naturalization Records*, 6.

67. 1861 Canadian Census, Canada West, Wellington County, Peel Township.

68. Archives of Ontario, R.G. 1, C1-1, Volume 42, Petitions 1827-1856 (Queen's Bush).

69. Ibid.

70. Elora Agency Applications, Applicants for Land, Peel Township, entry dated October 6, 1846, WCMA; Walker and Stratford-Deval, *Marriage Registers of Upper Canada/Canada West, Volume 9: Part 1, Wellington District, 1840-1852*, 32; 1851

Canadian Census, Canada West, Wellington County, Peel Township; 1861 Canadian Census, Canada West, Wellington County, Peel Township.

71. 1871 Canadian Census, Ontario, Wellington County, Peel Township.

72. Elora Agency Applications, Applicants for Land, Peel Township, entry dated March 13, 1846, WCMA; 1851 Canadian Census, Canada West, Wellington County, Peel Township.

73. 1861 Canadian Census, Canada West, Wellington County, Peel Township; Rowsell, *Gazetteer and Directory of the County of Wellington, 1867*, 66.

74. 1851 Canadian Census, Canada West, Waterloo County, Wellesley Township; 1871 Canadian Census, Ontario, Wellington County, Peel Township.

75. Archives of Ontario, R.G. 1, C1-1, Volume 42, Petitions 1827-1856 (Queen's Bush).

76. Elora Agency Applications, Applicants for Land, Peel Township, entry dated October 6, 1846; Archives of Ontario, R.G. 1, C1-1, Volume 42, Petitions 1827-1856 (Queen's Bush).

77. 1851 Canadian Census, Canada West, Wellington County, Peel Township.

78. Conversation with Elise Harding-Davis, September 1993; Archives of Ontario, R. G.1, C1-1, Volume 42, Petitions 1827-1856 (Queen's Bush); 1861 Canadian Census, Canada West, Wellington County, Peel Township.

79. Dan Walker and Fawne Stratford-Devai, *Marriage Registers of Upper Canada/Canada West, Volume 9: Part 2, Wellington District, 1852-1857* (Delhi: NorSim Research Publishing, 1997) 36; 1861 Canadian Census, Canada West, Wellington County, Peel Township; conversation with Elise Harding-Davis, September 1993.

80. 1861 Canadian Census, Canada West, Wellington County, Peel Township.

81. 1861 Canadian Census, Canada West, Wellington County, Peel Township.

82. Archives of Ontario, R.G. 1, C1-1, Volume 42, Petitions 1827-1856 (Queen's Bush).

83. Ibid, 1871 Canadian Census, Ontario, Wellington County, Peel Township.

84. 1861 Canadian Census, Ontario, Wellington County, Peel Township.

85. Elora Agency Applications, Land Applicants, Peel Township, entry dated June 16, 1845, October 6, 1846, WCMA; Robert W. Kerr, P.L.S. "Memorandum of the

Clerances [sic] of the Settlers," Held with Surveyors Letters, Township of Peel, Archives of Ontario; Archives of Ontario, R.G. 1, C1-1, Volume 42, Petitions 1827-1856 (Queen's Bush); 1861 Canadian Census, Canada West, Wellington County, Peel Township; Peel Township, Wellington County, Ontario Land Abstracts Index to Deeds, Volume 1, entry dated July 18, 1854, WCMA.

86. Archives of Ontario, R.G. 1, C1-1, Volume 42, Petitions 1827-1856 (Queen's Bush).

87, Walker and Stratford-Devai, *Marriage Registers of Upper Canada/Canada West, Volume 9: Part 2, Wellington District, 1852-1857*, 106.

88. Archives of Ontario, R.G. 1, C1-1, Volume 42, Petitions 1827-1856 (Queen's Bush).

89. 1861 Canadian Census, Canada West, Wellington County, Peel Township.

90. Ibid.

91. 1851 Canadian Census, Canada West, Wellington County, Peel Township; Archives of Ontario, R.G. 1, C1-1, Volume 42, Petitions 1827-1856 (Queen's Bush).

92. Ibid.

93. 1851 Canadian Census, Canada West, Wellington County, Peel Township.

94. Ibid.

95. Simpson, "Negroes in Ontario From Early Times to 1870," 863-864.

96. Elora Agency Applications, Land Applicants, Peel Township, entry dated October 6, 1846; Archives of Ontario, R.G. 1, C1-1, Volume 42, Petitions 1827-1856 (Queen's Bush).

97. 1832 Gore District Census and Assessment, Woolwich Township; 1833 Gore District Census and Assessment, Woolwich Township; Archives of Ontario, R.G. 1, C1-1, Volume 42, Petitions 1827-1856 (Queen's Bush); Hoffman, *Upper Canada Naturalization Records*, 9.

98. 1832 Gore District Census and Assessment, Woolwich Township.

99. 1861 Canadian Census, Canada West, Wellington County, Peel Township.

100. Ibid.

101. Elora Agency Applications, Applicants for Land, Peel Township, entry dated October 6, 1846, WCMA; Walker and Stratford-Devai. *Marriage Registers of Upper*

Canada/Canada West, Volume 9: Part 1, Wellington District, 1840-1852, 106; 1851 Canadian Census, Canada West, Wellington County, Peel Township; 1871 Canadian Census, Ontario, Wellington County, Peel Township.

102. Elora Agency Applications, Applicants for Land, Peel Township, entry dated October 27, 1846, WCMA; Archives of Ontario, R.G. 1, C1-1, Volume 42, Petitions 1827-1856 (Queen's Bush).

103. *Drayton Advocate,* Oct. 20, 1955.

104. *Drayton Advocate,* Oct. 20, 1955; Waterloo-Wellington Branch, Ontario Genealogical Society, *Glen Allan Union Cemetery,* 23.

105. Elora Agency Applications, Applicants for Land, Peel Township, entry dated October 6, 1846, WCMA; "List of Thos. Vipond's Receipt," March 6, 1850, AMAA.

106. 1851 Canadian Census, Canada West, Waterloo County, Galt; "List of Thos. Vipond's Receipt," March 6, 1850, AMAA; 1854 Galt Assessment Records, KPL.

107. *Guelph Weekly Mercury & Advertiser,* Oct. 24, 1907.

108. Archives of Ontario, R.G. 1, C1-1, Volume 42, Petitions 1827-1856 (Queen's Bush).

109. 1851 Canadian Census, Canada West, Wellington County, Peel Township.

110. Walker and Stratford-Devai. *Marriage Registers of Upper Canada/Canada West, Volume 9: Part 2, Wellington District, 1852-1857,* 27.

111. 1861 Canadian Census, Canada West, Wellington County, Peel Township.

112. Archives of Ontario, R.G. 1, C1-1, Volume 42, Petitions 1827-1856 (Queen's Bush).

113. French, *Men of Colour,* 25-26; *Colonial Advocate,* Aug. 2, 1832; Walker and Devai, *Marriage Registers of Upper Canada/Canada West, Volume 9, Part 1, Wellington District,* 15; Archives of Ontario, R.G. 1, C1-1, Volume 42, Petitions 1827-1856 (Queen's Bush); Hoffman, *Upper Canada Naturalization Records,* 9.

114. *Minutes of the Sixteenth Annual Conference of the African Methodist Episcopal Church,* 1, 9; *Minutes of the Seventh Session of the Annual Conference of the B.M.E. Church,* 13; Elora Agency Applications, Applicants for Land, Peel Township, entry dated June 28, 1845, WCMA; 1861 Canadian Census, Canada West, Wellington County, Peel Township.

115. Archives of Ontario, R.G. 1, C1-1, Volume 42, Petitions 1827-1856 (Queen's Bush).

116. 1851 Canadian Census, Canada West, Waterloo County, Wellesley Township; 1854 Wellesley Township Assessment Records, "List of Thos. Vipond's Receipt, March 6, 1850, AMAA.

117. 1861 Canadian Census, Canada West, Wellington County, Peel Township.

118. Archives of Ontario, R.G. 1, C1-1, Volume 42, Petitions 1827-1856 (Queen's Bush).

119. Ibid.

120. 1851 Canadian Census, Canada West, Waterloo County, Wellesley Township; Archives of Ontario, R.G. 1, C1-1, Volume 42, Petitions 1827-1856 (Queen's Bush).

121. Robert W. Kerr, P.L. S. "Memorandum of the Clerances (sic) of the Settlers," Held with Surveyors Letters, Township of Peel, Archives of Ontario; Archives of Ontario, R.G. 1, C1-1, Volume 42, Petitions, 1827-1856 (Queen's Bush); Payne, *History of the African Methodist Episcopal Church*, 203, 213.

122. 1861 Canadian Census, Canada West, Wellington County, Peel Township.

123. Archives of Ontario, R.G. 1, C1-1, Volume 42, Petitions, 1827-1856 (Queen's Bush).

124. Elora Agency Applications, Applicants for Land, Peel Township, entry dated October 6, 1846, WCMA.

125. "Copy of Thos. Vipond's Receipt," March 6, 1850, AMAA.

126. *Ibid.*

127. *Ibid.*

128. Conversation with Melba Jewell, May 4, 1998; *Kitchener-Waterloo Record*, July 17, 1997; McKenzie, *Upper Canada Naturalization Records, 1828-1850*, 64; Elora Agency Applications, Applicants for Land, Peel Township, entry dated October 3, 1845, WCMA; 1851 Canadian Census, Canada West, Wellington County, Peel Township; *Elora Observer and Salem and Fergus Chronicle*, June 14, 1867.

129. 1861 Canadian Census, Canada West, Wellington County, Peel Township; conversation with Melba Jewell, May 4, 1998.

130. Conversation with Melba Jewell, May 4, 1998.

131. *Ibid.*

132. 1861 Canadian Census, Canada West, Wellington County, Peel Township; 1871

Canadian Census, Ontario, Peel Township; Ontario Deaths Records, entry 0274622, Archives of Ontario; *Drayton Advocate*, Jan. 12, 1899.

133. 1861 Canadian Census, Canada West, Wellington County, Peel Township.

134. Waterloo-Wellington Branch, Ontario Genealogical Society, *Ten Cemeteries*, 12.

135. *Ibid.*

136. Elora Agency Applications, Applicants for Land, Peel Township, entry dated October 6, 1846; *Deutscher Canadier,* Aug. 4, 1848.

137. Elora Agency Applications, Applicants for Land, Peel Township, entry dated October 6, 1846, WCMA; Robert W. Kerr, P.L.S. "Memorandum of the Clerances [sic] of the Settlers," Held with Surveyors Letters, Township of Peel, Archives of Ontario; Archives of Ontario, R.G. 1, C1-1, Volume 42, Petitions 1827-1856 (Queen's Bush).

138. Elora Agency Applications, Applicants for Land, Peel Township, entry dated 14 October 14, 1845; Archives of Ontario, R.G. 1, C1-1, Volume 42, Petitions 1827-1856 (Queen's Bush); Hoffman, *Upper Canada Naturalization Records*, 12.

139. 1851 Canadian Census, Canada West, Wellington County, Peel Township; Elora Agency Applications, Applicants for Land, Peel Township, entry dated October 27, 1846, WCMA; Robert W. Kerr, P.L.S. "Memorandum of the Clerances [sic] of the Settlers," Held with Surveyors Letters, Township of Peel, Archives of Ontario; "List of Thos. Vipond's Receipt," March 6, 1850, AMAA; Archives of Ontario, R.G. 1, C1-1 Volume 42, Petitions 1827-1856 (Queen's Bush); Peel Township, Wellington County, Ontario, Land Abstract Index to Deeds, Volume 1, entry dated December 14, 1862, WCMA.

140. *Drayton Advocate*, Feb. 20, 1946.

141. Elora Agency Applications, Applicants for Land, Peel Township, entry dated October 6, 1846, WCMA; Archives of Ontario, R.G. 1, C1-1, Volume 42, Petitions 1827-1856 (Queen's Bush).

142. Elora Agency Applications, Applicants for Land, Peel Township, entry dated May 22, 1845, WCMA.

143. 1851 Canadian Census, Canada West, Wellington County, Peel Township; Hoffman, *Upper Canada Naturalization Records, Wellington District, 1842-1849*, 12. No Hillsborough, Vermont, has been found in any Vermont place name resources. However, in the early 1800s, a section of Starksborough in Addison County was known as Hillsborough. Esther Swift, *Vermont Place-names: Footprints of History* (Brattleboro, VT: Stephen Greene Press, 1977) 66.

144. 1851 Canadian Census, Canada West, Wellington County, Peel Township; 1861 Canadian Census, Wellington County, Peel Township.

145. *Guelph Weekly Mercury and Advertiser*, Oct. 24, 1907.

146. Elora Agency Applications, Applicants for Land, Peel Township, entry dated October 27, 1846; Archives of Ontario, R.G. 1, C1-1 Volume 42, Petitions 1827-1856 (Queen's Bush).

147. Dumas, *Dictionary of American Biography, Volume 15*, 443-444: *Pine and Palm*, May 18, 1861, July 6, 1861, Aug. 31, 1861, Sept. 7, 1861, Sept. 14, 1861, Sept. 21, 1861, Sept. 28, 1861, Oct. 19, 1861, Nov. 16, 1861, Nov. 30, 1861, Dec. 7, 1961; Winks, *Blacks in Canada*, 165.

148. *Guelph Weekly Mercury and Advertiser*, Oct. 24, 1907; Abstract Index to Peel Township, Wellington County Deeds, Volume 1, entry dated December 13, 1862, WCMA; *Pine and Palm*, June 22, 1861, July 6, 1861, Sept. 7, 1861; Miller, *Search for a Black Nationality*, 247.

149. Miller, *Search for a Black Nationality*, 242; *Pine and Palm*, Nov. 9, 1861.

150. Miller, *Search for a Black Nationality*, 242.

151. 1851 Canadian Census, Canada West, Wellington County, Peel Township.

152. 1861 Canadian Census, Canada West, Wellington County, Peel Township.

153. Ibid.

154. Archives of Ontario, R.G. 1, C1-1, Volume 42, Petitions 1827-1856 (Queen's Bush).

155. *Elmira Signet*, Sept. 29, 1910; 1832 Gore District Census and Assessment, Woolwich Township, 1832; 1833 Gore District Census and Assessment, Woolwich Township; 1851 Canadian Census, Canada West, Wellington County, Peel Township Census.

156. 1840 Gore District Census and Assessment, Woolwich Township.

157. *Elmira Signet*, Sept. 29, 1910; 1851 Canadian Census, Canada West, Wellington County, Peel Township; Elora Agency Applications, Applicants for Land, Peel Township, entry dated October 14, 1845, WCMA; Robert W. Kerr, P.L.\S. "Memorandum of the Clerances [sic] of the Settlers." Held with Surveyors Letters, Township of Peel, Archives of Ontario.

158. Walker and Devai, *Marriage Registers of Upper Canada/Canada West, Volume 9, Part 1, Wellington District, 1840-1852*, 106.

159. Abstract Index to Peel Township, Wellington County Deeds, Volume 1, entry dated March 29, 1862, WCMA.

160. Letter from Helen S. Hulse to the author, July 23, 1994; *Elmira Signet*, Sept. 29, 1910; 1861 Canadian Census, Canada West, Wellington County, Peel Township.

161. *Elmira Signet*, Sept. 29, 1910.

162. *Elmira Signet*, Sept. 29, 1910; Rowsell, *Gazetteer and Directory of the County of Wellington, 1867*, n.p., Glen Allan entry; Loomis, A.O. *Gazetteer and Directory of the County of Wellington for 1871/1872* (Hamilton, ON: The author, 1871) 107; *Union Publishing Company's Farmers and Business Directory for the County of Halton, Peel, Waterloo and Wellington, 1891* (Ingersoll, ON: Union Publishing Company, 1891) n.p., Glen Allan entry.

163. Ibid.

164. Hancocks, *County Marriage Registers of Ontario, Canada, 1858-1869, Volume 32, Waterloo County*, 49.

165. Stewart, Kitchen, Dietrich, *Maple Leaf Journal*, 106; Waterloo-Wellington Branch, Ontario Genealogical Society, *Ten Cemeteries*, 12.

166. Walker and Stratford-Devai, *Marriage Registers of Upper Canada/Canada West, Volume 9: Part 1, Wellington District, 1840-1852*, 63.

167. Archives of Ontario, R.G. 1, C1-1, Volume 42, Petitions 1827-1856 (Queen's Bush).

168. Ibid.

169. Ibid.

170. Ibid.

171. 1871 Canadian Census, Canada West, Wellington County, Peel Township.

172. 1851 Canadian Census, Canada West, Waterloo County, Waterloo Township; Archives of Ontario, R.G. 1, C1-1, Volume 42, Petitions 1827-1856 (Queen's Bush).

173. *Elmira Signet*, Oct. 5, 1893.

174. 1861 Canadian Census, Canada West, Wellington County, Peel Township.

175. Ibid.

176. Ibid.

177. 1851 Canadian Census, Canada West, Wellington County, Peel Township.

178. *Ibid,* 1861 Canadian Census, Canada West, Wellington County, Peel Township.

179. Robert W. Kerr, P.L.S. "Memorandum of the Clerances [sic] of the Settlers," Held with Surveyors Letters, Township of Peel, Ontario Archives; Elora Agency Applications, Applicants for Land, Peel Township, entry dated June 13, 1845; Archives of Ontario, R.G. 1, C1-1, Volume 42, Petitions 1827-1856 (Queens Bush); 1851 Canadian Census, Canada West, Wellington County, Peel Township; 1861 Canadian Census, Canada West, Wellington County, Peel Township.

180. 1861 Canadian Census, Canada West, Wellington County, Peel Township; Rowsell, *Gazetteer and Directory of the County of Wellington, 1867,* 69.

181. Elora Agency Applications, Applicants for Land, Peel Township, entry dated June 17, 1845, WCMA.

182. 1851 Canadian Census, Canada West, Wellington County, Peel Township; Elora Agency Applications, Applicants for Land, Peel Township, entry dated October 6, 1846, WCMA; 1861 Canadian Census, Canada West, Wellington County, Peel Township; 1871 Canadian Census, Ontario, Wellington County, Peel Township.

183. A.O. Loomis & Company, *Gazetteer and Directory of the County of Wellington for 1871-1872,* 107; 1871 Canadian Census, Ontario, Wellington County, Peel Township.

184. Elora Agency Applications, Applicants for Land, Peel Township, entry dated October 27, 1846, WCMA.

185. Elora Agency Applications, Applicants for Land, Peel Township, entry dated March 12, 1846, WCMA; Archives of Ontario, R.G. 1, C1-1, Volume 42, Petitions 1827-1856 (Queen's Bush).

186. 1851 Canadian Census, Canada West, Wellington County, Peel Township; Archives of Ontario, R.G. 1, C1-1, Volume 42, Petitions 1827-1856 (Queen's Bush).

187. Hancocks, *County Marriage Registers of Ontario, Canada, 1858-1869, Volume 32, Waterloo County,* 105; 1861 Canadian Census, Canada West, Wellington County, Peel Township.

188. *Berliner Journal,* Nov. 15, 1866, reprinted in the *Kitchener-Waterloo Record,* July 2, 1927.

189. 1851 Canadian Census, Canada West, Waterloo County, Wellesley Township; 1861 Canadian Census, Canada West, Elgin County, St. Thomas; Archives of Ontario, R.G. 1, C1-1, Volume 42, Petitions 1827-1856 (Queens Bush).

190. Elora Agency Applications, Applicants for Land, Peel Township, entry dated October 6, 1846, WCMA; 1851 Canadian Census, Canada West, Wellington County, Peel Township; Hoffman, *Upper Canada Naturalization Records, Wellington District, 1842-1849,* 14.

191. *Elora Observer and Salem and Fergus Chronicle,* June 14, 1867.

192. 1851 Canadian Census, Canada West, Wellington County, Peel Township; *Elora Observer and Salem and Fergus Chronicle,* June 14, 1867.

193. Elora Agency Applications, Applicants for Land, Peel Township, entry dated October 6, 1846, WCMA; Archives of Ontario, R.G. 1, C1-1, Volume 42, Petitions 1827-1856 (Queen's Bush).

194. Archives of Ontario, R.G. 1, C1-1, Volume 42, Petitions 1827-1856 (Queen's Bush).

195. *Ibid.*

196. *Ibid.*

197. *Ibid.*

198. 1851 Canadian Census, Canada West, Wellington County, Peel Township.

199. 1861 Canadian Census, Canada West, Wellington County, Peel Township.

200. 1851 Canadian Census, Canada West, Wellington County, Peel Township.

201. Ibid.

202. Archives of Ontario, R.G. 1, C1-1, Volume 42, Petitions 1827-1856 (Queen's Bush).

203. Josiah B. Jackson to Lewis Tappan, 4February 4, 1850, AMAA; "Copy of Thos. Vipond's Receipt," March 6, 1850, AMAA.

204. Archives of Ontario, R.G. 1, C1-1, Volume 42, Petitions 1827-1856 (Queen's Bush).

205. Elora Agency Applications, Applicants for land, Peel Township, entry dated June 16, 1845, WCMA; 1851 Canadian Census, Canada West, Wellington County, Peel Township; Payne, *History of the African Methodist Episcopal Church,* 203, 213; *Voice of the Fugitive,* Aug. 26, 1852; *Minutes of the Fifteenth Annual Conference of the*

African Methodist Episcopal Church, 3; 1861 Canadian Census, Canada West, Wellington County, Peel Township.

206. 1861 Canadian Census, Canada West, Wellington County, Peel Township.

207. "Copy of Thos. Vipond's Receipt," March 6, 1850, AMAA.

208. 1851 Canadian Census, Canada West, Wellington County, Peel Township; 1861 Canadian Census, Canada West, Wellington County, Peel Township; 1871 Canadian Census, Ontario, Wellington County, Peel Township; Elora Agency Applications, Applicants for Land, Peel Township, entry dated October 6, 1846, WCMA; Roswell, *Gazetteer and Directory of the County of Wellington, 1867*, 70; Walker and Stratford-Devai, *Marriage Registers of Upper Canada/Canada West, Volume 9: Part 1, Wellington District, 1840-1852*, 51; Waterloo-Wellington Branch, Ontario Genealogical Society, *Ten Cemeteries*, 12.

209. Archives of Ontario, R.G. 1, C1-1, Volume 42, Petitions 1827-18556 (Queen's Bush).

210. 1861 Canadian Census, Canada West, Wellington County, Peel Township.

211. "Plan of the Township of Wellesley, 1843," KPL; 1854 Wellesley Township Assessment Records, KPL.

212. 1851 Canadian Census, Canada West, Waterloo County, Wellesley Township; David Bowyer, *Baptism, Marriages and Burials, Church of St. John the Evangelist, Berlin, Canada West*, (Kitchener: Waterloo-Wellington Branch, Ontario Genealogical Society, 1985) 7, 8; Hancocks, *County Marriage Registers of Ontario, Canada, 1858-1869, Waterloo County*, 64.

213. *Berlin Chronicle*, Apr. 9, 1856; Snyder, *Hannes Schneider*, 210B.

214. *Dumfries Reformer*, Nov. 26, 1853; *Berlin Chronicle*, May 28, 1856, June 18, 1856, July 22, 1857, Sept. 16, 1857.

215. *Berlin News*, Jan. 1856 as reprinted in Snyder, *Hannes Schneider*, 210B.

216. Snyder, *Hannes Schneider*, 210B.

217. *Berlin Daily Telegraph*, Feb. 22, 1861, Jan. 24, 1862; Bowyer, *Baptisms Performed at St. John the Evangelist Church, Berlin, Canada West Now Kitchener, Ontario, 1858-1872*, 7, 8; City of Kitchener Cemetery Personnel, *A Walking Tour of Kitchener's Mount Hope Cemetery* (Kitchener, ON: City of Kitchener, 1984) 4; Telephone conversation with Mount Hope Cemetery staff, June 30, 1997.

218. 1862-1863 Berlin Assessment Records, KPL.

219. 1865-1870 Berlin Assessment Records, KPL; *Kitchener-Waterloo Record*, July 2, 1927.

220. 1870 United States Census, Michigan, Bay City.

221. Hancocks, *County Marriage Registers of Ontario, Canada, 1858-1869, Volume 32, Waterloo County*, 64; 30 Telephone conversation with Mount Hope Cemetery staff, June 30, 1997.

222. Telephone conversation with Mount Hope Cemetery staff, June 30, 1997; Sue Mansell, *Burials from the Parish Register of St. John the Evangelist, Church of England, Bernlin, Now Kitchener, Ontario, 1859-1890* (Kitchener: Waterloo-Wellington Branch, Ontario Genealogical Society, 1985) 1; Sue Mansell, *Marriages From the Parish Registers of the Church of St. John the Evangelist, Church of England, Berlin, Now Kitchener, Ontario, 1878-1889* (Kitchener: Waterloo-Wellington Branch, Ontario Genealogical Society, 1985) 3, 4; Last Will and Testament of Elizabeth Susand, entry GR-1582, Waterloo County Land Records Office, Kitchener, Ontario.

223. Archives of Ontario, R.G. 1, C1-1, Volume 42, Petitions 1827-1856 (Queen's Bush).

224. Ibid.

225. Ibid.

226. 1861 Canadian Census, Canada West, Wellington County, Peel Township.

227. Elora Agency Applications, Applicants for Land, Peel Township, entry dated October 6, 1846, WCMA; Archives of Ontario, R.G. 1, C1-1, Volume 42, Petitions 1827-1856 (Queen's Bush).

228. 1861 Canadian Census, Canada West, Wellington County, Peel Township.

229. Ibid.

230. Ibid.

231. 1861 Canadian Census, Canada West, Wellington County, Peel Township; Elora Agency Applications, Applicants for Land, Peel Township, entry dated March 27, 1846, WCMA; Roswell, *Gazetteer and Directory of the County of Wellington, 1867*, 70.

232. 1861 Canadian Census, Canada West, Wellington County, Peel Township.

233. Ibid.

234. Ibid.

235. Elora Agency Applications, Applicants for Land, Peel Township, entry dated June 27, 1845, WCMA.

236. Archives of Ontario, R.G. 1, C1-1, Volume 42, Petitions 1827-1856 (Queen's Bush).

237. Peel Township, Wellington County, Ontario Land Abstract Index to Deeds, Volume 1, entry dated September 13, 1853, WCMA; 1861 Canadian Census, Canada West, Wellington County, Peel Township.

238. 1861 Canadian Census, Canada West, Wellington County, Peel Township.

239. 1851 Canadian Census, Canada West, Wellington County, Peel Township; Elora Agency Applications, Applicants for Land, Peel Township, entry dated October 6, 1846, WCMA; 1861 Canadian Census, Canada West, Wellington County, Peel Township; Robert W. Kerr, P.L.S. "Memorandum of the Clerances [sic] of the Settlers," Held with Surveyors Letters, Township of Peel, Archives of Ontario.

240. Letter from Samuel White to Lewis Tappan, March 17, 1854, AMAA; Archives of Ontario, R.G. 1, C1-1, Volume 42, Petitions 1827-1856 (Queen's Bush); letter from Mary Teall to George Whipple, January 10, 1852, AMAA; *Guelph Weekly Mercury and Advertiser*, Oct. 24, 1907.

241. 1871 Canadian Census, Ontario, Wellington County, Peel Township; Waterloo-Wellington Branch, Ontario Genealogical Society, *Ten Cemeteries*, 11.

242. Hancocks, *County Marriage Registers of Ontario, Canada, 1858-1869, Volume 32, Waterloo County*, 148; 1861 Canadian Census, Canada West, Wellington County, Peel Township.

243. Elora Agency Applications, Applicants for Land, Peel Township, entry dated June 28, 1845, WCMA.

244. Elora Agency Applications, Applicants for Land, Peel Township, entry dated October 14, 1845, WCMA; Archives of Ontario, R.G. 1, C1-1, Volume 42, Petitions 1827-1856 (Queen's Bush).

245. Archives of Ontario, R.G. 1, C1-1, Volume 42, Petitions 1827-1856 (Queen's Bush).

246. 1861 Canadian Census, Ontario, Wellington County, Peel Township.

247. 1861 Canadian Census, Canada West, Wellington County, Peel Township.

248. Elora Agency Applications, Applicants for Land, Peel Township, entry dated January 5, 1846, WCMA; Archives of Ontario, R.G. 1, C1-1, Volume 42, Petitions 1827-1856 (Queen's Bush).

249. 1871 Canadian Census, Ontario, Wellington County, Peel Township.

250. 1851 Canadian Census, Canada West, Wellington County, Peel Township; Elora Agency Applications, Applicants for Land, Peel Township, entry dated October 6, 1846, WCMA; 1861 Canadian Census, Canada West, Wellington County, Peel Township; Peel Township, Wellington County, Ontario Land Abstract Index to Deeds, Volume 1, entry dated April 5, 1864, June 28, 1864, WCMA.

251. Archives of Ontario, R.G. 1, C1-1, Volume 42, Petitions 1827-1856 (Queen's Bush).

Appendix B: Petitions

1. Archives of Ontario, R. G. 1, C1-1, Volume 42, Petitions 1827-1856 (Queen's Bush).

BIBLIOGRAPHY

PRIMARY SOURCES:

Books:

Bibb, Henry, *Narrative of the Life and Adventures of Henry Bibb, an American Slave.* New York: Harper & Row, 1969 reprint ed.

Blassingame, John. *Slave Testimony: Two Centuries of Letters, Speeches, Interviews and Autobiographies.* Baton Rouge: Louisiana State University Press, 1977.

Brown, Paola, *Address Intended to be Delievered in the City Hall, Hamilton, February 7, 1851 on the Subject of Slavery.* Hamilton: The author, 1851.

Douglass, Frederick, *My Bondage and My Freedom.* New York: Miller, Orton & Mulligan, 1855.

Drew, Benjamin, *The Refugee: or the Narratives of Fugitive Slaves in Canada.* Toronto: Coles Publishing Company, 1981 reprint ed.

Dumond, Dwight, L., ed., *Letters of James Gillespie Birney, 1831-1857, Volume 2.* New York City: D. Appleton-Century Company, Inc., 1938.

Henson, Josiah, *An Autobiography of the Reverend Josiah Henson.* Reading: Addison-Wesley Publishing Company, 1969, reprint ed.

Loguen, Reverend Jermain Wesley, *The Reverend J.W. Loguen, as a Slave and as a Freeman.* Syracuse: J.G.K. Truair & Co., 1859.

Mohr, James, ed., *The Cormany Diaries: A Northern Family in the Civil War.* Pittsburgh: University of Pittsburgh Press, 1982.

Payne, Daniel, *Recollections of Seventy Years.* Nashville, TN: Publishing House of the A. M. E. Sunday School Union, 1888.

Sprague, Stuart, ed., *His Promised Land: The Autobiography of John P. Parker, Former Slave and Conductor on the Underground Railroad.* New York: W. W. Norton & Company, 1996.

Steward, Austin, *Twenty-Two Years a Slave, and Forty Years a Freeman; Embracing a Correspondence of Several Years While President of Wilberforce Colony, London, Canada West.* New York: Negro Universities Press, 1968, reprint ed.

Ward, Samuel Ringgold, *Autobiography of a Fugitive Negro: His Anti-slavery Labours in the United States, Canada and England.* New York: Arno Press, 1968 reprint ed.

Warren, Richard, *Narrative of the Life and Sufferings of Rev. Richard Warren, (A Fugitive Slave)* (Hamilton: Christian Advocate Book & Job Office, 1856).

Wayman, Rev. A.W., *My Recollections of African M. E. Ministers or Forty Years Experience in the African Methodist Episcopal Church,* Philadelphia: A. M. E. Book Rooms, 1881.

Manuscripts:

Amistad Research Center, Tulane University, New Orleans, Louisiana.
American Missionary Association Archives, Canada File.
American Missionary Association Archives, William Raymond Collection.

Archives of Maine, Portland, Maine
Will of Eleazer Coburn, 11 February 1845

Archives of Ontario, Toronto, Ontario
Archives of Ontario Land Records Index
Ontario Death Records
Ontario Marriage Records
Robert W. Kerr, P.L.S. "Memorandum of the Clerances [sic] of the Settlers."
Held with Surveyors Letters, Township of Peel
R.G. 1, C1-1, Volume 42, Petitions and Applications 1827-1856.(Queen's Bush)

Kitchener Public Library, Kitchener, Ontario
Henry S. Huber Vertical File
Winterbourne Women's Institute Tweedsmuir History

New Hampshire Historical Society, Concord, New Hampshire
Records of the Dover Ladies Anti-slavery Society Sewing Circle, 1835-1866

Simcoe County Archives, Minesing, Ontario
Minutes of the Bethesda Congregational Church, 1859-1865

D. B. Weldon Library, University of Western Ontario Library, London,
Ontario
Fred Landon Papers

Wellington County Museum and Archives, Fergus, Ontario
Abstract Index to Peel Township, Wellington County Deeds
Elora Agency Applications, Applicants for Land, Peel Township
Peel Township Vertical File
Robert W. Kerr, P.L.S. "Diary of the Time Occupied in Surveying the
Township of Peel, 1843"

Journals (American):

American Missionary, 1846-1853.

Journals (Canadian):

Canadian Baptist Magazine, 1841.
Ecclesiastical and Missionary Record, 1848.

Newspapers (American):

Colored American. New York, 1841.
Friend of Man. Utica, 1838-1842.
Hartford Daily Courant. Hartford, 1841.
Liberator. Boston, 1840.
Liberty Standard. Hallowell, 1842-1847.
National Anti-slavery Standard. New York, 1865.
North Star. Rochester, 1848.
Oberlin Evangelist. Oberlin, 1845-1848.
Pine and Palm. Boston and New York, 1861.
True Wesleyan. Cleveland, 1846-1848.
The African. St. Louis, 1843.

Newspapers (Canadian):

Berlin Chronicle. Berlin, 1856-1859.
Berliner Journal. Berlin, 1872, 1881.
Brantford Weekly Expositor. Brantford, 1900.
Colonial Advocate. Toronto, 1832.
Daily Mercury. Guelph, 1980.
Der Morgenstern. Berlin, 1841.
Drayton Advocate. Drayton, 1917, 1955.
Dumfries Reformer and Weekly Advertiser. Galt, 1863.
Elmira Signet. Elmira, 1910, 1935.
Elora Observer and Salem and Fergus Chronicle. Elora,1867.
Globe. Toronto, 1851-1853.
Guelph Herald. Guelph, 1847.
Guelph Weekly Mercury and Advertiser. Guelph, 1907.
Kitchener-Waterloo Record. Kitchener, 1927, 1977, 1979.
London Free Press. London, 1969.
Provincial Freeman. Toronto and Chatham, 1853-1857.
Reporter. Cambridge, 1974.
Voice of the Fugitive. Windsor, 1851-1852.
Toronto Mirror. Toronto, 1847.

Reports of Societies:

African Methodist Episcopal Church
Minutes of the Annual Conference of the Canadian Conference, 1853-1856.

American Missionary Association
Annual Reports, 1846-1853.

American Anti-slavery Society
Annual Report, 1837.

American and Foreign Anti-slavery Society
Annual Report, 1849-1850.

British Methodist Episcopal Church
Minutes of the Annual Conference, 1856-1865

Canadian Baptist Missionary Convention
Annual Report, 1857-1879.

SECONDARY SOURCES:

Books:

Ambrose, Rosemary, *Waterloo County Churches: A Research Guide to
    Churches Established Before 1900*. Kitchener, ON: Waterloo-Wellington
    Branch, Ontario Genealogical Society, 1993.
American Baptist Home Mission Society, *Baptist Home Missions in North
    America*. New York: Baptist Home Mission Society, 1883.
Beard, Augustus F., *A Crusade of Brotherhood: A History of the American
    Missionary Association*. New York: Krause Reprint Company, 1970
    reprint ed.
Bloomfield, Elizabeth, *Waterloo Township Through Two Centuries*. St.
    Jacobs: St. Jacobs Printery, 1995.
Bradford, Sarah H., *Harriet: The Moses of Her People*. Gloucester, MA: Peter
    Smith, reprint edition 1981.
Burke, Ronald K., *Samuel Ringgold Ward: Christian Abolitionist*. New York:
    Garland Publishing, Inc., 1995.
Campbell, James T., *Songs of Zion: The African Methodist Episcopal Church
    in the United States and South Africa*. New York: Oxford University
    Press, 1995.
Campbell, Stanley, *The Slave Catchers: Enforcement of the Fugitive Slave
    Law, 1850-1860*. Chapel Hill: University of North Carolina Press, 1970.
Cant, Hugh, *Historical Reminiscences of Galt and Other Writings*. Printed
    privately, 19 —.
Cheek, William and Cheek, Aimee, *John Mercer Langston and the Fight for
    Black Freedom, 1829-1865*. Urbana: University of Illinois Press, 1989.
Coburn, Louise Helen, *Skowhegan on the Kennebec*. Skowhegan, Maine:
    The author, 1941.
Cornelius, Janet Duitsman, *Slave Missions and the Black Church in
    Antebellum South*. Columbia: University of South Carolina Press, 1999.
Cumming, Ross, ed., *Historical Atlas of Wellington County, Ontario, 1906*.
    Guelph: Corporation of the County of Wellington, reprint edition, 1972.
DeBoer, Clara Merritt, *Be Jubilant My Feet: African American Abolitionists
    in the American Missionary Association, 1839-1861*. New York: Garland
    Publishing, Inc., 1994.

Dumas, Charles, ed., *Dictionary of American Biography* New York: Charles Scribner's Sons, 1936.

Dumond, Dwight L., ed., *Letters of James Gillespie Birney, 1831-1857, Volume 2.* New York: D. Appleton-Century Company, Inc., 1938.

Eaker, Madeline, ed., *The Heritage of Person County, 1981.* Roxboro, N.C.: Person County Historical Society, 1981.

English, John and McLaughlin, Kenneth, *Kitchener: An Illustrated History.* Waterloo, ON: Wilfrid Laurier University Press, 1983.

Fairchild, James, *Oberlin: The Colony and the College, 1833-1883.* Oberlin: E. J. Goodrich, 1883.

Fletcher, Samuel, *A History of Oberlin College From Its Foundation Through the Civil War.* Oberlin, OH: Oberlin College, 1943.

Franklin, John Hope and Schweninger, Loren, *Runaway Slaves: Rebels on the Plantation.* Oxford: Oxford University Press, 1999.

French, Gary E., *Men of Colour: An Historical Account of the Black Settlement on Wilberforce Street and in Oro Township, Simcoe County, Ontario, 1819-1949* Stroud: Kaste Books, 1978.

Friedman, Lawrence J., *Gregarious Saints: Self and Community in American Abolitionism, 1830-1870.* New York: Cambridge University Press, 1982.

Gagan, David, *Hopeful Travellers: Families, Land, and Social Change in Mid-Victorian Peel County, Canada West.* Toronto: University of Toronto Press, 1981.

Guillet, Edwin C., *The Pioneer Farmer and Backwoodsman, Volume 1 and 2.* Toronto: Ontario Publishing Company Ltd., 1963.

Hancocks, Elizabeth., *County Marriage Registers of Ontario, Canada, 1858-1869, Volume 32, Waterloo County.* Agincourt: Generation Press, 1996.

Hill, Daniel G., *The Freedom Seekers: Blacks in Early Canada.* Agincourt: Society of Canada Ltd., 1981.

Hoffman, Frances., *Upper Canada Naturalization Records, Wellington District, 1842-1849.* Kitchener: Waterloo-Wellington Branch, Ontario Genealogical Society, 1998.

Hornsby, Alton, Jr., *Chronology of African American History From 1492 to the Present.* Toronto: Gale Research, 1997.

Houston, Cecil. J. and William J. Smyth, *Irish Emigration and Canadian Settlement* Toronto: University of Toronto Press, 1990.

Hutchinson, Jean F., *History of Wellington County.* Grand Valley: Landsborough Printing Ltd., 1997.

Jeffrey, Julie, *The Great Silent Army of Abolitionism, Ordinary Women in the Antislavery Movement.* Chapel Hill: University of North Carolina Press, 1998.

Katz, Michael B., *The People of Hamilton, Canada West: Family and Class in a Mid-Nineteenth-Century City* Cambridge: Harvard University Press, 1975.

Litwack, Leon F., *North of Slavery: The Negro in the Free States, 1790-1860.* Chicago: University of Chicago Press, 1961.

Lesick, Lawrence T., *The Lane Rebels: Evangelicalism and Antislavery in Antebellum Americ.* Metuchen, NJ: Scarecrow Press, 1980.

Lewis, Elsie M., "Mary Ann Shadd Cary," in James, Edward T., ed., *Notable American Women, Volume 1.* Cambridge: Belknap Press of Harvard University Press, 1971.

Lovejoy, Joseph C., *Memoir of Rev. Charles T. Torrey, Who Died in the Penitentiary of Maryland Where he was Confined for Showing Mercy to the Poor.* New York: Negro Universities Press, reprint edition, 1969.

McKenzie, Donald, *Upper Canadian Naturalization Records, 1828-1850.* Toronto: Ontario Genealogical Society, 1991.

Mackay, Robert W., *The Canadian Directory.* Montreal: John Lovell, 1851.

Malone, Dumas, ed., *Dictionary of American Biography, Volume 18.* New York: Charles Scribner's Sons, 1936.

Mansell, Sue, *Burials from the Parish Register of St. John the Evangelist, Church of England, Bernlin, Now Kitchener, Ontario, 1859-1890.* Kitchener: Waterloo-Wellington Branch, Ontario Genealogical Society, 1985.

————. *Marriages From the Parish Registers of the Church of St. John the Evangelist, Church of England, Berlin, Now Kitchener, Ontario, 1878-1889.* Kitchener: Waterloo-Wellington Branch, Ontario Genealogical Society, 1985.

Martin, Christopher, *The Amistad Affair.* New York: Abelard-Schuman, 1970.

Martineau, Harriet, *Martyr Age of the United States of America with an Appeal on Behalf of the Oberlin Institute in Aid of the Abolition of Slavery.* Newcastle Upon Tyne, England: Newcastle Upon Tyne Emancipation and Aborigines Protection Society, 1840.

Meyler, Peter & David Meyler, *A Stolen Life: Searching for Richard Pierpoint.* Toronto: Natural Heritage, 1999.

Miller, Floyd, *The Search for a Black Nationality: Black Emigration and Colonization, 1787-1863.* Urbana: University of Illinois Press, 1975.

Nichols, Charles H., *Many Thousand Gone; the Ex-slaves' Account of their Bondage and Freedom.* Leiden: E. J. Brill, 1963.

Oberlin College, *Oberlin College Alumni Directory, 1960.* Oberlin, OH: The author, 1960.

Oro Township School Board and Oro Historical Committee, *A History of Oro Schools, 1836 to 1966,* Oro: The authors, 1967.

Payne, Daniel A., *History of the African Methodist Episcopal Church.* Nashville: Publishing House of the African Methodist Episcopal Sunday School Union, 1891.

Pease, William and Jane Pease, *Black Utopia, Negro Communal Experiments in America.* Madison: State Historical Society of Wisconsin, 1963.

Quantrell, Jim, *Time Frames: Historical Chronologies of Galt, Preston, Hespeler and Cambridge.* Cambridge: City of Cambridge Archives, 1993.

Reville, F. Douglas, *History of the County of Brant.* Brantford: Hurley Printing Company Ltd., 1920.

Rhodes, Jane, *Mary Ann Shadd Cary: The Black Press and Protest in the Nineteenth Century.* Bloomington: Indiana University Press, 1998.

Ripley, C. Peter, *The Black Abolitionist Papers, Volume II, Canada, 1830-1865.* Chapel Hill: University of North Carolina Press, 1986.

Robertson, Robert, *Denmark Vesey.* New York: Alfred A. Knopf, 1999.

Ross, Cumming, ed., *Historical Atlas of Wellington County, Ontario, 1906.* Guelph, ON: Corporation of the County of Wellington, reprint edition 1972.

Rowsell, Henry, *Gazetteer and Directory of the County of Wellington, 1867.* Toronto: The author, 1867.

Seibert, Wilbur H., *The Underground Railroad From Slavery to Freedom.* New York: Russell & Russell, 1898.

Shadd, Adrienne, "The Lord Seemed to Say Go: Women and the Underground Railroad Movement," in Bristow, Peggy, coordinator. *'We're Rooted Here and They Can't Pull Us Up': Essays in African Canadian Women's History.* Toronto: University of Toronto Press, 1994.

———, Afua Cooper and Karolyn Smardz-Frost, *The Underground Railroad: Next Stop, Toronto!* Toronto: Natural Heritage, 2002.

Shadd, Mary Ann, *A Plea for Emigration or, Notes of Canada West, in its Moral, Social, and Political Aspect: With Suggestions Respecting Mexico, West Indies and Vancouver's Island for the Information of Colored Emigrants.* Detroit: George W. Pattison, 1852.

Silverman, Jason H., *Unwelcome Guests: Canada West's Response to American Fugitive Slaves, 1800-1865.* New York: Associated Faculty Press, Inc., 1985.

———, "Mary Ann Shadd and the Search for Equality," in Hine, Darlene Clark, ed., *Black Women in American History: From Colonial Times Through the Nineteenth Century, Volume 4.* Brooklyn: Carlson Publishing Inc., 1990.

Slaney, Catherine, *Family Secrets: Crossing the Colour Line.* Toronto, Natural Heritage, 2003.

Smith, Charles, *A History of the African Methodist Episcopal Church.* New York: Johnson Reprint Corporation, 1968.

Snyder, Miriam H., *Hannes Schneider and his Wife Catharine Haus Schneider Their Descendants, 1534-1939.* Kitchener: Miriam Helen Snyder, 1945.

Stouffer, Allen P., *The Light of Nature and the Law of God: Antislavery in Ontario, 1833-1877.* Baton Rouge: Louisiana State University Press, 1992.

Stewart, Barbara; Phyllis Kitchen and Debbie Dietrich, *The Maple Leaf Journal: A Settlement History of Wellesley Township.* Waterloo: Corporation of the Township of Wellesley, 1983.

Sutherland, James, *County of Waterloo Gazetteer and General Business Directory for 1864.* Toronto: Mitchel & Company, 1864.

Ullman, Victor, *Look to the North Star: A Life of William King.* Toronto: Umbrella Press, 1969.

Uttley, W. V., *A History of Kitchener, Ontario.* Waterloo: Chronicle Press, 1937.

Walker, Clarence, *A Rock in a Weary Land: The African Methodist Episcopal Church During the Civil War and Reconstruction.* Baton Rouge: Louisiana State University Press, 1982.

Walker, Dan and Stratford-Deval, Fawne, *The Marriage Registers of Upper Canada/Canada West, Volume 9: Part 1, Wellington District, 1840-1852.* Delhi: NorSim Research and Publishing, 1997.

Walker, James, "African-Canadians" in Paul R. Magosci, ed., *An Encyclopedia of Canada's Peoples* (Toronto: University of Toronto Press, 1999) 139-176.

Walker and Miles Publishing Company, *Illustrated Atlas of Wellington County, Ontario, 1877.* Toronto: The authors, 1877.

Walters, Ronald G., *Antislavery Appeal: American Abolitionism After 1830.* Baltimore: John Hopkins University Press, 1976.

Waterloo-Wellington Branch, Ontario Genealogical Society, *Ten Cemeteries, Peel Township, Wellington County, Ontario.* Kitchener: Ontario Genealogical Society, 1984.

——, *Glen Allen Union Cemetery.* Kitchener: Ontario Genealogical Society, 1996.

Williams, Emma, *Historic Madison.* Jackson, TN: McCowat & Mercer Press, 1972.

Winks, Robin W., *Canada and the United States: The Civil War Years.* Baltimore: John Hopkins Press, 1960.

——, *The Blacks in Canada: A History.* New Haven: Yale University Press, 1971.

Wright, Richard, ed., *Encyclopaedia of the African Methodist Episcopal Church.* Philadelphia: Book Concern of the AME Church, 1947.

Wyatt-Brown, Bertram, *Lewis Tappan and the Evangelical War Against Slavery.* Cleveland: Case Western Reserve University Press, 1965.

Articles:

Baily, Marily, "From Cincinnati, Ohio to Wilberforce, Canada:; A Note on Antebellum Colonization," *Journal of Negro History,* 53 (October 1973).

Brantford Historical Society Publication Committee, "Prince Van Patten: A Loyal Servant of Joseph Brant," *Brantford Historical Society Quarterly* 2 (Winter 1995).

Brown, Lloyd, "Beneath the North Star: the Canadian Image in Black Literature," *Dalhousie Review* (1970).

Brown-Kubisch, Linda, "In Search of Freedom: Early Blacks in Waterloo County," *Waterloo Historical Society Annual Volume,* 80 (March 1993).

Cousins, Leone Banks, "Woman of the Year – 1842: The Early Life of Eliza Ruggles," *Nova Scotia Historical Quarterly* 6 (December 1976).

Devitt, A. W, "Blacks Celebrate Abolition of Slavery in Elmira," *Waterloo Historical Society Annual Volume* 49 (1961).

Hancock, Harold B., "Mary Ann Shadd: Negro Editor, Educator, and
    Lawyer," *Delaware History* 15 (April 1973).
Hembree, Michael F., "The Question of 'Begging': Fugitive Slave Relief in
    Canada 1830-1865," *Civil War History* 37 (December 1991).
Hill, Daniel G., "Negroes in Toronto, 1793-1865," *Ontario History* 55 (June
    1963).
Hite, Roger W., "Voice of a Fugitive: Henry Bibb and Antebellum Black
    Separatism," *Journal of Black Studies* 4 (March 1974).
Klinck, George, "The Early Days of Elmira," *Waterloo Historical Society
    Annual Volume* 15 (1927).
Knight, Claudette, "Black Parents Speak: Education in Mid-Nineteenth-
    Century Canada West," *Ontario History* 89 (December 1997).
Landon, Fred, "The Buxton Settlement in Canada," *Journal of Negro History*
    3 (October 1918).
———, "The Anti-Slavery Society of Canada," *Journal of Negro History* 4
    (January 1919).
———, "The Negro Migration to Canada After the Passing of the Fugitive
    Slave Act," *Journal of Negro History* 5 (January 1920).
———, "Henry Bibb, A Colonizer," *Journal of Negro History* 5 (October 1920)
———, "The Diary of Benjamin Lundy Written During His Journey
    Through Upper Canada January 1832," *Ontario Historical Society
    Papers and Records* 19 (1922).
———, "The Work of the American Missionary Association among the
    Negro Refugees in Canada West, 1848-1864," *Ontario Historical Society
    Papers and Records* 21 (1924).
———, "Social Conditions Among the Negroes in Upper Canada Before
    1865,"*Ontario Historical Society Papers and Records* 22 (1925).
———, "Amherstburg, Terminus of the Underground Railroad, "*Journal of
    Negro History* 10 (January 1925).
Landon, Fred, "Agriculture Among Negro Refugees in Upper Canada,"
    Journal of Negro History 21 (July 1936).
Lewis, James K., "Religious Nature of the Early Negro Migration to Canada
    and the Amherstburg Baptist Association," *Ontario History* 58 (1966).
Murray, Alexander, "The Provincial Freeman: A New Source for the
    History of the Negro in Canada and the United States," *Journal of
    Negro History* 43 (1959).
Myers, John, "American Antislavery Society Agents and the Free Negro,
    1833-1838," *Journal of Negro History* 52(July 1967).
Ogram, Grace, "Hawksville/Hawkesville on the Conestogo River," *Waterloo
    Historical Society Annual Volume* 74 (1986).
Padgett, Chris, "Hearing the Antislavery Rank-and-File: The Wesleyan
    Methodist Schism of 1843," *Journal of the Early Republic* 12 (Spring 1992).
Pease, William and Jane Pease, "Opposition to the Founding of the Elgin
    Settlement," *Canadian Historical Review* 38 (September 1957).

Riddell, William Renwick, "The Slave in Canada," *Journal of Negro History* 5 (July 1920).

Schantz, Orpheus, "Hawksville, A Pioneer Village of Waterloo County," *Waterloo Historical Society Annual Volume* 22 (1934).

Silverman, Jason H., "The American Fugitive Slave in Canada: Myths and Realities," *Southern Studies* 19 (Fall 1980).

Silverman, Jason H. and Donna J. Gillie, "'The Pursuit of Knowledge Under Difficulties': Education and the Fugitive Slave in Canada," *Ontario History* 74 (June 1982).

Uttley, W.V., "Woolwich Township – It's Early Settlement," *Waterloo Historical Society Annual Volume* 21 (1933).

Wade, Richard C., "The Negro in Cincinnati, 1800-1830," *Journal of Negro History* 39 (January 1954).

Waterloo Historical Society Publication Committee, "Biography: Reverend James Sims," *Waterloo Historical Society Annual Volume* 29 (1942).

———, "Wellesley Township and its Early Settlement," *Waterloo Historical Society Annual Volume* 30 (1943).

Wayne, Michael, "The Myth of the Fugitive Slave: The Black Population of Canada West on the Eve of the American Civil War: A Reassessment Based on the Manuscript Census of 1861," *Historie Sociale/Social History* 56 (November 1995).

Welter, Barbara. "The Cult of True Womanhood, 1820-1860." *American Quarterly* 18 (Summer 1966).

Winks, Robin, "Negro School Segregation in Ontario and Nova Scotia," *Canadian Historical Review*, 50 (June 1969).

Wright, Gerald, "Fugitive Negro Slaves," *Waterloo Historical Society Annual Volume* 67 (1979).

Yee, Shirley J, "Gender Ideology and Black Women as Community Builders in Ontario, 1850-70," *Canadian Historical Review* 75 (March 1994).

Dissertations/theses/student papers:

Cooper, Afua, "'Doing Battle in Freedom's Cause:' Henry Bibb Abolitionism, Race Uplift, and Black manhood 1842-1854," Ph.D. dissertation, University of Toronto, 2000.

DeBoer, Clara Merritt, "Role of Afro-Americans in the Origin and Work of the American Missionary Association, 1839-1877," Ph.D. dissertation, Rutgers University, 1973.

Murray, Alexander, "Canada and the Anglo-American Anti-slavery Movement: A Study in International Philanthropy," Ph.D. dissertation, University of Pennsylvania, 1960.

Simpson, Donald, "Negroes in Ontario From Early Times to 1870," Ph.D. dissertation, University of Western Ontario, 1971.

Spencer, Hildreth, "To Nestle in the Mane of the British Lion: A History of Canadian Black Education, 1820 to 1870," Ph.D. dissertation, Northwestern University, 1970.

Stevens, Elizabeth Cooke, "From Generation to Generation: The Mother and Daughter Activisim of Elizabeth Buffurn Chase and Lillie Chace Wyman," Ph.D. dissertation, Brown University, 1993.

Warner, Helen, "The Mennonite Heritage of the Huber Family: Oxford and Waterloo Counties, Ontario," Student essay, August 1990.

INDEX

About the Author

Linda Brown-Kubisch became interested in the Queen's Bush settlement while employed at the Kitchener Public Library in Kitchener, Ontario. The staff of the library's Grace Schmidt Room of Local History frequently received queries about this community's inhabitants. Realizing that virtually nothing was known about the settlement, she began to search for information from a wide variety of sources – a process that would take several years to complete.

Following her employment in Kitchener from 1987 to 1992, she moved to the United States, where she received a master's degree in history from the University of Missouri-Columbia, and then worked for a number of years as a reference specialist for the State Historical Society of Missouri. Linda wrote numerous historical and genealogical articles for both Canadian and American journals and published an entry in *Organizing Black America: An Encyclopedia of African American Associations* (New York: Garland Publishing, Inc.).

Most recently, Linda lived with her family in Covington, Louisiana, a small town north of New Orleans, and was employed as the genealogy specialist for the St. Tammany Parish Public Library. Linda Brown-Kubisch died at her home on December 20, 2003, after a courageous battle with cancer.